Instant Astrology

Also by Mort Gale

BIORHYTHM COMPATIBILITY
MOONPOWER

Mort Gale

INSTANT ASTROLOGY

A Warner Communications Company

To my children
Robert Ian
Neal Taylor
Alayne Leslie
who have taught me the importance of unconditional love

I want to thank Shirlee Kiley and Dr. Jacob Schwartz for sharing their astrological expertise with me during the preparation of this book. However, since I did not always listen to what they told me, I accept full responsibility for any shortcomings of the book.

I also want to thank Kathleen Malley—and my wife, Maureen—for continued support, encouragement, and patience. Thanks.

Warner Books Edition

Warner Books Inc., 75 Rockefeller Plaza, New York, N.Y. 10019

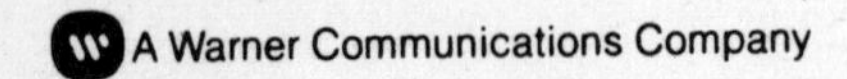

Cover design by Dennis Wheeler
Book design by Helen Roberts
First Printing: October 1980
Reissued: June 1982
10 9 8 7 6 5 4 3 2
Printed in the United States of America

Library of Congress Cataloging in Publication Data

Gale, Mort.
Instant astrology

Bibliography: p.
1. Astrology. 2. Horoscopes. I. Title.
BF1708.1.G335 133.5 80-15875
ISBN 0-446-37355-9 (U.S.A.)
ISBN 0-446-37361-3 (Canada)

Contents

Figures

Tables

Blank Worksheets

Preface

Two things stop most people from doing their own astrology. The first is learning what all the special words mean. The second is learning how to prepare a horoscope.

This book helps you overcome both difficulties.

First, it helps you to understand the language and basic ideas of astrology. Most of you know something about Sun signs and what they mean. You might know that Capricorns are hard workers, Scorpios are sexy, Virgos are perfectionists (or picky!), and so on. But do you know the difference between a Sun sign and a rising sign? Or the difference between a water sign and a fixed sign? You hear about conjunctions, oppositions, squares, and trines. But what are they, and what can they tell you about yourself? And can you explain the difference between the twelve houses and the twelve signs?

If you suddenly feel overwhelmed, hang in. You will soon understand all this, and much more. You will know what it means when someone tells you that his Mars is conjunct Venus in Taurus in his Fifth House. And you will know that your rising sign is the same as your Ascendant, and that both are at the cusp of your First House.

Learning the language of astrology is not as hard as you might think. It all depends on how you go about it. I will show you an easy way in Chapter One, where I begin by assuming that you know absolutely nothing about astrology. I will show you how to visualize the planets as they circle our rotating earth, so that you can "see" what all the astrological words mean. Trust me. You'll see.

After that, you will be ready to overcome the second major obstacle—preparing your own horoscope. Horoscopes are maps of where the planets are in the skies at a given time. A natal horoscope is a map of the planet positions at the time you were born. It usually takes careful calculations to come up with your horoscope. True, it's not too hard to do for those who enjoy that kind of work. But for those who dread mathematics or calculations, it seems to be impossible. Many an eager student has fallen off the sled trying to steer through sidereal time, read an ephemeris, convert longitude minutes of arc into hours of time, interpolate logarithms, or find house cusps for the latitude of birth.

Fortunately, you won't have to do any of that. Chapter Two shows you an easy way to prepare your horoscope. It's so easy that you can do one in less than ten minutes, without a single calculation. That's because I have replaced all the mathematics with a few look-up tables and worksheets that do practically all the work for you. It's as close as you can come to having an instant horoscope.

Once you have your horoscope you can do many things with it. Chapter Three shows you how to interpret the over-all distribution of the planets among the signs of the zodiac and among the houses. You will learn the meaning of the four elements—fire, earth, air, and water—and what it means if your planets are bunched up in the cardinal, fixed, or mutable signs. You will also learn about the house hemispheres, which can tell you at a glance if you are the kind of person who makes things happen or whether you just let things happen to you.

After this over-all interpretation of your horoscope, you will be ready to make more detailed interpretations of the astrological forces in your life. Each planet says something about you, depending on where it is in the zodiac, and on where it is among the houses of your horoscope. Chapter Four tells you the significance of the different planets in each of the signs and houses.

But you won't stop there. The planetary influences also depend on how the planets are aligned with each other. These alignments are called "aspects." Aspects tell you whether a planet's influence is strengthened or weakened by the action of other planets. Chapter Five tells you what it means when pairs of planets are in certain aspects with respect to each other. Here is where you learn what it means when Mars is conjunct Venus.

By this time you will be able to prepare your own "daily horoscope." Each day the planets move through the houses of your horoscope, or make aspects with the positions that the planets held in your natal (birth) horoscope. As the planets pass over (transit) your houses or the positions of your natal planets, they bring about influences that affect you during that period of time. Chapter Six shows you how to find the daily positions of the planets and compare them with your horoscope to determine which influences are affecting you at that time.

Chapter Seven "tells all" about what you can find out by comparing the horoscopes of two people. Since each person's horoscope tells you something about his or her personality, a comparison of the two horoscopes can tell you about their chances for a compatible relationship. Here you will learn how to check out your romantic or business companions to see whether you should develop the relationship or let it drop. You will need birth dates. So, if you don't have them yet, start figuring out how you can get them.

Chapter Eight is for those who want to know more about

some of the things that were passed over in the earlier chapters. I tried to keep unnecessary details from getting in your way as I went through the basics. However, if you are interested in more details or in how to learn more about astrology, this chapter is for you.

If you always wanted to do your own astrology, this book will finally get you started. It makes it easy for you to see what astrology is all about. And it makes it easy for you to do it.

Once you try it you will be amazed at how accurately astrology shows you your nature and your needs. And how helpful it is in alerting you to the changing flow of cosmic forces that affect your life.

The best way to get started is to turn the page.

Chapter One

Understanding Astrology

Astrology can tell you many interesting things about yourself just from the way the planets were arranged in the skies at the time you were born. Centuries of observations have shown that people born under similar celestial patterns seem to follow similar behavioral patterns.

The language of astrology grew from the need to describe these planetary patterns as they were seen from the earth. Let's see how we can visualize these patterns.

The Planets

Astrology deals with *ten* planets. Eight of these are the sister planets of the earth—Mercury, Venus, Mars, Jupiter, Saturn, Uranus, Neptune, and Pluto. The other two are the Sun and the Moon, neither of which is a planet. (A planet circles the Sun.) However, as seen from the earth, the Sun and Moon follow the same path as the planets. Astrologers, interested in the relationships between the positions of all ten objects, simply call them the "ten planets." That's what we will call them, even though we know that the Sun and Moon are not planets.

The path followed by the ten planets is called the ecliptic. You can visualize the ecliptic by imagining yourself looking out from a glass-enclosed observation tower located at the center of a giant circular racetrack. The tower represents the earth. The racetrack represents the ecliptic.

As you look out from your tower, you see all ten planets moving around the track in the same direction, from your right to your left. Since the planets move at different speeds, they are spread out all around the track. Faster moving planets circle the track several times a year, overtaking and passing slower moving planets that take centuries to make one lap.

Astrologers are interested in where each planet can be found on the track, and where they are with respect to each other. They use the signs of the zodiac to describe planet positions, and "aspects" to describe the relations between them. We'll look at these shortly, but first let's look at the planets themselves.

Planets represent different cosmic forces which affect your basic character traits and your changing urges and needs. They provide the energies which drive your physical, emotional, mental, and intuitional systems. These planetary energies are modified by the planet's position in the zodiac, and by its relationships (aspects) to the other planets.

Planets fall into three groups according to how long it takes them to make one trip around the track. The first group of planets takes less than two years to make a full cycle. These include the Sun, Moon, Mercury, Venus, and Mars. Since we experience the influence of these planetary cycles so often, we soon learn to recognize and control our reactions to them. These are the "personal planets." The key characterizations for them are as follows:

Sun	Identity, Purpose	(Individuality)
Moon	Feeling, Responsiveness	(Personality)

Mercury	Intellect, Communication	(Mentality)
Venus	Attraction, Harmony	(Affection)
Mars	Energy, Assertion	(Initiative)

You will learn more about the influences of these personal planets in Chapters Four and Five.

The second group of planets includes those whose cycles are measured in decades. These are Jupiter, at twelve years, and Saturn, at about twenty-eight years. The extended length of these cycles means that they are felt more as long-term inner urges than as immediate conscious needs. These urges determine how you view the world. The two "viewpoint planets" are characterized as follows:

Jupiter	Enthusiasm, Adventurousness	(Expansive)
Saturn	Caution, Restraint	(Conservative)

The third group of planets moves so slowly that its energies influence entire generations in essentially the same way—setting the culture-tone for long periods of time. Uranus makes a full cycle in about eighty-four years, a full lifetime, while Neptune and Pluto take about two centuries (164 and 247 years, respectively). The characteristics of these "transpersonal planets" are as follows:

Uranus	Independent, Intuitional	(Originality)
Neptune	Inspirational, Mystical	(Sensitivity)
Pluto	Regeneration, Obsession	(Control)

The influences of these transpersonal planets will vary between individuals depending on how they relate to the other planets of the horoscope, and how they fall into a person's natal houses. (Houses will be described shortly.)

As mentioned earlier, astrologers determine the influence of the planets from their positions in the zodiac. These positions are described in terms of the familiar "signs of the zodiac." Let's get more familiar with them.

The Signs of the Zodiac

When the ancients noticed the planets moving along the ecliptic path, they also noticed the background of fixed stars behind that path. It would be as though you noticed a background of billboards around your imaginary racetrack. You could then tell the positions of horses around the track just by identifying the billboard behind each horse. The ancients used the background of fixed stars in the same way. They divided their racetrack (the ecliptic) into twelve equal sectors. Each sector was named after the fixed-star group seen in that sector. Since several of these star groups had names of animals—Leo the lion, Aries the ram, Pisces the fish, etc.—the ancients referred to these sectors as the "little zoo." The Greek word for "little zoo" is *zodiac*.

The names and symbols for the twelve sectors of the zodiac are called the "signs of the zodiac." These are shown in Figure 1–1. The figure shows what the zodiac would look like if you saw it from high above the earth's North Pole. Imagine that you are looking down on your glass-enclosed observation tower (earth), located at the center of your imaginary racetrack (the ecliptic). The circle at the center of the figure represents the earth, and the outer circle represents the ecliptic (not to scale, of course).

Notice how the racetrack is divided into twelve equal sectors. Since the planets move around the track from right to left (counterclockwise as you look down on it), the sectors follow that same order around the track—Aries, Taurus, Gemini, Cancer, Leo, Virgo, Libra, Scorpio, Sagittarius, Capricorn, Aquarius, and Pisces. Aries is the starting point of the zodiac. That's because the Sun enters the sign of Aries on the first day of spring to start the round of seasons.

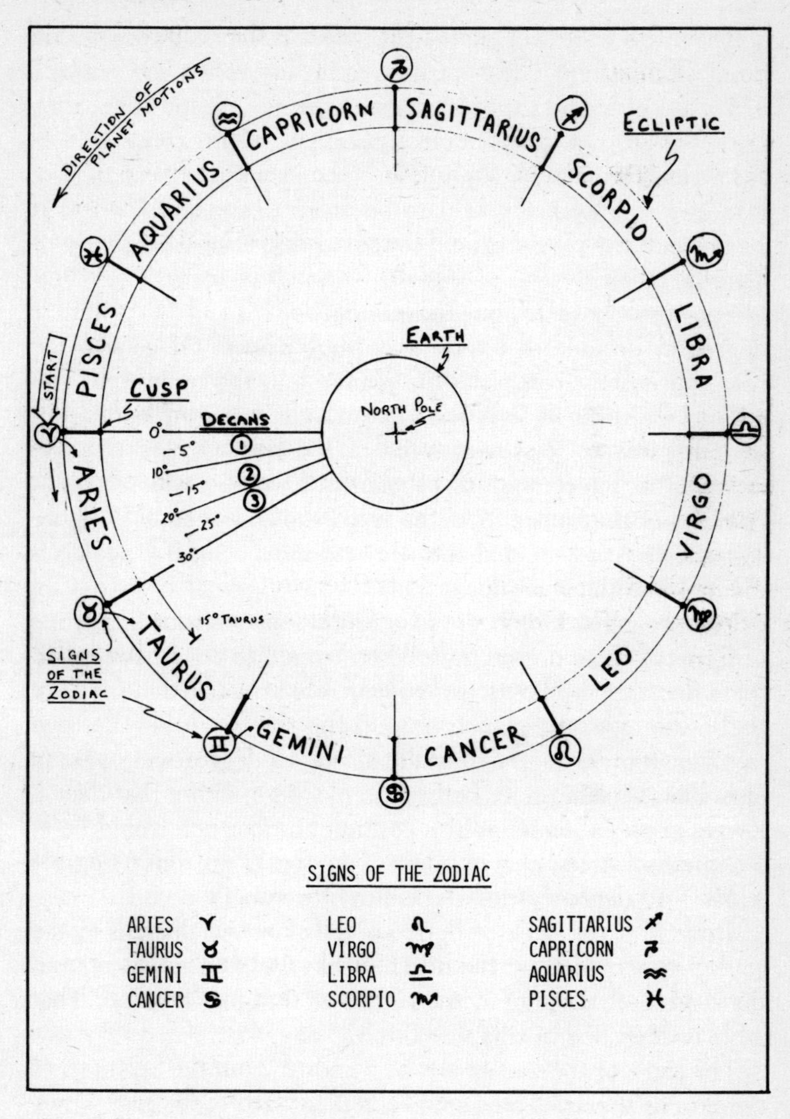

Figure 1–1. The Zodiac

The symbol for each sign of the zodiac is shown at the starting point of that sign. These starting points are called the "cusps." The cusp of each sign is 30 degrees further around the zodiac from the cusp of the previous sign. Each cusp is considered as the 0-degree mark for finding any planet within that sign. For example, if a planet is said to be at 15 degrees of Taurus, it means that the planet can be found 15 degrees past the cusp of Taurus.

You don't have to find the position of a planet to within 1 degree to be able to interpret its significance. Of course, the more accurately you place the planet, and the more time you take to interpret its significance, the more you can learn from your horoscope. However, some of the best astrologers make meaningful interpretations of planets found to within only a "decan" of the zodiac. A decan is a 10-degree segment; Figure 1–1 shows Aries divided into three decans. The full zodiac is divided into thirty-six decans.

You are going to find the planet positions for your horoscope in terms of these decans, numbered from 1 to 36. I have called these decans "Sky Positions," to help you visualize that they are the locations of the planets around the sky. Each Sky Position number represents the middle of its 10-degree-wide decan. However, a planet may be found anywhere within that decan. For example, a planet at Sky Position number one would be at 5 degrees of Aries, plus or minus 5 degrees (i.e., from 0 degrees Aries to 10 degrees Aries, the width of decan 1).

Table 1 at the back of the book tells you which signs of the zodiac are covered by the different Sky Position numbers, and the degree of the sign at the center of that Sky Position. That table is described in Chapter Two.

The signs of the zodiac are best known from the positions of the Sun as it moves through the zodiac once each year. These are the famous Sun Signs. Your Sun Sign is the sign of the zodiac through which the Sun was passing on the day you were born. The dates during which the Sun is in each sign differ by a few days depending on the leap years involved. The Sun is in the following signs of the zodiac on the dates shown:

ARIES	MARCH 22 to APRIL 20
TAURUS	APRIL 21 to MAY 21
GEMINI	MAY 22 to JUNE 21
CANCER	JUNE 22 to JULY 23
LEO	JULY 24 to AUGUST 23
VIRGO	AUGUST 24 to SEPTEMBER 23
LIBRA	SEPTEMBER 24 to OCTOBER 23
SCORPIO	OCTOBER 24 to NOVEMBER 22
SAGITTARIUS	NOVEMBER 23 to DECEMBER 22
CAPRICORN	DECEMBER 23 to JANUARY 20
AQUARIUS	JANUARY 21 to FEBRUARY 19
PISCES	FEBRUARY 20 to MARCH 21

You can't use these dates to find the positions of your planets because they move through the zodiac slower or faster than the Sun each year. Astrologers use a table (ephemeris) to find each planet's position in the signs. You will use my special tables to find them in the decans, or Sky Positions.

Significance of the Signs

The planets represent the energies which drive your physical, emotional, mental, and intuitional systems. These energies manifest themselves differently depending on the positions of the planets in the signs of the zodiac. Different signs channel the energies into different behavior patterns, which are then recognized as personality traits. In a word. the traits associated with each sign are as follows:

Aries—Outgoing	Gemini—Versatile
Taurus—Conservative	Cancer—Emotional

Leo—Authoritative
Virgo—Exacting
Libra—Helpful
Scorpio—Determined
Sagittarius—Optimistic
Capricorn—Cautious
Aquarius—Independent
Pisces—Impressionable

Other words could have been used in each case. Each sign actually represents a cluster of traits with both positive and negative attributes, depending on the intensity of their expression. The traits in each cluster appear in different combinations among all the signs of the zodiac. The difference between the signs depends on how these traits are combined in each sign.

The signs share common traits depending on how far apart they are from each other. Signs which are 120 degrees apart share the traits which affect your temperament (or how you approach life). Only three signs can be 120 degrees apart from each other (three times 120 degrees equals 360 degrees, or a full circle of the zodiac). Such a group of three signs is called a "triplicity." There are four triplicities in the twelve signs of the zodiac, each sharing a common temperament trait.

Ancient astrologers associated the temperaments of each of the four triplicities with the attributes of the four fundamental "elements" of the universe—fire, earth, air, and water. Signs in the fire triplicity are called the "fire signs," those in the earth triplicity are the "earth signs," etc.

The attributes of the signs in each triplicity are as follows:

Fire Signs (Aries, Leo, Sagittarius)
Enthusiastic, courageous, passionate, impulsive
Earth Signs (Taurus, Virgo, Capricorn)
Practical, materialistic, conservative, inhibited
Air Signs (Gemini, Libra, Aquarius)
Intellectual, adaptable, impractical, superficial
Water Signs (Cancer, Scorpio, Pisces)
Emotional, sensitive, placid, susceptible

These four groups of signs, fire, earth, air, and water, combine to form two major groups that represent two fundamental approaches to life, active or passive. The fire and air signs make up the active signs, while the earth and water signs make up the passive signs. It is unfortunate that the ancients called the active signs "masculine" and the passive signs "feminine." The intent was to designate the odd-numbered signs (Aries, Gemini, Leo, Libra, Sagittarius, and Aquarius) as imparting the aggressive traits of males, and the even-numbered signs (Taurus, Cancer, Virgo, Scorpio, Capricorn, and Pisces) as imparting the passive traits that were associated with women. Attempts to eliminate these sexist overtones in the gender classification of the signs include designations such as positive vs. negative, extroverted vs. introverted, outgoing vs. withdrawn, etc. As you can see, these don't help to de-sex the signs.

You will be checking for the distribution of planets among the masculine and feminine signs in your own horoscope when you get to Chapter Three.

Another grouping of traits occurs among signs which are 90 degrees apart from each other. There are four signs in each such group (four times 90 degrees equals 360 degrees of the full zodiac). A group of four signs is a "quadruplicity." There are three quadruplicities among the twelve signs of the zodiac. The quadruplicities, or "qualities" as they are more often called, are the cardinal, fixed, and mutable signs. They indicate the basic kinds of activity a person will be engaged in—getting things started, keeping them going, or steering them in different directions.

The attributes of the signs of each quality are as follows:

Cardinal Signs (Aries, Cancer, Libra, Capricorn)
Initiating, enterprising, ambitious, domineering
Fixed Signs (Taurus, Leo, Scorpio, Aquarius)
Determined, conventional, organizing, dogmatic

Mutable Signs (Gemini, Virgo, Sagittarius, Pisces)
Adaptable, imaginative, tutorial, critical

The cardinal signs are sometimes called the acute or movable signs, the fixed signs are sometimes called the grave signs, and the mutable signs are sometimes called the common or flexible signs.

You will interpret the distribution of your planets in the cardinal, fixed, and mutable signs in Chapter Three.

The significance attributed to each sign of the zodiac arises from its unique combination of the traits of its elements, gender, and qualities. No two signs share the same combination of these three traits, as you can see from the following list:

Sign	*Element*	*Gender*	*Quality*
Aries	Fire	Masculine	Cardinal
Taurus	Earth	Feminine	Fixed
Gemini	Air	Masculine	Mutable
Cancer	Water	Feminine	Cardinal
Leo	Fire	Masculine	Fixed
Virgo	Earth	Feminine	Mutable
Libra	Air	Masculine	Cardinal
Scorpio	Water	Feminine	Fixed
Sagittarius	Fire	Masculine	Mutable
Capricorn	Earth	Feminine	Cardinal
Aquarius	Air	Masculine	Fixed
Pisces	Water	Feminine	Mutable

Using this list, you can substitute the attributes for the element, gender, and quality of each sign to see how they combine to give that sign its special significance. For example, Aries is a fire sign (enthusiastic), masculine (active), and a cardinal sign (initiating). These three attributes show that Aries is an "outgoing" sign.

The interpretations given in the later chapters are based on combining the traits of the signs with the influences of the planets into typical behavioral profiles that are likely to arise from those traits and influences. These profiles describe your approach and responses to situations in business and family life. Although you may not be involved with the specific situations, you should be able to recognize your behavior pattern by imagining how you would react in that situation.

Rising Signs (Your Ascendant)

If you are like most people, you know your Sun sign but don't know your rising sign. But you have probably heard about rising signs, and you may know that they can be as important as your Sun sign in your horoscope. You may also know that your rising sign has something to do with the time of day that you were born.

Your rising sign is the sign of the zodiac that was just coming up over the eastern horizon at the moment you were born. If you were born at sunrise, your rising sign would be the same as your Sun sign. That's because your Sun sign tells you what part of the zodiac the Sun was in at that time. Since that was the part of the zodiac rising over the horizon at sunrise, it is also your rising sign. If you were born a few hours earlier, or a few hours later than sunrise, a different part of the zodiac would be rising, or ascending, over the eastern horizon. Another name for your rising sign is your "Ascendant."

You just saw that the Ascendant at sunrise is the same as the Sun sign. The Ascendant two hours after sunrise would be one sign past the Sun sign. That's because it takes that long for the earth's horizon to move another 30 degrees across the zodiac. Let me show you how you can see that.

Imagine yourself back in your glass-enclosed observation tower (earth), looking out at your zodiac racetrack. This time imagine that your tower rotates on its axis, making one full revolution each day. As you look straight out, say through one window, you will see all twelve signs of the zodiac pass across your window in one twenty-four-hour period. Every two hours another sign of the zodiac comes into view. Since the earth rotates counterclockwise (when one looks down on its North Pole), you will see the signs of the zodiac appear in their natural order, Aries, Taurus, Gemini, Cancer, Leo, Virgo, Libra, Scorpio, Sagittarius, Capricorn, Aquarius, and Pisces. Check this by looking back at Figure 1–1.

Actually, the time it takes the eastern horizon to pass through each sign is not exactly two hours. It depends on the time of year and your latitude on the earth. However, if you know where the Sun was at sunrise, and you know how long it was between sunrise and your time of birth, it is possible to figure out your rising sign, or Ascendant. Fortunately, you won't have to do that. I have provided an Ascendant look-up table that is good for any time of the year, and for any latitude between 30 and 50 degrees (that includes the continental United States). It gives you your Ascendant in terms of its Sky Position number in the zodiac. You will learn how to find your Ascendant in Chapter Two.

Your Ascendant is important for two reasons. First, like your Sun sign, it serves to establish a basic pattern in your life. Where the Sun establishes your character, or who you really are, your Ascendant determines your personality, or what you show the world as you deal with it. You will find interpretations of your Ascendant in Chapter Four. Briefly, the personalities that go with each Ascendant sign are as follows:

Aries—Outspoken
Taurus—Timid
Gemini—Talkative
Cancer—Sympathetic
Leo—Dignified
Virgo—Shy
Libra—Charming
Scorpio—Intense
Sagittarius—Expansive
Capricorn—Serious
Aquarius—Considerate
Pisces—Idealistic

The second reason for the importance of the Ascendant is that it establishes the position of your houses in the zodiac. That's because your Ascendant marks the beginning of your First House. Let's take a closer look at this sometimes confusing concept of houses.

The Twelve Houses

The twelve signs of the zodiac show the positions along the ecliptic where the planets can be found on any date. These planetary positions don't change very much during a single day. However, you just saw that the daily rotation of the earth brings the next sign of the zodiac up over the eastern horizon every two hours. After it rises, each sign moves slowly across the sky toward the western horizon, where it sets about twelve hours later. Visualize how the Sun rises in the east and sets in the west. That's how each sign of the zodiac rises and sets each day. Remember, the zodiac is fixed in space, it just seems to move across the sky because of the earth's rotation each day.

Astrologers found that the influence of a sign (and of the planets in any sign) depended on the hourly positions of the sign as it moved across the sky each day. And so they developed a system to identify those hourly positions with respect to the eastern horizon. This is where the system of the "Twelve Houses" comes in. Let's go back into your rotating observation tower to see how it works.

First, you must imagine your tower enclosed by twelve windows, numbered from one to twelve as shown in Figure 1–2. Each window provides a 30-degree view of the zodiac. As the tower (earth) rotates through the day, the windows look out on different parts of the zodiac. Astrologers call these twelve windows on the zodiac the "Twelve Houses." The arrangement shown in the figure is called the Equal House System, since each

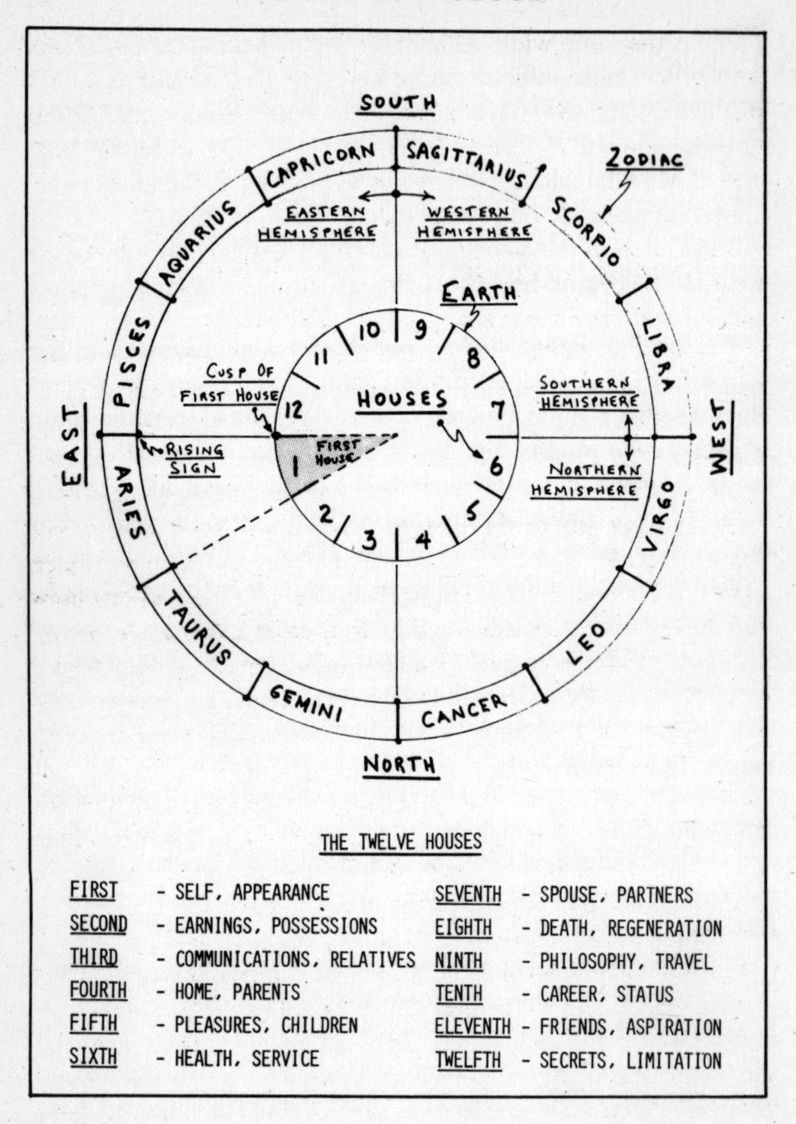

Figure 1–2. The Twelve Houses

house is the same width (30 degrees). It is gaining in popularity over other, more difficult systems which take account of the tilt of the ecliptic as seen from the earth. There is very little difference between these other systems (Placidus, Campanus, etc.) and the Equal House System at latitudes of the continental United States and Southern Europe.

Regardless of these differences, astrologers agree on where the First House begins, how the houses are numbered, and how they are to be interpreted.

The houses are numbered to show their relationship to the rising sign that effectively marks the start of your first day of life. Your rising sign (Ascendant) marks the cusp, or starting point, of your First House. The remaining houses are numbered consecutively around the earth in a counterclockwise direction, each showing where the eastern horizon will be in the zodiac during the next two-hour interval. The houses tell you which signs (and planets in those signs) come up over the eastern horizon during each successive two-hour interval to influence you on the first full day of your life. These influences are strengthened or weakened, depending on which signs and planets appear in those houses. You will find interpretations of the planets in your houses in Chapter Four.

Figure 1–2 shows the cusp of the First House lined up with the cusp of Aries, the first sign of the zodiac. This sets up a "Natural Chart," which shows how the characteristics of the houses are related to the characteristics of the signs of the zodiac. We will look at those shortly.

Normally the cusp of the First House can be anywhere in the zodiac, depending on the position of the Ascendant. In any given case, the chart shows the sign of the Ascendant on the outer circle, next to the cusp of the First House. You will learn how to prepare a chart for your houses in Chapter Two. If you don't know the time of your birth, and therefore cannot determine your Ascendant, you can still find your houses by using your Sun sign as the cusp of your First House. This is called a "Solar

Chart" and is based on the assumption that you were born at sunrise. Interestingly, statistics show that many people are indeed born near the hours of sunrise, making Solar Charts rather useful.

The interpretation of your horoscope is based in part on how the planets are clustered in different groups of houses. These groups are identified in terms of "hemispheres." Since the Ascendant is on the eastern horizon, the six houses (10, 11, 12, 1, 2, 3) on that side of the earth are in the Eastern Hemisphere. The six houses (4, 5, 6, 7, 8, 9) on the other side of the earth are in the Western Hemisphere. Notice in Figure 1–2 that these hemispheres are on sides of the chart opposite from where you would expect to find east and west on a standard map. That's because the horoscope is a map of the earth and the zodiac as seen by looking down on the North Pole. You can see that east is the direction of sunrise when the Sun is in Aries as the earth rotates toward it (Aries is the Ascendant in this Natural Chart).

The six houses across the bottom of the chart (1, 2, 3, 4, 5, 6) are in the Northern Hemisphere, while the six houses across the top (7, 8, 9, 10, 11, 12) are in the Southern Hemisphere. The reason for this is that the signs of the zodiac corresponding with those houses in the Natural Chart are respectively north and south of the earth's equator. If you were to look out your tower windows you would see that the zodiac is tilted so that it is higher at Cancer and lower at Capricorn. Therefore, the zodiac is north of the equator at Cancer and south of the equator at Capricorn.

You will learn how to interpret the significance of your planets in the different hemispheres in Chapter Three. But now let's look at the meanings of the houses themselves.

Significance of the Houses

The houses represent the different departments of life in which your planetary energies find their expression. For example, your character and personality, which are set up by your planets in the different signs, will be directed either into personal or public matters, depending on whether they fall into the houses of the Northern Hemisphere or Southern Hemisphere, respectively. Again, you will be self-sufficient if they fall into the eastern houses, or dependent on others if they fall into the western houses.

Each house represents a cluster of interests and activities just as each sign represents a cluster of traits and approaches for dealing with those activities. The spheres of interest of each house are as follows:

First—Self, appearance
Second—Earnings, possessions
Third—Communications, relatives
Fourth—Home, parents
Fifth—Pleasures, children
Sixth—Health, service
Seventh—Spouse, partnerships
Eighth—Death, regeneration
Ninth—Philosophy, travel
Tenth—Career, status
Eleventh—Friends, aspirations
Twelfth—Secrets, limitations

You can get a better insight into the meanings of the houses by thinking of them as falling into several different groups. This is what we did with the signs of the zodiac—elements, gender, qualities. I have already mentioned the hemisphere groupings which determine the over-all focus of your activities. If most of your planets fall into one of the hemispheres the significance is as follows:

Northern—A focus on private matters
Southern—A focus on public activities
Eastern—Activities are self-initiated
Western—Dependence on others' initiatives

Another useful grouping of the houses corresponds with the groupings of signs into the four elements. The houses can be grouped similarly into the fire, earth, air, and water *houses*. This arrangement follows from the fact that the attributes of each house correspond with the attributes of the sign on its house cusp in the Natural Chart shown in Figure 1–2. The significance of a cluster of planets in the fire, earth, air, and water houses is as follows:

Fire Houses—Life Identity (First, Fifth, Ninth)
Activities focus on achieving life's aspirations
Earth Houses—Material Wealth (Second, Sixth, Tenth)
Activities focus on meeting material needs
Air Houses—Relationships (Third, Seventh, Eleventh)
Activities focus on social contact and mind-sharing
Water Houses—Emotional (Fourth, Eighth, Twelfth)
Activities focus on achieving emotional tranquillity

Still another important house grouping corresponds with the qualities of the signs. Here the houses are grouped into angular, succedent, and cadent houses, corresponding with the cardinal, fixed, and mutable signs of the zodiac. Again, the houses are placed in these groups based on their correspondence with the signs on their cusps in the Natural Chart. The significance of a cluster of planets in the angular, succedent, or cadent houses is as follows:

Angular houses—Starting (First, Fourth, Seventh, Tenth)
Activities are self-starting for immediate effects
Succedent houses—Controlling (Second, Fifth, Eighth, Eleventh)
Activities are aimed at managing and controlling things
Cadent houses—Changing (Third, Sixth, Ninth, Twelfth)
Skills are acquired to improve relationships

The intensity of a planet's influence in a house depends on the sign of the zodiac that happens to fall on that house cusp in your horoscope. If cardinal signs are found in the angular houses, they strengthen the planetary energies flowing into the activities of those houses. The same strengthening occurs when fixed signs are in succedent houses and mutable signs are in cadent houses.

The interpretation of the significance of your planets in your houses, or of a companion's planets in your houses, will be given as brief behavior sketches that illustrate the interplay of character traits in the different spheres of life represented by those houses. Chapter Four tells you about your own planets, while Chapter Seven tells you how a companion's planets in your houses can affect your relationship.

Planetary Aspects

You just saw that the energies of the planets affect your character (who you really are), that their positions in the signs affect your personality (how you show yourself to the world), and that their positions in the houses show where you focus your interests and activities (self, friends, career, home, etc.).

These cosmic energies are also influenced by how the planets are positioned with respect to each other at any time. Some positions produce arrangements that reinforce those energies in helpful ways, while others bring about disruptive effects. These relations between planetary positions are called "aspects." You have heard about aspects if you have heard about oppositions and squares, or conjunctions and trines. Here's how to visualize what all this means.

Imagine yourself back in the observation tower looking at the planets spread out all around the track. Remember, they are spread out because they move around the zodiac at different speeds, the faster planets overtaking and passing the slower ones. Whenever a faster planet overtakes a slower one—when they are neck and neck—they are in "conjunction." This means that they are both at the same sign of the zodiac—0 degrees apart—as seen from the earth.

Whenever two planets are on opposite sides of the track from each other, they are in "opposition." This aspect places them six signs—180 degrees—apart from each other in the zodiac.

Two planets 90 degrees apart are in a "square" aspect to each other. Imagine one planet straight ahead of you with another planet directly to your left. If you pointed your arms to each planet, the angle between your arms would be 90 degrees. If there were another planet off to your right side, it would also be square to the planet in front of you, since it too would be 90 degrees from the planet in front.

Notice, however, that in this last case the planet to your right is in opposition to the planet on your left, since they are on opposite sides of the track. If you pointed your arms to the planet on the right and the one on the left, the angle between your arms would be 180 degrees, the angle of the opposition aspect.

I mention this so that you will know that a planet can make several aspects to other planets at the same time. The left planet was square to the front planet, while it was also in opposition to the right planet. You will learn a fast way to check for all the aspects of a planet when you get to Chapter Five.

In addition to the conjunction, opposition, and square, there are two other major aspects to be considered. These are the "sextile" and the "trine." The sextile occurs when two planets are two signs—or 60 degrees—apart. The trine occurs when two planets are four signs—or 120 degrees—from each other in the zodiac. Other aspects of 30 degrees (semisextile), 45 degrees (semisquare), 72 degrees (quintile), 135 degrees (sesquare) and 150 degrees (quincunx or inconjunct), are considered as minor aspects and will not be discussed in this book.

The effect of an aspect between two planets is strongest when the faster planet reaches the exact angle of the aspect. However, the effects can be felt over several degrees (called the "orb") depending on which planets are involved and on whether it is a major or a minor aspect. The important orbs cover about 10 degrees, or one Sky Position number. You will use an Aspect Finder in Chapter Five that gives the planetary aspects to within one Sky Position number, placing them within the orb of meaningful interpretations.

The interpretation of aspects is based in part on how the planets fall into signs with similar or conflicting elements and qualities. For example, the square aspect has planets in the same quality but in conflicting elements (e.g., fire and water), while in the trine aspect the planets are in the same element, but stimulated by different qualities.

The aspects are no longer described as good or bad, but rather as harmonious or inharmonious. Harmonious aspects can help matters along. Inharmonious aspects ("badly aspected planets") introduce stresses, many of which can actually help you grow if you learn to deal with them. Chapter Five shows you how to interpret the significance of the aspects between the planets in your horoscope. A brief description of the meaning of the major aspects is as follows:

Conjunction (0 degrees)

Neither harmonious nor inharmonious, this aspect merges and intensifies the energies of two planets. Inner tension can arise if the planets have conflicting natures.

Sextile (60 degrees, two signs apart)

Harmonious aspect that helps energies flow toward attainment of your goals, provided that you make some conscious effort to achieve them yourself.

Square (90 degrees, three signs apart)

Inharmonious aspect causing tensions and obstacles for you to overcome. It forces you to choose between your conflicting inner needs and urges.

Trine (120 degrees, four signs apart)

Harmonious aspect that brings the two energies into an easy interplay. This can create such beneficial consequences that things become too easy for you, making you lazy.

Opposition (180 degrees, six signs apart)

Inharmonious aspect creating inner tensions between your planetary urges. It also creates dynamic tensions with others, which you must reconcile if you want to maintain harmonious relationships.

The similarity of the sextile and trine, differing primarily in matter of degree, makes it possible to consider both aspects at the same time when making interpretations of their significance. The same can be said of the square and the opposition aspects. The interpretations in this book will consider the conjunction, sextile-trine, and square-opposition as three basic aspect-categories.

The influence of an aspect is modified somewhat depending on whether the faster planet is still overtaking the slower planet, or has already passed it but still falls within the orb of the aspect. If the faster planet is still closing in on the slower planet, it is called a closing (or applying) aspect. If the faster planet has already passed the slower planet, it is called a separating aspect.

Closing aspects intensify the influence of the aspect, while separating aspects exert less intense influences—making separating aspects less significant in their effects. The Aspect Finder in

Chapter Five will show you when an aspect is closing or separating. However, before you decide whether two planets are closing or separating, you must determine whether either planet is in retrograde motion. Let me explain retrograde motion, along with two other frequently used terms.

Retrograde Motion—Transits—Progressions

If you are sitting in a train alongside another train in a railroad station, you may see the other train begin to move backward. However, you won't know if that train is moving backward or yours is moving forward, especially if your train moves off smoothly and slowly. In the same way, the apparent motion between the earth and its sister planets makes it seem that the other planets are sometimes moving backward around the zodiac. Actually, the planets all move around the zodiac in the same direction at all times.

This apparent backward motion of the planets is called "retrograde" motion. It occurs in several stages. First the planet seems to stand still, then it backs up through the signs, stands still again, and then resumes its forward motion. The Sun and Moon are never in retrograde motion. The amount of time that a planet spends in retrograde motion depends on the planet's orbit, varying from about twenty-two days for nearby Mercury to about 160 days for distant Pluto. Chapter Two will show you how to determine when a planet is in retrograde motion.

A popular misconception is that a retrograde planet signifies something unpleasant. It's easy to see why. A retrograde planet prolongs the influence of that planet in its sign and house of a horoscope. If that influence happens to be an unpleasant one, the prolonged unpleasantness will be blamed on that retrograde condition. But in all fairness, if a retrograde planet is producing pleasant circumstances, that too will be prolonged by the retrograde planet.

Chapter Four will tell you the significance of retrograde planets in your horoscope, while Chapter Six will tell you how the retrograde planets affect you as they transit across your horoscope each day.

This brings up another astrological term that you might have heard about—"transits." Each day, as the planets move along in the zodiac, they make aspects with or pass over the positions of the planets in your natal horoscope. (A natal horoscope is the map of the planets in the sky at the time of birth.) The planets' passages over these natal positions are called "transits." They energize the promise of your natal horoscope. You will deal with transits in Chapter Six, where you will learn how to interpret your own daily horoscope based on how the planets transit over your natal horoscope.

You may also have heard the astrological term "progression." Progressions are revisions to your natal horoscope. Each planet is moved forward through the zodiac according to rules such as "1 degree for each year of life." This then provides the progressed horoscope, whose patterns then show the ongoing conditions in your life, at that age. We will not deal with progressed horoscopes in this book. I just thought you might like to know what they are.

Your Horoscope

The horoscope is your basic tool for doing astrology. It is a map of the positions of the planets in the zodiac at a particular time. If it is for your time of birth it is called your natal horoscope. In that case, the positions of the planets would be shown around the zodiac with your Ascendant's sign placed at the left side of the chart. This then shows the planets in the houses as well as in the signs.

Once your planets are arranged on your horoscope wheel, you can begin its interpretation by counting the planets in the different groups of signs and houses. Following that, you can look up the meaning of each planet in its sign and house. Here you may notice that some of the interpretations seem to go against the others. This is to be expected. Most of us are under conflicting influences which we spend our lives trying to resolve.

After you become familiar with the interpretation of your planets in the signs and houses, you can examine the significance of the aspects made between your natal planets. Here again you must recognize that you are at the center of forces which may be pulling you in different directions. The horoscope is useful in showing you these forces.

After you have interpreted your natal horoscope you can go further. You can use it to examine the influences of the transiting planets as they move through the skies each day. Here you must determine the positions of the planets for a particular time of interest and place them on your horoscope wheel, along with your natal planets. A comparison of the transiting planets with your natal planets and with your signs and houses shows you the forces at work at that time.

Finally, you can use your natal horoscope along with the horoscope of an interesting companion to determine how compatible you might be with each other. You will learn how to prepare such a compatibility horoscope, and how to interpret it, in Chapter Seven. If there are any problems between you, your compatibility horoscope will show you the probable causes of those problems.

There you have it. All you need to know about the planets, signs, houses, rising sign, aspects, transits, and other terms used by astrologers when they do astrology. You are now ready to take the first step in doing your own astrology.

Chapter Two

How to Find Your Planets

The first step in doing astrology is to find out where the planets were in the skies on the day you were born. This chapter shows you how you can do that in less than ten minutes. That's because you won't have to do any calculations. A set of look-up tables gives you all the information you need. To make it even easier, special worksheets guide you through the tables, and help you to identify the important relationships between the planets.

The fastest way to learn how to use these tables is to do your own horoscope as you follow me through a typical example. Once you see how it's done, you won't have any trouble doing it yourself.

Finding the Planets' Sky Positions

You can find the positions of all the planets by using Tables 1 through 14 at the back of the book, along with Worksheet I—Planet Positions. A supply of these worksheets is also provided at the back of the book. But you can see what they look like in Figure 2–1. Please look at it now.

NAME: Jackie Kennedy Onassis
DATE: July 28, 1929 TIME: 4 P.M. ☑ DAYLIGHT SAVING

PLANET	ROW LETTER	KEY NUMBER	SKY POSITION		RETRO. (✓)
SUN			(1)	(SU) 13	
MOON	(2) U	(3) 22	(4)	(MO) 4	
MERCURY	(5) GG	(6) 10	(7)	(ME) 13	–
VENUS	(8) GG	(8) 1	(9)	(VE) 9	–
MARS	(10) DD	(10) 19	(11)	(MA) 17	–
JUPITER		(12) 7	(13)	(JU) 8	–
SATURN			(14)	(SA) 27	✓
URANUS			(14)	(UR) 1	✓
NEPTUNE			(14)	(NE) 16	–
PLUTO			(14)	(PL) 11	–
ASCENDANT			(15)	(AS) 25	

Figure 2–1. Worksheet I—Planet Positions

Notice the numbered spaces in each of the columns. These numbers tell you which table to use for getting the information for those spaces. The letters in the column headed "Sky Position" are the abbreviations you can use for the planets listed in the first column.

Let's get started. Get a copy of Worksheet I from the back of the book. Write your name and birth date on the top. If you know your time of birth, write that also.

I will work through the tables using Jackie Kennedy Onassis's birth date, July 28, 1929, at 4:00 P.M., Eastern Daylight Saving

Time. You should follow me through each step, and then do the same thing, using your own birth date instead of Jackie's. Let's begin.

Finding Your Sun (Table 1)

The position of the Sun is found from Table 1: Sun—Sky Positions. Please look at it now. Notice the dates in the first column, followed by the Sky Position numbers in the second column. You will recall from Chapter One that these Sky Positions are the 10-degree sectors of the zodiac, the decans numbered from 1 to 36. Each sign of the zodiac (shown in the last column) is covered by 3 decans. The "DEG." column shows where each decan is centered in its sign, as described in Chapter One. For example, decan 1 covers Aries from 0 to 10 degrees, centered at 5 degrees.

Notice that the dates on each line cover a ten-day interval. The Sky Positions on each line tell you where the Sun can be found during that ten-day interval. Jackie Kennedy's birth date, July 28, falls on the line for the interval JUL 24–AUG 2. During that period of time, the Sun can be found in Sky Position 13, which is in the sign of Leo.

Now look up the Sun's Sky Position for your own birth date. After you find it in Table 1, write it in space #1 on your worksheet. Write only the position *number*, not its sign in the zodiac. We will deal with the signs of the zodiac when we get to Worksheet II. For now, we only want to find the Sky Position numbers for each of your planets.

Finding Your Moon (Tables 2, 3, and 4)

The Moon's Sky Position is found in three easy steps. First you find a Row Letter, then a Key Number, and finally a Sky Position. You start with your birth date.

Table 2: Moon Row Letters: Find the Moon's Row Letter at the intersection of the *line* on which you find your birth *year*, and the *column* in which you find your birth *month*. For Jackie, the Moon's Row Letter for July 1929 is U, at the intersection of line 1929 and the JUL column.

Now, find the Moon's Row Letter for your own birth date. After you find it in Table 2, write it in space #2 on your worksheet.

Table 3: Moon Key Numbers: Find the Moon's Key Number at the intersection of the *line* for the Moon's *Row Letter*, and the *column* for your *day* of birth. For Jackie, the Moon's Key Number is at the intersection of Row Letter "U" and column "28" (for July 28). That Key Number is "22."

CAUTION: Be sure to read the *day* of the month from the *top row* of Table 3. The numbers along the other rows of the table are Key Numbers, not dates.

Now, find your Moon's Key Number by using your Moon's Row Number and your day of birth in Table 3. When you find it, write it in space #3 on your worksheet.

Table 4: Moon—Sky Positions: Find the Moon's Sky Position at the intersection of the *line* for the birth *date*, and the *column* for the Moon's *Key Number*. Jackie's date, July 28, and her Key Number, 22, intersect at a Sky Position of 4. Notice that July 28 falls on the date line JUL 24–AUG 2. That was the same date line you used for finding her Sun's Sky Position. The zodiac symbol following each date shows you the Sun sign for that date.

Now, find your own Moon's Sky Position from Table 4, and write it in space #4 on your worksheet.

Finding Your Mercury (Tables 5, 6, and 7)

Mercury's Sky Position is found in three steps also. First you find the Row Letter leading to the Key Number, which then takes you to the Sky Position.

Table 5: Mercury Row Letters: Find Mercury's Row Letter at the intersection of the *line* on which you find your birth *year*, and the column in which you find your birth *month*. Jackie's Row Letter for July 1929 is "GG," at the intersection of line 1929 and column JUL.

Find Mercury's Row Letter for your birth date from Table 5 and write it in space #5 on your worksheet.

Table 6: Mercury Key Numbers: Find Mercury's Key Number at the intersection of the *line* for its *Row Letter*, and the column for your *day* of birth. Jackie's Key Number for Mercury is 10, at the intersection of Row Letter GG and day 28 (for July 28). Notice in Table 6 that each column represents two days, as shown by the two dates at the top of each column.

Now find Mercury's Key Number for your own birth date, and write it in space #6 on your worksheet.

Table 7: Mercury—Sky Positions: Find Mercury's Sky Position at the intersection of the *line* for the birth *date*, and the *column* for Mercury's Key Number. Jackie's Sky Position for Mercury is 13, at the intersection of the date line JUL 24–AUG 2, and the column for Key Number 10.

Use Table 7 to find your Mercury Sky Position, and write it in space #7 on your worksheet.

Retrograde Motion

You will recall from Chapter One that the planets may appear to be moving backward as seen from the earth. During such times the planets are said to be in *retrograde motion*. The interpretation of a horoscope can be enhanced if you know which planets are in retrograde motion at a given time.

The Sky Position tables tell you when a planet is in retrograde motion. When a Sky Position number falls into one of the shaded areas of a table, the planet is in retrograde motion at that time. Look at Table 7 now to see what these shaded areas look like. Areas of retrograde motion are also shown on Tables 9, 11, 13, and 14, for the other planets. (NOTE: The shaded areas of the other tables are to help you look up the numbers more easily.)

When you find a Sky Position number in a shaded area, place a check mark on your worksheet in the last column (RETRO), next to that Sky Position number. If your Sky Position does not fall into a shaded area, place a dash in that space to show that you did not forget to check it.

Now, go back to Table 7 and check your Mercury Sky Position to see if it fell into a retrograde area. If it did, check your worksheet accordingly. Otherwise, place a dash mark next to your Mercury Sky Position.

Finding Your Venus (Tables 8 and 9)

Venus's Sky Position is also found by first finding its Row Letter and Key Number for your birth date.

Table 8: Venus Row Letters and Key Numbers: Your Row Letter and Key Number for Venus are both in the same table. Row Letters are in the upper part of the table, while the Key Numbers are in the bottom.

You should have no trouble finding Row Letters by now. Just find the intersection of the *line* for the *year*, and the *column* for the *month* of birth. Look at Table 8 and find Jackie's Row Letter for Venus at the intersection of the 1929 line and the JUL column. Her Row Letter is GG (it's just a coincidence that this is the same as her Row Letter for Mercury).

Now, use Table 8 to find your own Venus Row Letter. When you find it, write it in space #8, in the Row Letter column of your worksheet.

Your *Key Number* is found at the intersection of the *Row Letter* line and the *day-of-the-month* column on the lower part of Table 8. Notice that each day-of-the-month column represents a six-day interval between the two dates shown at the top of each column.

Look at Table 8 and find the Key Number for Jackie's Venus.

It's at the intersection of Row Letter GG and the column that includes the 28th. You should have found Key Number 1 (day 28 falls in the column 25–31).

Now find your own Key Number for Venus and write it on your worksheet in the Key Number column in space #8.

Table 9: Venus—Sky Positions: Find Venus's Sky Position at the intersection of the *line* for the birth *date*, and the *column* for Venus's *Key Number*. Venus's Sky Position for Jackie's date of July 28 is found at the intersection of the line JUL 24–AUG 2 and her Venus Key Number, 1. That Sky Position is 9.

Now find your own Venus Sky Position from Table 9 and write it in space #9 on your worksheet. Be sure to check for retrograde motion if your Sky Position falls in a shaded area on Table 9. Otherwise, write a dash in the space following the Sky Position.

Finding Your Mars (Tables 10 and 11)

As you have probably guessed by now, Mars's Sky Position is found from its Key Number, which in turn is found from its Row Letter.

Table 10: Mars—Row Letters and Key Numbers: Again, as with the Venus table, both the Row Letter and Key Number are on the same table. However, in this case the Row Letter is listed next to your *year* of birth, rather than at the intersection of the year and month. If you look at the top part of Table 10, you can see that Jackie's Row Letter for Mars is DD, right next to her birth year, 1929.

Find the Row Letter for Mars for your own birth year, and write it in the Row Letter column of your worksheet, in space #10.

Once you have your Row Letter, you can find your Mars Key Number in the bottom part of Table 10. The *Key Number* is at the intersection of the *line* for your *Row Letter*, and the column for your *month and day* of birth.

Please look at Table 10 now so that you can see how it differs from the other tables. Notice that the columns for the months are divided into two columns. The first half is for dates from the 1st to the 15th of the month. The second half is for dates from the 16th to the end of the month.

Now see if you can find Jackie's Key Number. Her Mars Row Letter was DD, and she was born on July 28. Notice that the intersection of the line for Row Letter DD and the column containing July 28 (i.e., column 16–31) shows the Key Number to be 19.

Find your own Mars Key Number from Table 10 and write it in the Key Number column of your worksheet, in space #10.

Table 11: Mars—Sky Positions: Find Mars's Sky Position at the intersection of the *line* for the birth *date* and the *column* for Mars's *Key Number*. Jackie's Sky Position for Mars is at the intersection of the line JUL 24–AUG 2 and the column for her Mars Key Number, 19. Her Mars Sky Position is 17. Since that number is not in a shaded area of the table, her Mars is not in retrograde motion.

Now find your own Mars Sky Position, using your Mars Key Number along with your date of birth. Write it in space #11. If it is not in retrograde motion, write a dash in the last column, next to the Sky Position.

Finding Your Jupiter (Tables 12 and 13)

Jupiter moves so slowly that its position can be found in two steps; from its Key Number to its Sky Position.

Table 12: Jupiter Key Numbers: If you look at Table 12 you will see that Jupiter's Key Number is found at the intersection of the *line* for the birth *year* and the *column* for the birth *month*. You should notice that each of the columns represents three months.

You can see that Jackie's Key Number for July 1929 is 7.

Find your own Key Number for Jupiter by using your birth date in Table 12, and then write it in space #12 on your worksheet.

Table 13: Jupiter—Sky Positions: Find Jupiter's Sky Position at the intersection of the *line* for the birth *date*, and the *column* for Jupiter's *Key Number*. For Jackie that would be on the line JUL 24–AUG 2, and the column 7. Therefore, her Jupiter was in Sky Position 8. It was not retrograde.

Now find your own Jupiter Sky Position from Table 13, and write it in space #13 on your worksheet. Be sure to check it for retrograde motion if it falls in a shaded area of Table 13.

Finding Your Saturn, Uranus, Neptune, and Pluto (Table 14)

The four "outer planets"—Saturn, Uranus, Neptune, and Pluto—move so slowly that their Sky Positions can be found in a single step, using Table 14. If you look at Table 14 you can see the list of years, followed by a column for each of these planets. The numbers in the columns are the Sky Positions for those planets during the year shown.

The Sky Positions for these outer planets during Jackie's birth year 1929 are as follows: Saturn, 27, Uranus, 1, Neptune, 16, and Pluto, 11.

Now notice the four charts on the lower part of Table 14. There is one chart for each of the outer planets. These charts help you to determine when those planets are in retrograde motion.

Please look at Table 14. Each of the horizontal spaces represents a ten-year interval. Your birth year falls into one of these intervals. For example, if you were born in 1929, your birth year would be represented by an imaginary horizontal line close to the bottom of the space marked 1921–1930. If you were born in

1925, your birth year would be represented by an imaginary line halfway across that same interval.

The columns on these charts represent the months. The first of each month is at the left side of each column, while the end of the month is at the right edge. July 28 would be near the right edge of the July column.

If the intersection of your birth-year line and your birth-month column falls in a shaded area on any of these charts, that planet was in retrograde motion on the day you were born.

Let's check Jackie's case on Table 14. You can see that 1929 would be near the bottom of the interval for 1921–1930, and July 28 would be near the right edge of the July column. That intersection, the imaginary horizontal line for 1929 and the right edge of the July column, falls in a shaded area on the chart for Saturn. Therefore, Jackie's Saturn was in retrograde motion when she was born. The same holds true for the chart for Uranus. However, that intersection of 1929 and July 28 on the Neptune and Pluto charts falls into the clear areas, showing that these two planets were in direct motion when she was born.

Now find the Sky Positions of the four outer planets on Table 14 for your birth year. Write them in the proper spaces on your worksheet (space #14 on the line for each planet). Be sure to check the charts on that table to see if any of your outer planets were in retrograde motion. Note that with a check mark or dash mark in the last column of your worksheet, next to their Sky Positions.

Finding Your Ascendant (Table 15)

You will recall from Chapter One that your Ascendant is the part of the zodiac that was just rising on the eastern horizon at the time of your birth. We will represent your Ascendant by the Sky Position number of that part of the zodiac.

Table 15 shows the Sky Position number of the Ascendant for

each hour of the day throughout the year. You will find the table at the back of the book.

Notice that morning and afternoon hours are listed across the top row. These are Standard Time. If you were born during Daylight Saving Time, subtract one hour from your birth time before using this table.

The Sky Position for your Ascendant is found at the intersection of the *line* for your *date* of birth and the *column* for your *hour* of birth. Jackie was born at 4 P.M. Eastern Daylight Saving Time. Since this table is for Standard Time, we must subtract one hour from her birth time. Therefore we look for the intersection of her birth date, July 28, and the column for 3 P.M. Notice that her Ascendant was in Sky Position 25. That is in Sagittarius (see Table 1). Again, we are looking only for the Sky Position numbers at this time, not for their signs in the zodiac.

Few people will know their exact birth time, and therefore will guess it to the nearest full hour. However, if you know your exact birth time, use the hour column that comes closest to it. For example, if you were born between 8:00 and 8:30, use the Sky Position you find in the column for eight o'clock. If you were born between 8:30 and 9:00, use the Sky Position number shown in the nine o'clock column.

If you were born exactly on the half hour, say at 8:30, use either the eight o'clock column or the nine o'clock column for your Ascendant's Sky Position number and then see how your horoscope interpretation turns out. If it seems wrong to you, use the other Sky Position number.

Notice in some cases that the Sky Positions between adjacent columns in Table 15 may skip a number. For example, on the first row (JAN 1–10) the Sky Position for 4:00 A.M. is 24, while the Sky Position for 5:00 A.M. is 26—skipping over 25. In such cases, use the intermediate Sky Position number to represent the Ascendant for someone born at the half hour (4:30 A.M. in this case). Notice on Table 15 that if you were born on March 22, at 11:30 A.M., your Ascendant would be in Sky Position 11.

Now look up your Ascendant's Sky Position number in Table 15 and write it in space #15 on Worksheet I. Once you have found your Ascendant, you are finished with this worksheet and are ready to move on to the next one. But before you do, here is a summary of the tables used for finding the Row Letters, Key Numbers, and Sky Positions for each of the planets:

Planet	*Row Letters*	*Key Numbers*	*Sky Positions*
Sun	——	——	Table 1
Moon	Table 2	Table 3	Table 4
Mercury	Table 5	Table 6	Table 7
Venus	Table 8	Table 8	Table 9
Mars	Table 10	Table 10	Table 11
Jupiter	——	Table 12	Table 13
Saturn/Uranus/ Neptune/Pluto	——	——	Table 14
Ascendant	——	——	Table 15

Your Planets in the Signs

After finding your planet positions you must see how they are distributed among the signs of the zodiac. I have made that easy for you by providing a special worksheet. It is called Worksheet II—Planets in the Signs and Houses. You can find a supply at the back of the book. Get one now and write your name and birth date at the top. Figure 2–2 shows Worksheet II partially completed for Jackie's planets.

Notice that there are several parts to the worksheet, each identified by a letter. That makes it easier for me to take you through the steps in filling it out. Let's start with Section A—Planet Sky Position.

Section A—Planet Sky Position: This section helps show you the placement of your planets among the signs of the zodiac.

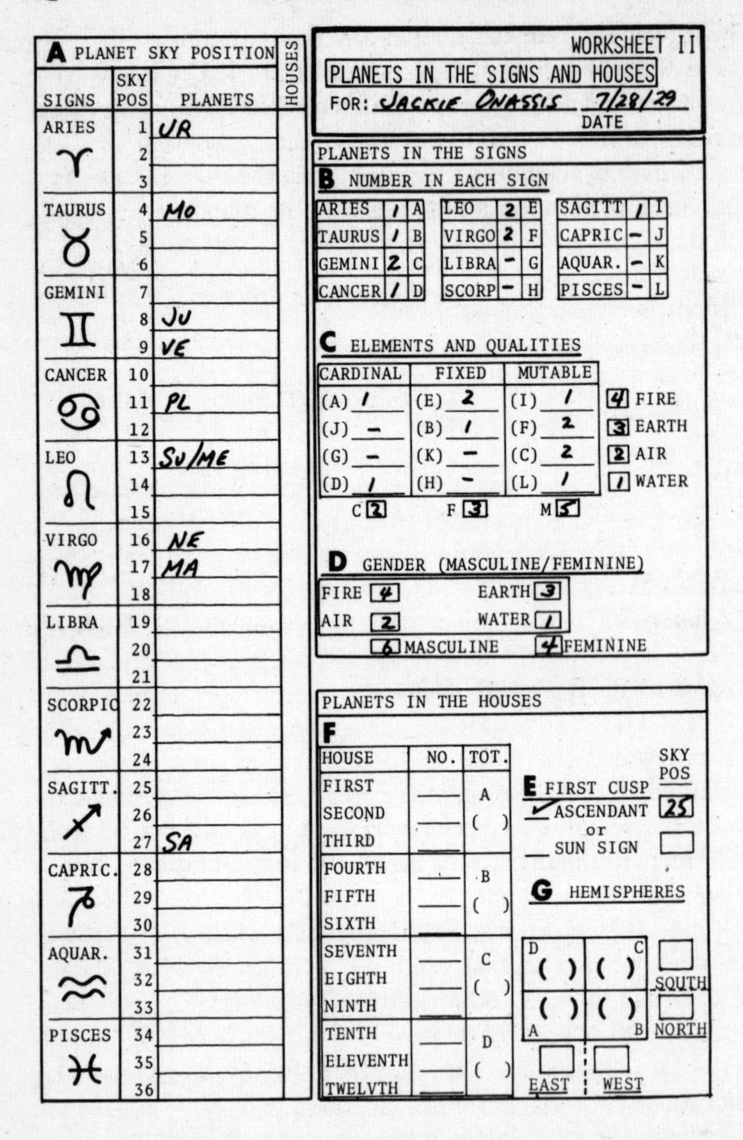

A PLANET SKY POSITION

SIGNS	SKY POS	PLANETS	HOUSES
ARIES ♈	1	UR	
	2		
	3		
TAURUS ♉	4	MO	
	5		
	6		
GEMINI ♊	7		
	8	JU	
	9	VE	
CANCER ♋	10		
	11	PL	
	12		
LEO ♌	13	SU/ME	
	14		
	15		
VIRGO ♍	16	NE	
	17	MA	
	18		
LIBRA ♎	19		
	20		
	21		
SCORPIO ♏	22		
	23		
	24		
SAGITT. ♐	25		
	26		
	27	SA	
CAPRIC. ♑	28		
	29		
	30		
AQUAR. ♒	31		
	32		
	33		
PISCES ♓	34		
	35		
	36		

WORKSHEET II

PLANETS IN THE SIGNS AND HOUSES

FOR: JACKIE ONASSIS 7/28/29
DATE

PLANETS IN THE SIGNS

B NUMBER IN EACH SIGN

ARIES	1	A	LEO	2	E	SAGITT	1	I
TAURUS	1	B	VIRGO	2	F	CAPRIC	–	J
GEMINI	2	C	LIBRA	–	G	AQUAR.	–	K
CANCER	1	D	SCORP	–	H	PISCES	–	L

C ELEMENTS AND QUALITIES

CARDINAL	FIXED	MUTABLE	
(A) 1	(E) 2	(I) 1	4 FIRE
(J) –	(B) 1	(F) 2	3 EARTH
(G) –	(K) –	(C) 2	2 AIR
(D) 1	(H) –	(L) 1	1 WATER
C 2	F 3	M 5	

D GENDER (MASCULINE/FEMININE)

FIRE 4 EARTH 3
AIR 2 WATER 1
6 MASCULINE 4 FEMININE

PLANETS IN THE HOUSES

F

HOUSE	NO.	TOT.
FIRST		A
SECOND		( )
THIRD		
FOURTH		B
FIFTH		( )
SIXTH		
SEVENTH		C
EIGHTH		( )
NINTH		
TENTH		D
ELEVENTH		( )
TWELVTH		

E FIRST CUSP — SKY POS
✓ ASCENDANT 25
or
SUN SIGN

G HEMISPHERES

D ( ) ( ) C — SOUTH
A ( ) ( ) B — NORTH
EAST | WEST

Figure 2–2. Worksheet II—Planets in the Signs and Houses

The information for this section comes from the worksheet that you just finished, so keep it in front of you as we go on.

You are going to write the initials of each of your planets on the line number in Section A corresponding with its Sky Position as shown on Worksheet I. Begin by finding your Sun's Sky Position. After you find it, write the letters SU next to that number in the column in Section A. Jackie's Sun was in Sky Position 13, as shown in Figure 2–2.

Next, find your Moon's Sky Position number and write the letters MO next to that number in Section A. Continue down the list of planets on Worksheet I until you have written the initials of all the planets next to their Sky Position numbers in Section A of Worksheet II.

DO NOT WRITE the initials for your Ascendant in this section. However, while it is conveniently in front of you, write the Ascendant's Sky Position number in the space provided in Section E of Worksheet II.

When more than one planet falls in a given Sky Position, write the initials of each of the planets on that line of Section A, as shown for Jackie's Sun and Mercury on line 13 in Figure 2–2.

When you finish, you should have ten planets listed in Section A of Worksheet II.

You can see the signs of the zodiac listed to the left of the three Sky Positions corresponding with each of those signs. These are to help you with the next step.

Section B—Number in Each Sign: This section is a tally of how many planets you have in each of the signs of the zodiac. All you have to do is count the planets in Section A and write the totals next to each of the signs in Section B.

Start by counting the number of planets on lines 1, 2, and 3 in Section A. Write that sum in the space after Aries, in Section B. If there are no planets in Aries, place a dash mark in that space.

Next count the number of planets in Taurus (lines 4, 5, and

6). Write that total in the space after Taurus in Section B. If there were none, place a dash mark in the space.

Continue counting the number of planets in each of the three-space intervals for each sign of the zodiac. Where there is more than one planet on a line, be sure to count them all for your total in that sign-interval.

Write the total number of planets in each sign, in the space next to each sign in Section B. Once you have all the totals in Section B, they must be transferred to Section C.

Section C—Elements and Qualities: This section helps you to find how the planets are distributed among the fire, earth, air, and water signs (the elements), and among the cardinal, fixed, and mutable signs (the qualities). You do that by adding up the number of planets in each sign, as they are arranged in Section C. Let me show you how to do that.

Each of the lettered spaces in Section C corresponds with a letter next to a total written in Section B. The easiest way to transfer these totals to Section C is as follows. Move from space to space across the rows of Section C, each time looking up the number that corresponds with that space's letter, as shown in Section B. For example, you would write the totals for space A, E, I, J, B, F, etc., as you moved across the rows of Section C (see Figure 2–2). Place a dash mark in those spaces for which there are no totals for those letters in Section B.

Once you have transferred all the totals from Section B to Section C, you must add them up across the rows and down the columns. Write these row and column sums in the spaces provided on the worksheet. Notice that the totals across the rows tell you the number of your planets in each of the elements, while the totals down the columns tell you the distribution of your planets among the qualities.

Section D—Gender (Masculine/Feminine): This section tells you how your planets are distributed among the masculine and feminine signs. All you do is write the sums of the planets in the elements, as found in Section C, and add up these numbers as shown on the worksheet. The total of fire and air signs are the masculine signs, while the total of earth and water signs are the feminine signs.

Your Planets in the Houses

The next step, after finding the distribution of your planets among the signs, is to see how they are distributed among the twelve houses. You will recall from Chapter One that your Ascendant marks the beginning of the first house. And that, for our Equal House System, each successive house starts 30 degrees later (3 decans, or 3 Sky Position numbers). With that in mind, let me show you how to identify your natal houses and find out which planets were in each house.

The first step is to find the starting position of your first house. If you found your Ascendant from Table 15, you already have the Sky Position for the beginning of your first house. (It was the last Sky Position you found on Worksheet I, and the one you wrote into Section E on Worksheet II.)

But what do you do when you don't know a time of birth, and therefore can't find your Ascendant? In such a case you use the Sky Position of your natal Sun as the beginning of your first house. That assumes you were born around sunrise. Statistics show that more people are born nearer to sunrise than at other hours of the day. A horoscope that is set up on the basis of your Sun's Sky Position is called a Solar Chart.

If you must set up a Solar Chart, check the "Sun Sign" box in Section E of Worksheet II, and write in the Sky Position of your Sun in the space provided there.

Section F—Planets in the Houses: This section is a tally of how many planets you have in each of your natal houses. Before you can count them, you must first mark off the houses in the last column of Section A. Here's how to do that.

You must first draw a circle around the Sky Position of your Ascendant in the column of numbers in Section A. Your Ascendant's Sky Position should be in Section E of the worksheet. If you don't have an Ascendant, circle the Sky Position of your natal Sun.

Now draw a line across the top of the space you just circled, extending it across the narrow space of the last column (Houses). Figure 2–3 shows how such a line is drawn across the last column, at the top of a space that was circled for an Ascendant Sky Position of 20.

The line you just drew marks the beginning of your first house. Your second house begins three lines below that. Draw a line across the last column at that third line, as shown in Figure 2–3. Write the number 1 in the last column, between the two lines you just drew. Planets which fall between these two lines are in your first house

Continue to draw lines across the last column at every third line. When you reach the bottom of the column, continue the count down the top of the column (see Figure 2–3). After you have drawn all the lines, go back to number the spaces from 1 to 12, starting from the 1 you already wrote in.

These numbered three-space intervals in the last column show the boundaries of your natal houses.

Once you have these boundaries for your houses, it is a simple matter to count how many planets fall within those boundaries in Section A, and to write those totals in the space provided for them in Section F.

CAUTION: When you count the planets in the houses, be sure to use the boundaries made by your lines in the last column, rather than the lines across the first column that you used for counting the number of planets in the signs.

When there are no planets in a house, show that by placing a dash mark next to that house in Section F.

After you have tallied the number of planets in each of the houses, find the four sums identified as A, B, C, and D in Section F (see Figure 2–3).

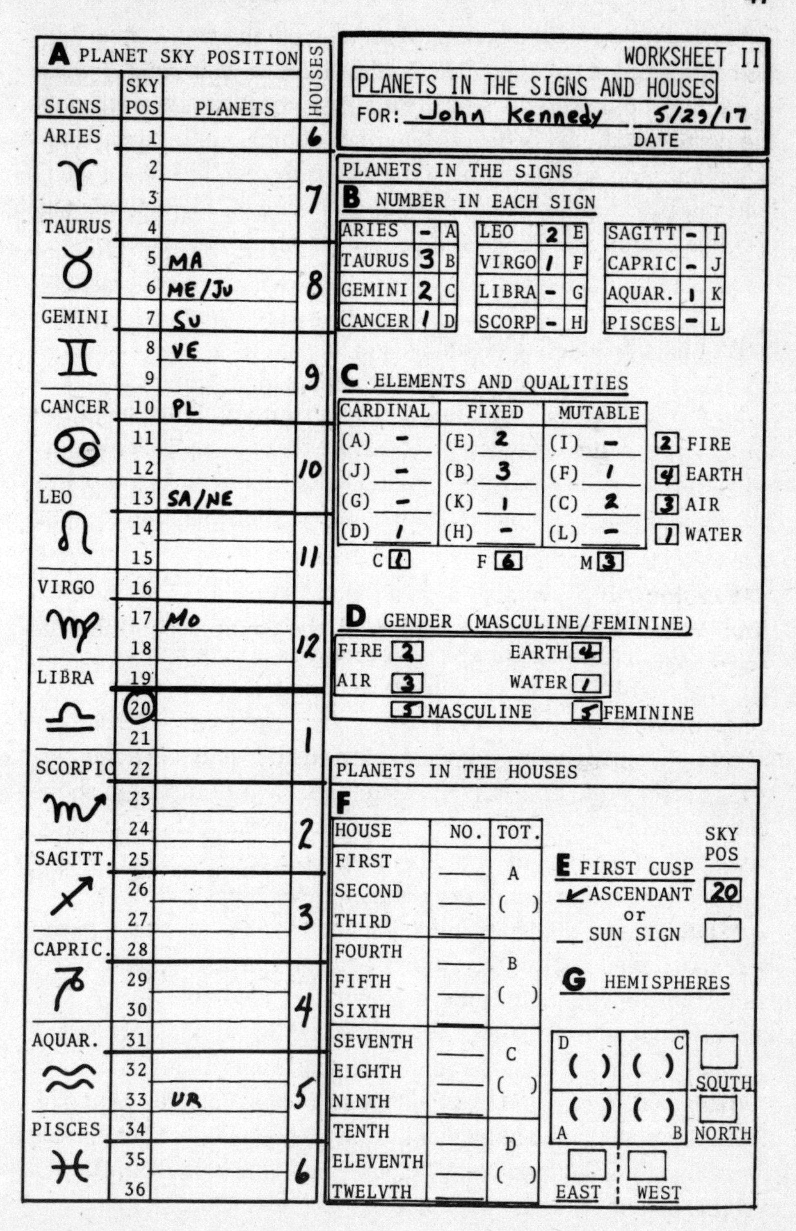

A PLANET SKY POSITION

SIGNS	SKY POS	PLANETS	HOUSES
ARIES	1		6
♈	2		
	3		7
TAURUS	4		
♉	5	MA	
	6	ME/JU	8
GEMINI	7	SU	
♊	8	VE	
	9		9
CANCER	10	PL	
♋	11		
	12		10
LEO	13	SA/NE	
♌	14		
	15		11
VIRGO	16		
♍	17	MO	
	18		12
LIBRA	19		
♎	(20)		
	21		1
SCORPIO	22		
♏	23		
	24		2
SAGITT.	25		
♐	26		
	27		3
CAPRIC.	28		
♑	29		
	30		4
AQUAR.	31		
♒	32		
	33	UR	5
PISCES	34		
♓	35		6
	36		

WORKSHEET II

PLANETS IN THE SIGNS AND HOUSES

FOR: John Kennedy 5/29/17
DATE

PLANETS IN THE SIGNS

B NUMBER IN EACH SIGN

ARIES	-	A	LEO	2	E	SAGITT	-	I
TAURUS	3	B	VIRGO	1	F	CAPRIC	-	J
GEMINI	2	C	LIBRA	-	G	AQUAR.	1	K
CANCER	1	D	SCORP	-	H	PISCES	-	L

C ELEMENTS AND QUALITIES

CARDINAL	FIXED	MUTABLE	
(A) -	(E) 2	(I) -	2 FIRE
(J) -	(B) 3	(F) 1	4 EARTH
(G) -	(K) 1	(C) 2	3 AIR
(D) 1	(H) -	(L) -	1 WATER
C 1	F 6	M 3	

D GENDER (MASCULINE/FEMININE)

FIRE 2 EARTH 4
AIR 3 WATER 1
5 MASCULINE 5 FEMININE

PLANETS IN THE HOUSES

F

HOUSE	NO.	TOT.
FIRST	___	A
SECOND	___	( )
THIRD	___	
FOURTH	___	B
FIFTH	___	( )
SIXTH	___	
SEVENTH	___	C
EIGHTH	___	( )
NINTH	___	
TENTH	___	D
ELEVENTH	___	( )
TWELVTH	___	

E FIRST CUSP — SKY POS
✓ ASCENDANT 20
or
___ SUN SIGN [ ]

G HEMISPHERES

D ( )	C ( )	[ ] SOUTH
A ( )	B ( )	[ ] NORTH
[ ] EAST	[ ] WEST	

Figure 2–3. Setting Up the Houses on Worksheet II

Section G—Hemispheres: This section shows the distribution of your planets among the hemispheres of your natal houses.

Each of the lettered totals in Section F must be transferred to the correspondingly lettered box in Section G. After you have done that, add up the numbers across each row and down each column, placing the totals in the spaces shown. Those totals tell you how many planets you have in each of the hemispheres.

The Horoscope Wheel

Your Worksheet II contains all the information you need for interpreting your horoscope. However, there is another way to show this information which makes it easier to see how transiting planets fall on your natal horoscope, or how a companion's planets fall on yours. That other way is to use the familiar Horoscope Wheel. Figure 2–4 shows a Horoscope Wheel filled out for *John* Kennedy, who was born at 3:00 P.M., EST, on May 29, 1917—his Ascendant's Sky Position was 20 (mid-Libra). You can find blank Horoscope Wheels at the back of this book.

Here's how to use it. First notice that the blank Horoscope Wheels do not have numbers written in the spaces around the rim of the wheel. You have to write your own numbers in these spaces, starting from the space at the left marked ASC. Find the Sky Position number of your Ascendant (or your Sun Sign if you have no Ascendant), and write it in the ASC space.

After you have written your Ascendant's Sky Position number, write the next higher number in the space below it. Continue writing higher numbers, moving around the wheel in a counterclockwise direction. When you get to 36, make the next number 1, and continue until all the spaces are filled.

After you have numbered all the spaces on the rim, you can place the planets on the wheel in the spaces corresponding with their Sky Position numbers. Be sure that you keep the planets within their proper spaces, as shown in Figure 2–4.

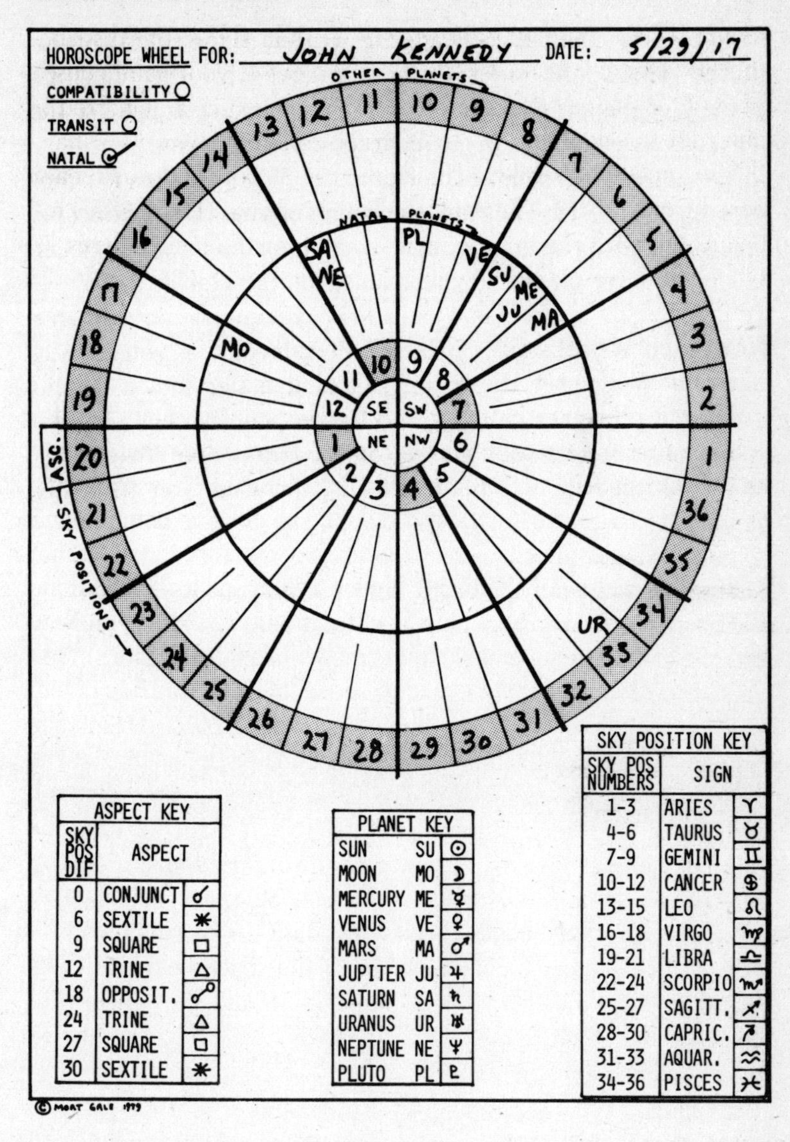

ASPECT KEY		
SKY POS DIF	ASPECT	
0	CONJUNCT	☌
6	SEXTILE	✱
9	SQUARE	□
12	TRINE	△
18	OPPOSIT.	☍
24	TRINE	△
27	SQUARE	□
30	SEXTILE	✱

PLANET KEY		
SUN	SU	☉
MOON	MO	☽
MERCURY	ME	☿
VENUS	VE	♀
MARS	MA	♂
JUPITER	JU	♃
SATURN	SA	♄
URANUS	UR	♅
NEPTUNE	NE	♆
PLUTO	PL	♇

SKY POSITION KEY		
SKY POS NUMBERS	SIGN	
1-3	ARIES	♈
4-6	TAURUS	♉
7-9	GEMINI	♊
10-12	CANCER	♋
13-15	LEO	♌
16-18	VIRGO	♍
19-21	LIBRA	♎
22-24	SCORPIO	♏
25-27	SAGITT.	♐
28-30	CAPRIC.	♑
31-33	AQUAR.	♒
34-36	PISCES	♓

Figure 2–4. Horoscope Wheel for John Kennedy

Notice that the natal planets are written in the middle circle of the wheel. The outer circle is reserved for the transiting planets, or planets in a companion's horoscope. You will use the outer circle when you get to Chapters Six and Seven.

The innermost circle of the Horoscope Wheel is already numbered from 1 to 12. These are the houses of your natal horoscope, beginning with the first house at your Ascendant's Sky Position. Once you have placed all your planets on the Horoscope Wheel you can easily see which houses they occupy. Remember, the Horoscope Wheel simply presents the information you already have on Worksheet II—it just makes it easier to see certain important planetary patterns, and to compare two horoscopes.

The other information you see on the Horoscope Wheel, such as the Aspect Key, will be described later when you are ready to use it.

You are now ready to begin interpreting your horoscope.

Chapter Three

Your First Look at the Horoscope

Once you have filled out Worksheet II, Planets in the Signs and Houses, you are ready to make a preliminary analysis of your horoscope. This analysis is based on the way the planets are distributed among the signs and houses. I'm not talking about where particular planets are found in specific signs or houses. You will look at those in the next chapter. Right now you are going to look at how the planets are clustered in the different kinds of signs, and in the different groups of houses. You will be surprised at how much you can learn about yourself from such a simple inspection of your horoscope.

Planets in the Elements—Fire, Earth, Air, and Water

You will recall from Chapter One that the signs of the zodiac are grouped into four basic elements: fire, earth, air, and water. The number of natal planets in each of these elements indicates how you approach life—enthusiastically, practically, intellectually, or emotionally.

Most people will have two or three planets evenly distributed among all four elements, signifying a balanced approach to life. However, if you find *four or more* planets in one element, it signifies that the characteristics of that element are overemphasized in your life. Conversely, if you find *no planets* in one or more of the elements, the characteristics of those elements are underemphasized. Either case indicates the need to make an effort to compensate for the excess or deficiency, so as to bring about a better balance in your life.

The characteristics associated with each of the elements are described briefly in the following paragraphs. These characteristics will show up, more or less, according to the number of planets you have in each of the elements. You can find how many planets you have in each element by looking in Section C of your Worksheet II.

Uniform Distribution (Balanced)

If you have two or three planets in each of the elements you are a well-balanced person. Enthusiasm will be tempered by practicality, and logic will be balanced by emotions. You can get very excited about planning a vacation, or you can cancel a vacation without remorse if it becomes necessary to do so. You think things out carefully before coming to a decision; but you can also make a decision impulsively. You live your life in the here-and-now, unconcerned by memories of the past or by warnings about the future.

Fire-Sign Emphasis (Enthusiastic)

If you have four or more planets in the fire signs you approach life with high hopes. That's because you have developed a deep sense of self-worth, in spite of those occasional setbacks. You make decisions quickly and easily, especially when you follow your hunches rather than try to think things out logically. You have many creative urges, but need considerable freedom to express them. The slightest restraints turn you off. You are always on the lookout for opportunities to lead, and often find them. Your willing followers are attracted by your exuberance and enthusiasm for new projects. However, when you undertake a new project, you should finish it quickly. Otherwise you will lose interest and go looking for new challenges. You can easily become a central figure in a large organization since higher ups quickly recognize your leadership potential.

Earth-Sign Emphasis (Practical)

If you have four or more planets in the earth signs, you are dependable, strong-willed, and would rather keep to yourself. Yours is always the practical approach in getting things done. You may be a slow starter, but you will stick to something until you can show concrete results. And you usually do. Your great skill at managing money and other physical resources makes you an excellent executive. You could do very well at organizing and operating a large enterprise. A major problem would be in overcoming your stubborn resistance to change. Friends consider you to be conservative; others say you are obstinate. In either case, you resist change until it can be shown that it makes sense on the basis of practical considerations. You will always find a way to accumulate what you require for your physical needs, which too often become more important to you than other needs. You take excellent care of your body and your personal surroundings.

Air-Sign Emphasis (Intellectual)

If you have four or more planets in the air signs, you are an "idea person" who focuses on the larger things in life. Your agile mind scoops up thousands of facts and quickly sorts out the significant from the insignificant. You're on the lookout for anything that can make life more meaningful for mankind. (You're less concerned about any one person.) You can think fast and clearly, and you can organize your life down to the smallest detail. Once you understand something (and you can understand almost anything!) you take special joy in communicating it to anyone who will listen. Objectivity is your passion. You use your mind like a surgeon's knife to cut away any irrelevancy. Unfortunately, many of your "irrelevancies" are the emotional enrichments of life. But emotions only confuse you; especially your own.

Your friends find your objectivity to be more like indifference or detachment. You often have to think and rethink something, again and again, before you are willing to make a commitment. Yet you work well with all sorts of people because you don't get deeply involved with them.

Water-Sign Emphasis (Emotional)

If you have four or more planets in the water signs, you are especially sensitive to everything going on around you. You seem to be able to tune in to what people are thinking or feeling. You also seem to know what's going to happen next, like when the phone is going to ring. Your strongest feelings are about your family and home. Too often you take on the moods and feelings of those around you, leading to confusion and feelings of insecurity. For your own sense of purpose in life you have to guard against developing a dependence on others. You spend too much time remembering the past. That's because you want to ignore the stressful present and the fearful future. You are always on the lookout for opportunities to use your active imagination. You love to design party settings, or decorate your own home. You would thrive in a job where you had to create a new ad campaign, design a store window or a landscape, or help in restoring a colonial village.

Most of your decisions are based on your hunches and feelings rather than logical considerations. But after you make your decision, you are never quite sure that it was the right one.

If you feel that you would like to get a "second opinion" about what your elements have to say about you, you can do so by looking at the element associated with your Ascendant. You can find the sign of your Ascendant from Section E on your Worksheet II. The element for that sign can be found from this list:

FIRE SIGNS: Aries, Leo, Sagittarius
EARTH SIGNS: Taurus, Virgo, Capricorn
AIR SIGNS: Gemini, Libra, Aquarius
WATER SIGNS: Cancer, Scorpio, Pisces

The Ascendant's element can be more important than the elements for Uranus', Neptune's, or Pluto's signs. That's because these planets have more to say about group behavior than your individual behavior. The Ascendant's sign plays a major role in setting up the urges which motivate your own daily behavior. If there seems to be a tie in the decision as to which element predominates your horoscope, let your Ascendant be the tie-breaker.

Masculine or Feminine?

You recall from Chapter One that the masculine signs are the fire and air signs, while the feminine signs are the earth and water signs. (You will also recall that I don't know how to avoid the sexist overtones of these very ancient designators.) A count of your planets in the masculine and feminine signs can show if you prefer to take the initiative in your life or to wait for the right moment before making your moves.

You can find the number of planets among the masculine and feminine signs in Section D of your Worksheet II. Compare your distribution with the brief descriptions below.

Evenly Distributed (Balanced)

If you have no more than six planets in either the masculine or feminine signs, you are a well-balanced person. You are well aware of your inner needs and you know how to take care of them. You are patient and can endure unpleasant circumstances, yet you have the courage to change them forcefully when necessary. Although you enjoy being the center of the stage, it doesn't bother you to step aside to let someone else have a turn in the limelight. Your occasional bouts with depression don't bother you because you know that you will soon be back up there, feeling like a million.

Masculine Signs Dominant (Outgoing)

If you have seven or more planets in the masculine signs, you are an outgoing person with a charming gift of gab. You are a self-starter concerned with setting things right in the world. However, you are more of an idealist than a practical doer. You depend on your charm and humor to win people over, rather than on persuasive arguments. Your motives are seldom in question, but your impractical approaches are. That's unfortunate, since you have the ability to take something from the planning stage to its completion. The problem is that you don't usually stay with a project long enough to finish it. Your love of excitement and new challenges lead you to other things, and often to the edge of exhaustion. You must learn to take the time to recharge your batteries. It would help even more if you learned to tap into your normally neglected emotional reserves. That would really bring you into balance and bring stability to your daily living.

Feminine Signs Dominant (Reserved)

If you have seven or more planets in the feminine signs, you are serious about everything you do. You are motivated by your need for security, and you take special pains to see that nothing threatens your income, family, or possessions. You are a defender of the traditional values such as honesty, hard work, and responsible behavior. You need to be under some sort of stress before you can feel comfortable. That's because you thrive on hard work which can show off your abilities in getting things done under difficult circumstances. You are also good at carrying emotional burdens without whimpering.

You don't go out of your way to change the world around you. Instead, you bide your time and wait for the right moment to try to improve matters, avoiding confrontations wherever possible. However, if pressed, you can assert yourself with surprising vigor. You get your strength from the faith in your beliefs, and from your determination to endure any difficulty if it will help you to achieve your goals in life.

Planets in the Qualities—Cardinal, Fixed, Mutable

You will recall from Chapter One that the signs of the zodiac are also grouped into three "qualities" called the cardinal, fixed, and mutable signs. A count of your planets in each of these three groups can show whether your actions are more toward initiating, supporting, or steering activities toward their successful conclusions.

You can find your planets in the cardinal, fixed, and mutable signs at the bottom of Section C on your Worksheet II. When you do, compare your distribution with the following descriptions.

Evenly Distributed (Balanced)

If you have no more than four planets in the cardinal, fixed, or mutable signs, your activities are well balanced between getting things started and helping to keep them going or keeping them on the track against changing circumstances. You can come up with new ideas, yet you do not become so attached to them that you can't change your mind in the face of new circumstances or unforeseen problems. You can be just as effective as a team player or a team leader; you handle both positions equally well.

Cardinal Signs Dominant (Decisive Initiator)

If five or more planets fall in the cardinal signs, you are a self-motivated, ambitious, and enterprising realist who likes nothing better than to be in on the ground floor of a promising new business or organization. Your ability to act decisively stems from your quick perception of the potentials for action in any situation. You become impatient with delays imposed by what you feel to be needless concerns for the future consequences of your decisions. Your boundless ambitions are often frustrated by your restless nature and your inability to cope with unexpected problems. If almost all your planets are in the cardinal signs, you should guard against butting into everyone's business where, by this time, you should recognize that you are not welcome.

Fixed Signs Dominant (Determined Supporter)

If you have five or more planets in fixed signs, you have already chosen your goal in life. The problem is that your goal is so far in the future that you can't see how your daily struggles are getting you any closer to it. Since you are a "one-idea person" with an intense sense of purpose, you have to guard against falling into the stubborn pursuit of a "one-track life." On the positive side, you have enormous powers of concentration and will stay with something long after everyone else has given up and left the scene. Yours is the kind of determination that often seeks out some cause to support. The more noble the cause, the more you enjoy your self-sacrifice, dedication, and perseverance in support of that cause. Choose your causes wisely.

Mutable Signs Dominant (Adaptable Mediator)

If you have five or more planets in the mutable signs, you are a chameleon who can change your colors to suit any surrounding or circumstance. Your motto is "I'd rather switch than fight." The ease with which you can recall past experiences gives you the distinct advantage of having all that experience at your fingertips for solving present problems. At best, your friends think of you as versatile, or perhaps changeable. At worst, they are more likely to call you unreliable. With your intellectual outlook, you prefer to think of yourself as flexible and resourceful. You do have that knack for keeping things moving and for stepping in to resolve difficulties as they arise between others. That's because of your inner need for a harmonious environment.

Your only problem is that you find it hard to accept responsibility. Perhaps that's because you spend so much time enjoying memories of the past that you resent the time it would take to deal with the problems of the future.

This completes your inspection of how the planets are distributed among the different kinds of signs. You are now ready to look at how they are distributed among the houses. We're not interested in seeing which planets fall in which houses; that comes up in Chapter Four. All we want to see is how your planets are distributed among the four hemispheres.

Planets in the Hemispheres—East, West, North, South

In Chapter One you saw that the distribution of planets among the houses could be characterized by how many are found in each hemisphere, east, west, north, and south. The number of natal planets in each hemisphere can tell you if you are self-reliant or dependent on others, and whether you are a social or a private person.

You can find the distribution of your planets among the hemispheres in Section G on your Worksheet II. When you find it, compare your distribution with the following descriptions.

Uniform Distribution (Balanced)

If you have five or six planets in each of the hemispheres, you are a balanced person. You don't find it hard to live with the conditions imposed on you by others. But then, too, you don't find it hard to change things when you feel that others are crowding you. You like your privacy, but you also need friends. You can enjoy yourself by being alone with a good book, or by working on a committee to raise funds for a worthy cause. You have learned how to go along with the wishes of others without sacrificing your own best interests.

Eastern-Hemisphere Dominance (Self-Reliance)

If you have seven or more planets in the eastern hemisphere, it signifies that you insist on making your own choices about your goals and your life styles. Your determination and stubborn self-reliance often lead you into confrontations with parents, higher-ups, and friends who feel that they know better what you should do and how you should do it. But you need your freedom of choice more than you need their approval. Above all, you must feel that you are in control of your circumstances.

Your self-starting impulses often lead you into starting more than you can handle. But that's a price you are willing to pay in your efforts to become master of your own destiny.

Western-Hemisphere Dominance (Dependence)

If you have seven or more planets in the western hemisphere, it signifies that you willingly accept, and often seek out, the advice and opinions of others in matters affecting your own life. Not that you can't decide these things for yourself—it's just that your own happiness depends on meeting the needs and wishes of others in your life whom you care about. It isn't important to you that you choose your own path—only that you gain the approval of family and friends for how well you do your thing in following that path. This need for approval makes you vulnerable to a few who might see it as an opportunity for taking advantage of your need to please them. Fortunately, experience teaches you how to protect yourself from such abuse. More often, your cooperative nature brings you the well-earned rewards of success in both personal and business relationships.

Northern-Hemisphere Dominance (Privacy)

If you have seven or more planets in the northern hemisphere, you prefer to keep to yourself. You are happiest when you can attend to your own affairs without worrying about how your actions are going to affect the lives of those around you. This leads you into a narrow range of interests centered around domestic matters. Your friends think of you as an introvert, leading a life of self-imposed loneliness. Little do they know that you prefer your loneliness to the hassles of making connections to a more social life style. You do your best work when you work behind the scenes. The limelight turns you off.

You deal with the world strictly on the basis of your "gut feelings." That becomes a problem because those feelings are often thrown into confusion by sudden changes in your circumstances. That's why you find yourself in those gloomy moods so often. You will have to learn how to turn to others for help in overcoming these bouts with the blues. You can become more sociable without losing your privacy.

Southern-Hemisphere Dominance (Sociability)

If you have seven or more planets in the southern hemisphere, you are energetic in your pursuit of a wide range of interests. These interests are usually focused on social issues rather than personal pursuits. In fact, you are annoyingly aloof when it comes to personal relationships. It is difficult for you to share your inner life with someone else. That's because you are hardly aware of your own inner feelings. They are less interesting to you than what's going on out in the "real world"—that's where the action is, and that's where you want to be! Your interest and dedication come to life when you can link up with some global cause. You thrive on the causes which promise to bring about the greatest social change. Chances are good that you are into energy, ecology, and the nuclear threat.

Your involvements will not include antisocial behavior since you have a strong need to maintain the appearance of respectability. That goes hand in hand with your need for recognition of your natural leadership abilities. These leadership abilities are often recognized and rewarded soon after you have had the opportunity to demonstrate them.

Your Scout Planet

The Scout Planet in your natal horoscope is the last planet to come up over the eastern horizon before the Sun comes up. That relationship makes it important because transiting planets will meet and activate the Scout Planet just before they meet and activate your natal Sun.

You can see your Scout Planet on your Horoscope Wheel by looking for the first planet you come to as you move *clockwise* from the Sun's position. Or you can find the Scout Planet on Worksheet I by finding the planet with the next lower Sky Position number than the Sun's Sky Position. If the Sun is at a low Sky Position number, say 3, and there are no planets at Positions 1 or 2, look for planets in Sky Positions 36, 35, 34, etc., until you come to the first planet.

The following brief descriptions tell you the effects of each planet when they act as Scout Planets. These descriptions are adapted from the work of Frances Sakoian and Louis S. Acker as described in their book *Predictive Astrology* (see Bibliography).

If there is more than one Scout Planet in the same Sky Position, read the interpretation of each one. (Note: There is a space on Worksheet IV for recording your Scout Planet).

The Moon as Scout Planet

You are especially responsive to the demands of practical matters at home or at business. You cope with problems by falling back on the dependable values you learned during childhood. You also depend on your feelings and intuitions to help you in making important decisions.

Mercury as Scout Planet

You have to know everything about something before you can deal with it. So you study books and magazines and you talk to everyone, just to learn all you can. You are attentive to your appearance, and aware of the impression you make on others. You think things out carefully before you act.

Venus as Scout Planet

You are diplomatic in your dealings with friends and business associates. These dealings focus on improving family relationships, business partnerships, or contractual arrangements. You always seem to attract people who can make favorable changes in your surroundings or circumstances.

Mars as Scout Planet

You meet your obstacles head on, and think nothing of challenging whoever or whatever stands in your way. You always manage to trigger a confrontation just before you feel it's time for a change in your life. You live your life fully aware of your personal ambitions and long-range goals.

Jupiter as Scout Planet

You express yourself through generous gestures that accurately reflect your compassion for other people. Your optimistic outlook gives others the confidence to join in your idealistic pursuits or your personal adventures. These usually involve creative efforts to expand the potential for a better life for all.

Saturn as Scout Planet

You are a well-organized person with strong ambitions and a deep sense of responsibility. You are systematic and practical in dealing with daily activities. You depend on an older person for advice and guidance, especially in the matter of your career. Your determination leads to success.

Uranus as Scout Planet

You view the world from an unusual perspective. You have a link to hidden forces, which gives you a deeper understanding of the mysteries of life. Unusual things happen to you, often very abruptly and unexpectedly. You have unique ways of getting things done, which causes people to think of you as being an eccentric.

Neptune as Scout Planet

You are tuned in to the silent messages all around you. Fortunately, you have learned to respect and use your keen intuitions for sorting out the surrounding confusion. Your intuitive abilities can cause difficulties when you try to share your perceptions with others. Don't force your point.

Pluto as Scout Planet

You like to do things secretly, not letting anyone know what you are up to. Perhaps that's because your own keen perceptions let you see into everyone else's hidden thoughts. You just don't want them to see into yours! You are always on the lookout for ways to improve yourself, or for that better idea that will spell success.

These, then, are the kinds of things you can learn about yourself from an over-all look at your horoscope. But it is only the beginning. There's much more. Each piece adds to the picture, sometimes confirming and sometimes conflicting with earlier indications. Conflicting indications do not show "errors" in the horoscope; rather, they reveal the conflicts that we all experience and try to overcome. The horoscope is a useful tool for showing us where these conflicts may be coming from.

The next chapter will add to your picture by showing you how the planets influence you by their appearance in the different signs and houses of your horoscope.

Chapter Four

Planets in the Signs and Houses

As you saw in Chapter One, the planets influence your character (what you are), the signs influence your personality (what you show others), and the houses influence the thrust of your activities (what you focus on). This chapter shows you how the influence of the planets merges with the influence of the signs, and then how they in turn merge with the influence of the houses.

You will need to know where the planets were in the signs and houses at the time you were born. If you have not already done so, find those positions by using the methods described in Chapter Two. When you have found them, transfer the information to Worksheet IV—Summary of Natal Planets. You will find copies of that worksheet at the back of the book. Fill in only those columns that show the signs and house positions of each planet. You will add the planetary aspects when you get to the next chapter.

This chapter is arranged so that you can look up the influence of each planet, first in its sign and then in its house. The order of the planets is the same as the order you find them in on your worksheet, beginning with the Sun.

A final section shows you the influence of your rising sign, or Ascendant.

The Sun

The Sun's position in the zodiac is your familiar Sun sign. The Sun sign shows you how you express your creative urges through conscious acts of will. The following brief profiles describe how your character and personality are reflected in typical behavior patterns.

Sun in Aries. You are action-oriented, with your sights set on achieving a leadership position in life. Your impatience and impulsiveness often leave a wake of unfinished projects. All your clouds have silver linings.

Sun in Taurus. You are purposeful, practical, and plodding; all toward acquiring possessions, pleasures, and security. You must guard against being owned by the things you own, and against holding grudges too long.

Sun in Gemini. You are a nonconformist, seeking new and exciting life styles, especially if you can talk about them! You are easily depressed and need several ongoing interests to keep you happy. Learn to relax.

Sun in Cancer. Your sensitivity to everything going on around you makes you susceptible to wide mood swings. Your greatest joy comes from taking care of family and home matters, or from sharing an emotional experience with a trusted friend.

Sun in Leo. You need others on whom you can bestow your generosity, and with whom you can feel a reciprocal affection. You are a natural leader, but you must learn how to delegate work to others. Vanity makes you touchy.

Sun in Virgo. You are conscientious, practical, and thorough in providing services to others. You are a stickler for detail, even though your interests are wide-ranging. Avoid being too picky with others' faults.

Sun in Libra. You are always trying to make peace and bring harmony into your surroundings at work and at home. Your gentle ways and sense of fairness, backed by your ability to communicate, usually win out in the end.

Sun in Scorpio. You are strong-willed, with a desire for power, often used to exercise control over others. You are sensitive and secretive. You can satisfy your intense desires by your determination and endurance to finish what you start.

Sun in Sagittarius. You are enthusiastic about life but become restless with its routine. You need the continuous excitement of new knowledge or new experiences. You often overlook the practical matters of daily living.

Sun in Capricorn. You are ambitious in setting your goals, and usually attain them by following a careful and practical approach. You carefully avoid the frivolous in the responsible discharge of your duties. Even your fun is serious.

Sun in Aquarius. You are unconventional, always thinking of others first, but in a detached sort of way. That detachment gives you the freedom you need to do your own thing. You are always on the lookout for a better idea.

Sun in Pisces. You are tuned in to the feelings of people all around you. Which is why you need that time to unwind by yourself in pleasant surroundings. You try to help others achieve emotional balance, but only on your terms.

Now look at your Worksheet II to see where the Sun was among the houses of your horoscope. The house occupied by your natal Sun represents the area of activity in which you consciously control your creative energies. These are the activities in which it is important to you to be recognized for your individuality. The following brief behavioral profiles show how your natal Sun affects you when it is found in the different houses of a horoscope.

Sun in First House. You focus your energies on the attainment of a leadership position, especially one that promises power and visible status. You have the strength and determination to succeed at anything you set out to do.

Sun in Second House. You direct your efforts into any activity which promises to bring you financial independence. However, you are more interested in the prestige of being wealthy than in using your wealth wisely.

Sun in Third House. You are out to make your mark in life in any activity that can show off your brilliant mind. You prefer difficult subjects; love to talk, teach, and travel. You are close to your brothers and sisters.

Sun in Fourth House. Your early life is a struggle to acquire a showplace home, preferably on land of your own. Things get easier later as you settle down to enjoy your close family in serene surroundings.

Sun in Fifth House. Your activities center on the pursuit of pleasures—shared with other people—preferably through artistic or romantic exchanges. Your need for dominance also makes you fond of children.

Sun in Sixth House. Your activities must make allowance for your delicate health, and may even center on providing health services to others. You are proud of your work, but need to be recognized and rewarded for it by higher-ups.

Sun in Seventh House. Your activities depend on maintaining close relationships with partners, mate, and friends. You have to guard against dominating those relationships in your search for higher status.

Sun in Eighth House. You are drawn to spiritual concepts that can serve as a basis for your self-improvement efforts. Your interests focus on the larger themes of life. Wealth finally comes to you, but largely through the efforts of others.

Sun in Ninth House. You prefer those activities that require you to move from place to place, and that require you to use your intuition in dealing with problems. You have strong moral convictions, some of which are narrow.

Sun in Tenth House. It makes little difference to you what you do so long as it gives you a chance to climb to the top, where you can receive all the honor and recognition you feel you deserve. You certainly work hard enough to earn it.

Sun in Eleventh House. Whatever you do, you always get help from friends or from a group that shares your novel ideas and interests. You may be interested in humanity, but you often lose sight of the needs of specific individuals.

Sun in Twelfth House. Your activities center on serving the needs of others, often from behind the scenes. You prefer to work in large organizations, especially if they have to do with helping sick or troubled people.

The Moon

The Moon's position in the zodiac shows your unconscious emotional reactions to situations based on your early childhood experiences and family training. The following profiles show how those old responses affect your reactions to new situations.

Moon in Aries. You have a quick temper with anyone who tries to tell you what to do. Learn to pause before you react. Actually, you just take things too personally. Fortunately, you quickly forget your last outburst.

Moon in Taurus. You need someone to get you started on projects—but you can finish them easily if no one hurries you. You like good food, creature comforts, and security—both the financial and emotional kind.

Moon in Gemini. As soon as something comes into your mind it goes right out your mouth, usually into a telephone (or even at an innocent bystander!). You propel yourself into a variety of things with unnerving bursts of nervous energy.

Moon in Cancer. Your feelings run deep, especially with family ties. Your sensitivities border on being psychic. That can depress you unless you get out with others. You like to work, but only if it is creative rather than physical work.

Moon in Leo. You have a strong need for love and admiration, and you do all you can to earn and deserve them. You enjoy most people and don't mind showing it. Your need to be at stage center sometimes leads you to push others offstage.

Moon in Virgo. You prefer to work behind the scenes, doing all you can to be helpful in your own conscientious way. You enjoy hard work, especially attending to all those details that others often overlook or purposely avoid doing.

Moon in Libra. You want everything around you to match your own gentle manner and romantic spirit. And so you make many unnecessary compromises, just to please other people. Your boat won't be overturned if you make a few waves.

Moon in Scorpio. You can be very stubborn about getting your way, resorting to subtle manipulations of others if necessary. Jealousy, revenge, and divorce often loom large in your dark private broodings. Learn to let up.

Moon in Sagittarius. You enjoy all that life offers, and you cheerfully endorse it to anyone who will listen. Your restlessness sets you off in search of high adventure, either for the mind or the body, or for both.

Moon in Capricorn. You take everything so seriously that you come across to others as a cold fish. You try to offset your shyness and insecurity by setting ambitious goals, which you then set out to reach by hard work and dedication.

Moon in Aquarius. You enjoy many friendships, especially when you can keep them from becoming attachments. You want freedom to explore new solutions to the problems of the human condition. Be selective in the causes you choose to follow.

Moon in Pisces. Talk about being sensitive! You take the prize. You even know what people think and feel before they do. But that only makes you more compassionate, and adds fuel to your fantasies. Try not to be so gullible.

Now look at your Worksheet II to find where your natal Moon was among the houses of your horoscope. The house position of the Moon reveals which activities are most affected by your unconscious responses to the events and circumstances surrounding those activities. The following profiles show how the Moon affects you when it is found in the different houses.

Moon in First House. You seek out all opportunities for achieving personal recognition. Your need for approval leads you to try almost anything—first this and then that—whatever anyone asks. That makes it easy for others to use you.

Moon in Second House. Your activities center on obtaining whatever it takes to assure your material comforts in a home setting. You enjoy the business world, but you become uneasy if things stray too far from your comfortable routine.

Moon in Third House. You enjoy things that take your mind away from the monotony of life. You can easily become dependent on people whose ideas fire your imagination. Your brothers, sisters, and neighbors are important in your life.

Moon in Fourth House. Your activities center on hearth and home. Nothing is more important to you than a happy home life. You always try to upgrade your home surroundings, either by a wise move or by a clever bit of redecoration.

Moon in Fifth House. You are fond of pleasures and gambling of any kind—financial or romantic. Your emotional attachments are based on romantic fantasies which seem to change midway during an affair. You love children.

Moon in Sixth House. You find it hard to stay on the same job (or to keep the same employees) for any length of time. Your health is a factor in many of your activities, and often becomes the primary focus of your attention.

Moon in Seventh House. You spend most of your time extending or mending your relationships with other people. In marriage you seem to choose a father or mother substitute who will fill your early emotional needs.

Moon in Eighth House. Your interests seem to vary between the otherworldly (psychic, occult) and the very worldly (inheritances, taxes, insurance). Your financial success is linked to your marriage partner.

Moon in Ninth House. You look for new ways to bring the older traditions back into your life and home. These are the traditions you learned at your parents' knees. You have to guard against bringing back dogma instead of meaningful values.

Moon in Tenth House. Your activities are an extension of your parents' efforts to achieve a higher position in society. Women play an important part in bringing you to the attention of the general public. Perhaps even politics.

Moon in Eleventh House. Your activities focus on building up a large circle of friends and acquaintances who can then share in your far-out schemes for the improvement of the lot of mankind. After that, perhaps the galaxy.

Moon in Twelfth House. Sometimes you feel that you have been dealt a heavy number from the bottom of the deck. You are torn between wanting to help others and not knowing how to help yourself. So you live inside yourself, alone.

Mercury

Mercury's position in the zodiac shows how you think things out and then communicate your ideas and decisions to others. It also reveals how you make decisions and what you consider before making a decision. Here are brief profiles of the way your natal Mercury affects your life. First check to see if Mercury was in retrograde motion at the time of your birth. (Transfer retrograde checks from Worksheet I to Worksheet IV—Summary of Natal Planets.)

Mercury in Retrograde Motion. If Mercury was in retrograde motion in your horoscope, you tend to mull things over slowly and carefully before you decide what to do. And even then you reconsider everything before you communicate your ideas or decisions to anyone else.

Mercury in Aries. You think fast and make decisions quickly—sometimes just to get it over with. You defend your ideas and decisions more because they are yours than because of the merits they might have on their own.

Mercury in Taurus. Your thoughts focus on the practical aspects of every issue. You arrive at your decisions slowly, and you stand by them regardless of the arguments offered against them. Try to be less stubborn.

Mercury in Gemini. You arrive at your decisions by following logical thought processes based on your objective perceptions of the surrounding circumstances. You are curious about everything, and find it easy to understand it all.

Mercury in Cancer. Your decisions are based on your selective perception of factors that focus on the subjective and emotional side of an issue. Your memory is excellent. It is your link with the comfortable feelings of the past.

Mercury in Leo. Your thoughts run deep, tending to focus on the larger, more dramatic issues at hand. You make up your mind slowly and are reluctant to change it once you have taken your position on a matter. Work toward humility.

Mercury in Virgo. Your thoughts are precise, going right to the heart of the issue at hand. You acquire the knowledge and skills necessary for a career that offers sensible and practical services for the general public.

Mercury in Libra. Your thoughts are usually about thinking—how do others think? why do they do what they do? etc. Your decisions are so fair-minded that you would rather risk being indecisive than being wrong.

Mercury in Scorpio. Your thoughts are so private that they sometimes remain a secret even to you. You can penetrate into the hidden motives of others to size up the issues at hand accurately. Then you tell it like it is, sparing no one.

Mercury in Sagittarius. Your mind is always looking for the patterns hidden in the things all around you. You care less about the facts than about what they might mean. One way or another, you either discover or invent meaning.

Mercury in Capricorn. Your thoughts focus on the practical aspects of the problem at hand. You arrive at your decisions by a methodical evaluation of each step needed to reach your ambitious goals. Guard against depression.

Mercury in Aquarius. Your thoughts are unbiased by personal considerations, since you trust in the higher order of Truth. You can accept your intuitive decisions without requiring a rational support for your choices.

Mercury in Pisces. You often wonder where your decisions come from, since you don't recall giving them much thought. Most of your decisions come up from the depths of your intuition, or from the subliminal suggestions aimed at you by other people.

Now check your Worksheet IV to see where Mercury falls in the houses of your horoscope. The house in which you find your natal Mercury shows which area of activity is strongly affected by the way you think and the way you communicate with others. It also shows which activity gives you your food for thought, and from which you learn the most. The following brief profiles show how Mercury affects you from the different house positions.

Mercury in First House. Your daily activities usually require that you express yourself by talking as well as by writing. You especially enjoy those activities that give you a chance to compete with others in selling your ideas.

Mercury in Second House. You gravitate toward jobs that can make use of your gift of gab as well as your clever pen. You often learn-to-earn, and then buckle down to a well-planned practical career in the business world.

Mercury in Third House. Your activities center around your abilities to communicate effectively with others, mostly right off the top of your head. You are a problem solver, and you probably have very large phone bills to show for it.

Mercury in Fourth House. Your home is usually the base of your business operations. You are well educated and use books or references in your professional life. You gravitate into real estate or the environmental sciences.

Mercury in Fifth House. Your activities are aimed at producing creative literature, either for artistic or financial purposes. That can include creative stock market or financial reports. You also enjoy educating youngsters.

Mercury in Sixth House. Your activities are as much concerned with acquiring new skills as they are with using them. You enjoy difficult subjects such as engineering or medicine. Regardless of your profession, you are methodical.

Mercury in Seventh House. You seek out opportunities to work in cooperation with others, preferring partnerships to private practice. You care about the ideas of other people, which makes you an excellent arbitrator.

Mercury in Eighth House. Your interests tend toward the mysteries of the occult. You take special precautions to keep your activities to yourself. You have an almost morbid interest in and fascination with the subject of death.

Mercury in Ninth House. Your interests focus on matters having to do with advanced learning. You are especially fascinated by how society arrived at its present condition. You would be off on a trip at the drop of a hat—anyplace, anytime.

Mercury in Tenth House. Your interests in education are very practical—to help you get ahead in your career. You have very clear career goals and the ability to organize the details of your life so that you can achieve those goals.

Mercury in Eleventh House. Your activities are centered on the exchange of ideas with friends and with groups in general. You are not on any special mission in life, but you keep yourself open to help humanity at large.

Mercury in Twelfth House. Your activities center on extending your understanding of the mysteries of life. Your thoughts on the subject are fueled by your deeply intuitive insights. You find it hard to learn through formal education.

Venus

Venus's position in the zodiac shows how you give of yourself and how you express your feelings for others. It also reveals how you attract the good things in life, both the material and the spiritual. The following profiles show how your natal Venus affects your life. But first check to see if Venus was retrograde in your horoscope (see your Worksheet IV).

Venus in Retrograde Motion. If Venus was retrograde in your natal horoscope, it signifies that you become emotionally frustrated easily, and that you are susceptible to feelings of loneliness. You have especially strong needs to be loved and to belong.

Venus in Aries. Your affections are so easily aroused—and your responses are so immediate—that you seem to be aggressive or flirtatious. Your need for excitement in your romantic involvements may get you involved in several at once.

Venus in Taurus. You are a slow starter when it comes to romance. You need someone like yourself who enjoys physical contact and who will reciprocate your fidelity. You love the arts, music, and the things that grow from the earth.

Venus in Gemini. Your need for variety in your romantic relationships makes it hard for you to focus your attentions on one partner. You prefer parties, cruises, or other gatherings that offer you opportunities to meet like-minded adventurers.

Venus in Cancer. Your relationships tend to be tenacious, especially when they promised to fulfill your needs for material and emotional security.

Venus in Leo. When you are attracted to someone, she or he soon knows it. Your dramatic display of affection extends from the playful to the lavish. You are a born romantic who needs someone to play opposite you in an extended courtship.

Venus in Virgo. You approach the affairs of the heart with cool analytical curiosity. Unfortunately, most partners are put off by your lack of spontaneity and your tendency to apply your highly critical standards to all forms of behavior.

Venus in Libra. Your need for emotional harmony makes you sociable and sensitive to the needs of others, whom you soon learn to please. You enjoy mature intellectual stimulation as well as the aesthetic pleasures of the arts.

Venus in Scorpio. You become so deeply involved in your own emotional desires and sexual needs that you often dominate your relationships. Your jealous nature often backs you off into an "all or nothing" corner. You're too proud.

Venus in Sagittarius. You approach your romantic affairs with a touch of the ideal—seeking opportunities for the sincere display of your generosity. However, your affections are sometimes more impulsive than dependable.

Venus in Capricorn. Your emotional needs are tightly tied to your needs for status and security. You have difficulty in expressing your feelings in public, although you really do enjoy being sensual with your partner when you are alone.

Venus in Aquarius. You march to a different drummer when it comes to the affairs of the heart. You prefer sharing intellectual to emotional stimulations with your partners. You are friendly with almost everyone, in an impersonal way.

Venus in Pisces. You are so in love with love that you never think to ask your partner's intentions in a relationship. Your strong need for affection often places you in the position of being used or rejected by a thoughtless partner.

Now check your Worksheet IV to see where Venus falls in the houses of your horoscope. The house of your natal Venus shows which activity serves as your outlet for romantic and artistic feelings, and for establishing close relationships with other people. The following profiles show you the influence of Venus in the different houses.

Venus in First House. Your good looks and cheerful disposition assure your acceptance in the social and business worlds. You enjoy artistic activities but are lazy about pursuing them. Your happy childhood leads to an early marriage.

Venus in Second House. Your activities focus on the acquisition of wealth, which you spend on objects of art or adornment. It is not unusual for you to spend more than you earn. You attract people who like to spend money on you.

Venus in Third House. You approach your artistic interests in an intellectual way, expressing yourself most effectively in both the spoken and printed word. You enjoy good relations with family and friends. Travel turns you on.

Venus in Fourth House. Your contact with others centers around your domestic scene. You take special pride in decorating your home with the finest things you can afford. You have strong ties to your parents. Properties bring you wealth late in life.

Venus in Fifth House. Your activities center on the pursuit of pleasure. Your affectionate nature and sunny disposition lead you into many pleasant love affairs, one of which ends in a happy marriage with lovely, loving children.

Venus in Sixth House. Your outlets for romantic and social activities usually center around your working world. You get along very well with co-workers, and you may marry someone you work with. You love clothes—and pets.

Venus in Seventh House. Your emotional needs are soon met in an early and happy marriage. Your financial needs are also met by your marriage, or by your careful choice of a compatible partner. You find it easy to deal with the public.

Venus in Eighth House. Your financial gains are keyed to your choice of partners, both in business and marriage. Your need for affection may lead you to a dependence on sexual gratifications. Those needs may make you overly possessive.

Venus in Ninth House. Your contact with others usually centers on your pursuit of the higher values in life. Your religious interests and your love of travel often bring you together with the important people in your life.

Venus in Tenth House. Your activities focus on the pursuit of an ambitious artistic career. Your choice of a friend or marriage partner is based on his or her possible value to you as a helper for your professional or social advancement.

Venus in Eleventh House. Your need for close contacts with others is served by your involvement in clubs and other group activities. Your warmth toward others is warmly returned, providing you with lasting friendships, and a mate.

Venus in Twelfth House. You prefer your solitude to the open pursuit of friendships. Whatever contacts you do seek are usually made by subtle or secretive overtures. Although you are lonely, you have compassion for the needs of others.

Mars

The position of Mars in the zodiac shows how you use your physical energies in expressing your needs. It affects your sex drive, ambitions, and endurance, and your aggressive urges. The following behavior profiles show how Mars affects you in the different signs. But first check your Worksheet IV to see if Mars is retrograde in your horoscope.

Mars in Retrograde Motion. If your natal Mars was retrograde, it shows that you usually look before you leap. It also shows that you bottle up your angers and frustrations rather than release them in controlled confrontations. You may also avoid work and repress your sexual urges.

Mars in Aries. You are impulsive and ambitious. Your enthusiasm is contagious and often inspires others to follow your lead. You like to take risks. You enjoy vigorous activities and physical sex. Learn to control your impatience.

Mars in Taurus. You are determined to earn a lot of money. You're able to follow a carefully planned career that depends on your pride in craftsmanship and your perseverance. You would like to get married early in life and enjoy sex.

Mars in Gemini. You have a quick mind and prefer the direct (outspoken!) approach in dealing with people. You enjoy matching wits with a worthy intellectual rival. You are resourceful but restless—sexually superficial at times.

Mars in Cancer. You are moody because of your emotional dependence on others. You resent restraints, yet you seek the security of an authoritative surrounding. You are protective toward family and friends. Sexually refined.

Mars in Leo. You enjoy the leadership roles that your initiative and self-confidence often earn for you. You love the excitement of competition. You are honest and fearless in dealing with others. Yours is a warm sexuality.

Mars in Virgo. You love your work, especially when it demands a delicate craftsmanship or systematic planning and attention to detail. Your methodical methods can irritate your fellow workers. You have a need for gentle sex.

Mars in Libra. You have an easygoing way about you. Your need to avoid bickering makes you an excellent team worker. You seek partners who are more outgoing than you, but who will appreciate your needs. You prefer sensuous sex.

Mars in Scorpio. You have a forceful approach that comes across as a blunt indifference to the feelings of other people. You have intense desires and a powerful sex drive—the combination makes you both possessive and jealous.

Mars in Sagittarius. You dissipate your energies in the pursuit of a variety of interests. If you ever become interested in one particular thing, you could achieve wonders with it. But you lose interest before then. Variety in sex.

Mars in Capricorn. You can carefully control the intense flow of your energies directed toward the fulfillment of your ambitious goals in life—to acquire wealth and status. Everything you do has a practical purpose. Strong sex drive.

Mars in Aquarius. You spread your energies across a variety of group activities, each of which aspires to some higher humanitarian objective. You need the freedom to follow any path that might open. You share your sexuality with many.

Mars in Pisces. You often feel restless for no apparent reason. This comes from repressed resentments stemming from your reluctance to confront people whom you disagree with. Your sexual desires are based on romantic fantasies.

Now check your Worksheet IV to see where Mars falls in the houses of your horoscope. The house position of your natal Mars shows where your energies are expended toward the satisfaction of your needs and desires. The following brief profiles show how Mars affects you in the different houses.

Mars in First House. You have to be where the action is. You are competitive and work very hard to achieve your goals—which means achieving public recognition. You need the freedom to follow your own path to success. Control your temper.

Mars in Second House. Your activities are centered on the acquisition of wealth—which you often lose just as fast as you earn it. You must be out on your own, competing with giants for your share of the action.

Mars in Third House. You have a keen mind which enjoys the test of intellectual competition or the challenge of emergency situations. You would enjoy the political scene or investigative journalism. You quarrel with siblings.

Mars in Fourth House. You have to be boss in your own home—which is why you left home at an early age. You enjoy fixing up around the house. You are probably a leader in some "Save the Environment" campaign. Interest in land.

Mars in Fifth House. Your activities center on the pursuit of love and other pleasures. There is a sense of urgency in finding your sex partner. You are a natural disciplinarian, causing problems with children. Gambler.

Mars in Sixth House. You are the hard worker who quickly comes to the attention of higher-ups in an organization. You dislike people who shirk work. Your pride in demonstrating your superior skills may lead to friction with co-workers.

Mars in Seventh House. Your aggressive attitudes create difficulties with partners in particular and the public in general. You often get involved with people just like yourself. An early marriage gives you time to adjust to your mate.

Mars in Eighth House. You have intense emotional needs and desires. You often get involved in dealing with other people's money, either in legal disputes involving an inheritance, or with the finances in a partnership.

Mars in Ninth House. Your activities center around the pursuit of higher wisdom—often requiring that you travel widely. You inspire others to improve themselves, mostly by setting good examples for them to follow.

Mars in Tenth House. Yours is a search for fame and fortune. Your energies are directed toward reaching the top, regardless of the career you choose. The more competitive the career, the more you rise to the challenge, and win.

Mars in Eleventh House. Your energies flow out toward your many friends in the various groups you join. You can be an effective organizer of their joint efforts, but your impulsive behavior usually causes discontent and defections.

Mars in Twelfth House. You want to do your own thing from behind the scenes—perhaps because you want to avoid confrontations. You prefer to be lost in the ranks of a large organization. Even your sexual relations are kept undercover.

Jupiter

Jupiter's position in the zodiac shows how you express your need to grow. It shows your interests in the higher values of life and how you share those interests with others. Here are brief profiles of how your natal Jupiter affects your life. But first check your Worksheet IV to see if Jupiter was retrograde in your horoscope.

Jupiter in Retrograde Motion. If Jupiter was retrograde in your horoscope it signifies that you are slow to make changes in your life style and cautious about accepting the newest codes of morality. Your strong moral convictions are rooted in the deep soil of your impressionable childhood.

Jupiter in Aries. You need the freedom to express your enthusiasm for the higher values in life. Your optimistic approach and your self-assurance inspire confidence in others, who then select you for leadership positions in worthy causes.

Jupiter in Taurus. You understand that material wealth is just the means toward the end of improving the quality of life. However, that doesn't stop you from the enjoyment of the creature comforts that life has to offer.

Jupiter in Gemini. You enjoy stretching your mind to learn as much as you can about many different subjects. This diversity of interests keeps you from specializing in any one field. You soon become restless with a routine job.

Jupiter in Cancer. You make a sincere effort to extend sympathy and understanding to people with problems. You are generous to everyone you meet—but especially to those in your own household. Your home is a haven to many.

Jupiter in Leo. You enjoy the drama of religious ceremonies. You would like to be the leader in the pomp and circumstance of parades and lodge meetings. You are generous, loyal, and love children. Your weakness is gambling.

Jupiter in Virgo. You try hard to develop your technical and analytical abilities. Your concern with details comes in conflict with your interest in the over-all aspects of a project. You are almost compulsive about cleanliness.

Jupiter in Libra. You try your very best to spread yourself around like oil on troubled waters. You want recognition for your virtues and often get it in the praises of your virtuous mate. You thrive in harmonious surroundings.

Jupiter in Scorpio. You have a need to extend your control over the people in your life. Perhaps that's because you are involved with them in financial and legal matters. You have a passion for possessions, and for physical pleasures.

Jupiter in Sagittarius. You are overly generous with everyone you meet. You keep looking for a better philosophy to help guide you through life. You take pleasure in sharing your ideas with others. Lady Luck always arrives just in time.

Jupiter in Capricorn. Your conduct is always above reproach, whether in your social or business life. You can be trusted in the most responsible positions—which you often hold as a result of your drive for power and status.

Jupiter in Aquarius. You strive to become one with everyone, regardless of race, religion, color, or creed. Your tolerance for different values and life styles often leads you to try them for yourself. You push equality campaigns.

Jupiter in Pisces. You have a happy-go-lucky approach to life. However, you are overly sensitive and tend to fall back on your fantasies rather than confront difficulties. You are charitable toward those who you think are the underdogs.

Now check your Worksheet IV to see where Jupiter falls into the houses of your horoscope. The house occupied by your natal Jupiter shows where you find opportunities to move out into the world. It shows how you express your generosity and where you are likely to receive unexpected rewards. Here are some profiles of how Jupiter affects you in each of the houses.

Jupiter in First House. You have an optimistic outlook and the self-confidence that inspires others to select you as their leader. You love the pleasures of life and are fond of travel. You are lucky to enjoy the benefits of good health.

Jupiter in Second House. You have a keen business sense, always coming out ahead of the others in your financial dealings. You have to guard against impulsive extravagance in your generous moods, and against gambling or other self-indulgence.

Jupiter in Third House. You try to expand your mental horizons through reading and travel. You would do well in teaching, writing, or other forms of communications. You do your best to keep up with the latest trends.

Jupiter in Fourth House. You enjoy a congenial family life, surrounded by the benefits of financial security. Your parents may leave you properties, adding to your accumulation of wealth in later life. You love to be in splendid surroundings.

Jupiter in Fifth House. Your activities center on bringing education and pleasure to others, especially the children. Your romantic interests often involve someone with money or position. You play the stock market, or you gamble.

Jupiter in Sixth House. You have a strong need to provide practical service to the community at large. You are immersed in matters of health and healing, including an interest in unorthodox or spiritual healing. You are very cooperative.

Jupiter in Seventh House. You are open-handed and fair-minded in your dealings with other people. Your marriage is based on high moral standards with someone of social position or wealth. You do well in activities dealing with the public.

Jupiter in Eighth House. You find it challenging to handle other people's money. You may experience financial gain through marriage, a partnership, or an inheritance. You are interested in survival after death, and other spiritual matters.

Jupiter in Ninth House. You establish your high moral standards early in life. You are interested in understanding the basis of social order, and seek your answers in the halls of higher learning. You are active in religious groups.

Jupiter in Tenth House. You are headed for a successful social life and professional career. You bring spiritual values into your business dealings, quietly doing good deeds which later bring you rich rewards. You deserve them.

Jupiter in Eleventh House. You are warm and generous to many people, most of whom share your deep concern for humanitarian interests. The cooperative spirit of your friends makes it possible for you to undertake ambitious tasks.

Jupiter in Twelfth House. Your interests center on activities that permit you to work alone, preferably from behind the scenes. You are fascinated by psychic subjects, meditation, and introspection. You are always helped when in need.

Saturn

Saturn's position in the zodiac shows how you try to establish and protect your position in life. It also shows how you face responsibility and seek recognition for your efforts. The following profiles describe how Saturn's sign of the zodiac affects your life. But first check your Worksheet IV to see if it was retrograde in your horoscope.

Saturn in Retrograde Motion. If Saturn was in retrograde motion in your horoscope, it shows that your search for success is based on conservative planning. You build on the solid ground of your past experiences rather than gambling on untested skills or adventurous impulses.

Saturn in Aries. You always seem to be up against it—with no one to fall back on but yourself. These circumstances may be good for building character, but they only toss you between feelings of determination and feelings of despair.

Saturn in Taurus. You recognize your need to buckle down if you want to earn enough money to feel secure. You are practical in managing your affairs. You seem to work best when you are under a great deal of pressure to perform.

Saturn in Gemini. You are always in charge of yourself as you systematically move ahead in your career. You particularly enjoy working with complex subjects that challenge your intelligence. But you do take things too seriously!

Saturn in Cancer. You find it difficult to relate to the feelings of your family. This troubles you because it deprives you of the emotional security of those close ties. You protect yourself by drawing up into your lonely shell.

Saturn in Leo. You are almost compulsive in your drive to get ahead, lest someone think that you are mediocre. You have leadership abilities and always aim for the top position, where your success will be visible to everyone.

Saturn in Virgo. You meet your responsibilities as though your life depended on it. You are meticulous in your attention to detail, and distrustful of others who are less thorough than you. Guard against nagging others.

Saturn in Libra. Your actions are guided by your compulsion for honesty and fair play. You have a strong sense of social responsibility, which often earns you the high esteem of the general public. You're a good organizer.

Saturn in Scorpio. You try to remain free of emotional dependencies, which you recognize as the cause of your jealousies. Your shrewd mind is at its best when you make your financial deals—your secret ways serve you well.

Saturn in Sagittarius. You need freedom of action to express your independent views. You direct all your efforts toward the improvement of your mind and your work habits. You aim at achieving some sort of intellectual distinction.

Saturn in Capricorn. Your ambitions are directed toward the attainment of practical goals, which almost always require long-term commitments. You are dedicated, self-sufficient, sometimes pessimistic, but always sure of success.

Saturn in Aquarius. You resent restraints on your freedom of action or thought. You can deal with intellectual topics or personal matters, giving each the benefit of your full attention. Your originality spawns new discoveries.

Saturn in Pisces. You have a hard time living in the present. Echoes of bad experiences from your past activate your fears and imagination—blocking you from dealing with the daily demands of your life. And so you become moody.

Now check your Worksheet IV to see where Saturn falls in the houses of your horoscope. The house occupied by your natal Saturn shows how you confront and overcome the obstacles in your life. It shows how you are achieving maturity by disciplined and responsible actions. The following profiles show how Saturn affects you from each of the houses.

Saturn in First House. You are a no-nonsense person who has the patience, perseverance, and self-control to overcome most obstacles. You take on heavy responsibilities with the complete confidence that you can handle them all alone.

Saturn in Second House. Your activities are centered around the acquisition of material wealth. This often places you in the position of responsibility for handling money. You are concerned about saving enough money for your old age.

Saturn in Third House. Whatever you do, you do it in a deliberate and disciplined way—you even talk slowly so you can think about each word you say. You would do well in methodical work involving research on difficult subjects.

Saturn in Fourth House. You are always enmeshed in family responsibilities, often stemming from the problems of older people. That makes you worry about problems in your own old age—it gets worse as you get older, unless you stop.

Saturn in Fifth House. You have a deep sense of responsibility toward the care of children—especially in the matter of their education. Your romantic life is beset with obstacles, many of which are because of your "reserve."

Saturn in Sixth House. You take your job seriously and actually enjoy the hard work that it entails—provided that you are left alone to do it your own way. You would make an excellent supervisor since employees would respect you.

Saturn in Seventh House. You have a deep sense of responsibility in meeting your commitments to other people. You work hard, holding up your share of the load in any partnership. You marry someone like yourself, late in life.

Saturn in Eighth House. Somehow you always find yourself involved in taking care of the financial affairs of other people. Although you handle those affairs responsibly, you always seem to have trouble with your own financial affairs.

Saturn in Ninth House. Your activities focus on religion, science, and other serious studies. In each case you bring your practical criteria to bear in your judgments of the value of an idea or teaching. You seek public recognition.

Saturn in Tenth House. You choose ambitious goals that require dedication and commitment to a hard career. Your drive for success is sparked by your need for status as much as it is by your intense desire for financial rewards.

Saturn in Eleventh House. You feel a deep sense of obligation to your friends and your organizations. You prefer the comradeship of older people whose influence often helps you to advance in your social position as well as your career.

Saturn in Twelfth House. You do your best work when you can be away from other people. You keep your feelings and your problems to yourself—that's why you get into those deep depressions. You have to learn to let others into your life.

Uranus

Uranus's position in the zodiac shows something about the motivation, goals, and originality of those born in each seven-year period during which Uranus is in each of the signs. The following profiles describe how Uranus affects your life when it falls in the different signs. But first check your Worksheet IV to see if Uranus was retrograde in your horoscope.

Uranus in Retrograde Motion. If Uranus was retrograde in your natal horoscope, it signifies that you spend a lot of time reviewing the past rather than dealing with the present or future. You feel that the only way to make progress is to avoid making the same mistakes over again. Your past often does make an unexpected appearance in your life.

Uranus in Aries. You are a trailblazer who needs the freedom to explore new approaches to old problems. Your impulsiveness, along with your unconventional approach, leads people to consider you either rebellious or eccentric.

Uranus in Taurus. You are a financial maverick in business—creating new approaches for ways to use money. Your intensity is disruptive, and can lead you into positions which you then have to defend with unyielding stubbornness.

Uranus in Gemini. You are very bright and often come up with exciting new ways to get something done. However, your restlessness keeps you from staying with one thing long enough to see it through to completion. You are intuitive.

Uranus in Cancer. You look for newer ways to express your feelings—bypassing the restraints of traditional taboos. This may lead to an early departure from your parents' home. You have to guard against emotional instabilities.

Uranus in Leo. You can be creative in either the arts or sciences. You create your own social, moral, and professional standards, which you then insist that everyone else must follow. Your belief in free love is one example.

Uranus in Virgo. You often come up with creative solutions to problems at work. You enjoy things that demand your careful attention to detail. Your talents are useful in either the scientific or business enterprises.

Uranus in Libra. You are a charming person who can, at times, become disruptive because of your need to experiment with new approaches. You enjoy the arts and often get intuitive insights or psychic flashes. You can write well.

Uranus in Scorpio. You have difficulty in keeping up with recent changes, which seem to be coming along too quickly. You are intensely emotional and may suffer from fits of violent temper. You are resourceful and decisive.

Uranus in Sagittarius. You are still trying to bridge the gap between the rational rules of science and the mysteries behind conventional religions. You may have already become dogmatic, but your curiousity forces you to keep an open mind.

Uranus in Capricorn. Your primary interests are still toward securing a greater stability for society—based on choices that respect the primary criterion of practicality. You are an excellent leader with an authoritative bearing.

Uranus in Aquarius. You have a strong mind. You use it along with your penetrating intuitions to explore the mysteries of the occult. You are independent and willing to accept new ideas once they pass your test of worthiness.

Uranus in Pisces. You are more interested in what goes on inside you than what's going on around you. You have interesting dreams which you later interpret in your meditations. You enjoy your spiritual experiences.

Now check your Worksheet IV to see where Uranus was among the houses of your horoscope. The house position of Uranus shows where you may expect abrupt and unusual changes in your life. These areas are also those in which you find opportunities to exercise your intuitions and originality. The following profiles show how Uranus affects your life from its house position in your horoscope.

Uranus in First House. You like to play the role of "lone wolf"—often in a nervous and restless way. You are interested in promoting new ideas, especially if they offer exciting changes in the status quo. You change jobs often.

Uranus in Second House. Your financial circumstances are seldom under control. You never seem able to protect yourself against sudden surprises. Your originality gives you opportunities for unusual ways to make more money.

Uranus in Third House. You seem to have a psychic antenna that keeps you well informed about what's going on. You are interested in the unusual—especially occult teachings. You have a strong need for intellectual friends.

Uranus in Fourth House. Your early home life involved tension and upheaval—leading you to abrupt change of residence. In later life your home becomes a meeting place for close friends. You need them for emotional security.

Uranus in Fifth House. Your romantic relationships are as unusual for their sexual focus as they are for their uncertain durations. Your children are likely to be unusual—either being very gifted or very troubled, or both.

Uranus in Sixth House. You are likely to be nervous and high-strung. That works a hardship on those whom you work with—leading to a mutual on-the-job irritability. You resent routine assignments. Take care of your health.

Uranus in Seventh House. Your view of marriage accepts the newest arrangements in cohabitation—with or without the benefit of clergy. Your own marriage is likely to be a sudden (temporary?) arrangement with an eccentric partner.

Uranus in Eighth House. You are fascinated with the latest talk about life after death, and other occult mysteries. You seem to have an inner awareness about such things. Your fortune changes suddenly through a marriage or partnership.

Uranus in Ninth House. You have an independent mind. You can come up with such original insights that it borders on genius. Your enthusiasm can sometimes get out of hand, leading people to consider you a crank. Guard against accidents.

Uranus in Tenth House. You are so different from everyone else that you have to be your own boss. Your independence and unusual interests lead you to unconventional careers. You have to have absolute freedom in all you do.

Uranus in Eleventh House. You are open-minded and will accept whatever seems reasonable to you, regardless of what others may think. You prefer to deal with a wide spectrum of friends rather than a select few. You seek social justice.

Uranus in Twelfth House. You feel that you have to play all your cards close to the chest to protect yourself from treachery. Your enjoyment of secrecy may lead you into confidences whose betrayal can cost you your reputation.

Neptune

Neptune's position in the zodiac influences the collective outlook of all those born within the same thirteen-year period during which Neptune remains in one sign. The following profiles show the mystical and inspirational influences felt by each generation. However, first check your Worksheet IV to see if Neptune was in retrograde motion in your natal horoscope.

Neptune in Retrograde Motion. If Neptune was in retrograde motion in your natal horoscope it signifies that you are keenly aware of your intuitive insights and introspections. You are willing to reconsider your basic beliefs on the basis of a continuous evaluation of your innermost feelings.

Neptune in Aries. This generation was interested in the exploration of mystical concepts and in spiritual regeneration.

Neptune in Taurus. This generation sought to make practical use of its idealistic beliefs. Money was to be put to the services of higher values in life.

Neptune in Gemini. This generation focused its interests on intellectual pursuits, as expressed in writing and the arts.

Neptune in Cancer. This generation sought religious experiences for its emotional gratification, encountering mystical experiences along the way.

Neptune in Leo. This generation expresses itself through its interest in the performing arts, romantic gestures, and extravagance in the pursuit of pleasure.

Neptune in Virgo. This generation was confronted with difficulties in meeting material needs, leading to excessive emotional stresses in early life.

Neptune in Libra. This generation faces the stresses of changing social and moral standards, and is torn between the desire for conformity and the impulse for novelty.

Neptune in Scorpio. This generation must resolve the struggle between its strong sexual desires and its equally strong need for spiritual regeneration.

Neptune in Sagittarius. This generation will find new ways to bring occult teachings into the mainstream of traditional religions.

Neptune in Capricorn. This generation will be born into economic and political confusion, leading to a renewal of higher spiritual values.

Neptune in Aquarius. This will be the first generation of the twenty-first century to enter into the period of peace on earth and good will toward all of humanity.

Neptune in Pisces. This will be a generation of mystics and spiritual leaders, bringing the Age of Aquarius to its first fruition.

Now check your Worksheet IV to see where Neptune falls among the houses of your natal horoscope. The position of Neptune in its house shows where you channel your spiritual energies into daily life. There is where you get your hunches, where you tune in, and where you give yourself unselfishly. The following profiles show how Neptune influences your life.

Neptune in First House. You are intuitive to the extent of almost knowing what someone will do next. You love art and music, and all the finer things in life. You are a visionary with impractical goals and objectives.

Neptune in Second House. You want to use your money for humanitarian causes, often spending on impulse. Yet you have unusual ways for making more money—which you do to the point of accumulating wealth. Avoid becoming extravagant.

Neptune in Third House. You probably know that some of your best thoughts reach you from other sources during moments of inspiration. In that same vein, you act as a channel for sharing your knowledge and information with everyone else.

Neptune in Fourth House. Your home is a center for the spiritual growth of all who live there or meet there—strangers are always welcome. You have to keep such an openness from stressing your own family relationships.

Neptune in Fifth House. You have a flair for the dramatic and a love of luxurious things. Your romantic relationships can be adventures in mutual seduction. You can expect your children to be especially sensitive.

Neptune in Sixth House. You have latent psychic abilities which can be easily developed—placing you in the position of having to choose wisely in how you will use them. You have a psychic link with pets and animals.

Neptune in Seventh House. Your marriage is based on an almost platonic relationship with someone steeped in occult beliefs. Yours is an unselfish love that approaches a spiritual union. Be on your guard against deceptions.

Neptune in Eighth House. Your marriage partner brings you unusual access to financial gains. You both are likely to encounter spiritualistic experiences that provide you with first-hand evidence for the existence of higher beings.

Neptune in Ninth House. You have many intuitional insights and frequent forebodings of things that indeed come to pass. Your impressionable mind can lead you into following a cult, or worse yet, starting one of your own!

Neptune in Tenth House. You use your intuitions as just another skill to help you achieve success in your career. You have leadership abilities and will probably achieve fame or public recognition for your personal achievements.

Neptune in Eleventh House. Your high spiritual values attract many friends with similar high values and ideals. You have to guard against the deception and treachery that may arise in such a large group of diverse people.

Neptune in Twelfth House. You often feel that you are connected with higher sources—leading you to prefer the privacy of secluded surroundings. That does not preclude your need for a special soulmate, of this world or the next.

Pluto

Pluto's position in the zodiac influences the entire generation of people born within the same twelve- to thirty-two-year period during which Pluto remains in one sign. The following profiles show how Pluto affects the human need for regeneration and control in each generation. But first check your Worksheet IV to see if Pluto was retrograde in your horoscope.

Pluto in Retrograde Motion. If Pluto was in retrograde motion in your natal horoscope it signifies that you prefer subtle approaches toward achieving your goals. Your effort at self-improvement is a private matter rather than a public display.

Pluto in Aries. This was a pioneering generation capable of overcoming personal hardships in their search for a better life.

Pluto in Taurus. This was the generation that brought in the Industrial Revolution as the basis for economic expansion based on production of material goods.

Pluto in Gemini. This generation brought about the most dramatic changes in society by introducing a flood of discoveries and inventions.

Pluto in Cancer. This generation is concerned with the conflicts over land and food, and with the many rivalries that threaten both the family and national security.

Pluto in Leo. This generation focuses on the struggle for power and world leadership—especially on the complex problems arising from the proliferation of nuclear power.

Pluto in Virgo. This generation is concerned with the reexamination of our social systems to see if they can be made to work by a more sensible use of our technologies.

Pluto in Libra. This new generation will work to restore economic and ecological balances, and to establish a society based on law and order, and justice for all.

Pluto in Scorpio. This generation will face the awesome decisions that determine whether the human race will be over, or on the threshold of its regeneration.

Pluto in Sagittarius. This will be the first generation of the twenty-first century, responsible for transforming religions into more effective vehicles for higher spiritual values.

Pluto in Capricorn, Aquarius, and Pisces. The times that

Pluto enters these signs are well beyond the year 2000, and beyond the scope of this book.

Now check your Worksheet IV to see where Pluto falls in the houses of your natal horoscope. Pluto's house position shows where you feel the need for self-renewal, and how you go about expressing that need. The following profiles show how Pluto affects your life from its house position in your chart.

Pluto in First House. You feel a strong need to be alone, especially after you fail in yet another attempt at social interaction. Your life is one crisis after another, each one testing you to make that effort just one more time.

Pluto in Second House. You are resourceful in making money, especially when you can use other people's resources. Your activities give you ample opportunity to learn how to overcome greed and selfish interests. Learn from them!

Pluto in Third House. You have a searching mind that seeks out the basics behind the important issues of life. You have strong beliefs and original ideas which you freely share with others. You have problems with brothers and sisters.

Pluto in Fourth House. Your need to dominate the domestic scene may be the cause of all your family alienations. You should take those conflicts as opportunities to learn how to cooperate with other people. You love the earth.

Pluto in Fifth House. You express your creative urges through art and strong emotional involvements. You are domineering in romantic relations—causing fits of jealousy. You love the excitement of speculation or gambling.

Pluto in Sixth House. You are concerned with matters of health, and may find yourself in the health-care business. You may even be an unorthodox healer yourself! You expect too much of others. You must learn to be more tolerant.

Pluto in Seventh House. Your life seems to be one continuous round of dealings with other people, partners or your mate. You turn these dealings into mini-conflicts by your need to dominate each situation as it comes up.

Pluto in Eighth House. You have a powerful will which often causes crisis situations that you then have to defuse. Your intense focus turns everything into a black-or-white decision. You have a morbid concern about death.

Pluto in Ninth House. You have strong interests in reforming the social order into a more idealistic system. Your insights are excellent but are too philosophical to provide a basis for a practical course of action.

Pluto in Tenth House. You are independent and almost ruthless in your drive to achieve success. You are often misunderstood, causing crises that may force you to resign. You have powerful friends and powerful enemies.

Pluto in Eleventh House. You try to bring about changes by enlisting the cooperation of large numbers of friends. Your ideas are visionary but are often motivated by a personal advantage rather than by a humanitarian objective.

Pluto in Twelfth House. You are interested in the inner workings of the mind. You find it easy to meditate and explore the mysteries of life. However, you suffer from emotional tensions that manifest themselves as intense jealousies.

Your Ascendant (Rising Sign)

Your Ascendant is the sign of the zodiac that was rising over the eastern horizon at the moment you were born. You can find the sign of your Ascendant from your Worksheet II (which you should have put on Worksheet IV).

The interpretation of your rising sign follows very closely the interpretation of the Sun's position in that same sign. The influence of the sign is the same in both cases. The difference is that in one case it affects your inner character (Sun sign) while in the other case it affects your personality, or what you show the public (rising sign).

You can read the interpretation of your Sun sign and then the interpretation of the Sun in your rising sign to see how your inner character and your outer personality compare with each other.

Or you can read these brief profiles of the significance of your Ascendant.

Aries Ascendant. You are outspoken in your energetic approach to life. You act decisively in your determination to succeed. You forgive and forget. You are ardent in love.

Taurus Ascendant. You may seem timid and slow-moving to others, but that's your way of getting things done properly. You need to own beautiful things. You pick on your lover.

Gemini Ascendant. You are intellectually competitive and can talk circles around anyone on almost any topic. You need frequent changes to feel alive. You are a refined lover.

Cancer Ascendant. Your sympathetic nature links you to the changeable moods of others. You are overly sensitive to criticism. You are a sensuous lover—but jealous.

Leo Ascendant. Your dignified manner does not conceal your generous good nature or your need for open affection. You can become overbearing. You are a passionate lover.

Virgo Ascendant. Your shyness is a screen to keep others from discovering your intense needs—to be perfect in all details of your work, and to enjoy sex to the fullest.

Libra Ascendant. Your charm is your key to the inner circles of beautiful people who exude refinement and dignity. You feel lost when alone. You need excitement with your love.

Scorpio Ascendant. Your intense behavior conceals the fact that you are a sentimentalist who loves seclusion. You reach your goals as much by guile as by guts.

Sagittarius Ascendant. Your expansive optimism is contagious—spreading hope and enthusiasm among your many friends. You are passionate and aggressive in love.

Capricorn Ascendant. Your serious approach to life makes you seem melancholy most of the time. Behind that undemonstrative exterior lies a lustful sensuality.

Aquarius Ascendant. Your consideration and concern for others extends to people in general rather than to someone in particular. You prefer a brother-sister type of love.

Pisces Ascendant. Your idealistic dream world is full of bumps and bruises as your trusting nature is exploited again and again. You are a sentimentalist about love.

A more detailed interpretation of the significance of your Ascendant would consider the consequence of how the signs fall in each of the houses. For example, with an Aries Ascendant you would have Taurus in the Second House, Gemini in the Third House, etc. (see Figure 1–2 in Chapter One). You would then see how the characteristics of Taurus affect the affairs of the Second House, how Gemini's characteristics affect the affairs of the Third House, and so on.

As you can see, this method of interpreting the Ascendant considers the effect of every sign in every house, starting with your rising sign in the first house. A Scorpio Ascendant would feel Scorpio in the First House, while the Fifth House feels the sentimentality of Pisces (Pisces is five signs farther along in the zodiac from Scorpio in the First House).

More About These Interpretations

Most often you will find that the interpretations of the planets in the signs and houses fall into a consistent pattern that reveals your basic character and behavior pattern. However, if you find that there is a wide difference between the interpretations of the planets, you may wonder which planet offers you the most accurate description.

The interpretations given by the Sun and Moon are the most important indicators in your horoscope. Following that, your Ascendant offers important insights into your personality. These then are the three most important indicators.

The order of importance of the remaining planets depends on where they fall in your horoscope, and on the "planetary rulers" of your Sun sign and your rising sign. Each sign of the zodiac is "ruled" by a planet. The planet that rules your Sun sign has special importance, as does the planet that rules your rising sign.

The planets that rule each sign are as follows:

Aries—Mars	Libra—Venus
Taurus—Venus	Scorpio—Pluto
Gemini—Mercury	Sagittarius—Jupiter
Cancer—Moon	Capricorn—Saturn
Leo—Sun	Aquarius—Uranus
Virgo—Mercury	Pisces—Neptune

You should pay special attention to the interpretations offered for the planets that rule your Sun sign and your rising sign (Ascendant).

Other planets that take on special importance are those that stand alone at the four "angles" of your horoscope. These are the cusps of your Tenth House (the zenith, midheaven or M.C.), your First House (Ascendant), your Seventh House (Descendant), and your Fourth House (nadir, or I.C.). Planets found near these angles are more influential than those found elsewhere.

If the interpretations of your house positions seem to be wrong for you, read the preceding or following house descriptions to find which fits you better. You may have to change the position of the Ascendant on your chart to bring it into line with the correct house interpretation. That means you would move each of the planets one house in either direction on your Worksheet IV.

Now that you have seen the significance of the planets in the signs and houses, it's time to see what you can learn from their positions with respect to each other.

Let's look at their aspects.

Chapter Five

Your Natal Aspects

Your natal aspects show where the planets were with respect to each other in the zodiac at the time you were born. Each natal planet could have been in any one of five major aspects with respect to the other nine planets. You saw in Chapter One that these aspects—conjunctions, sextiles, squares, oppositions, and trines—bring the energies of the planets into harmonious or inharmonious combinations. This chapter describes how the aspects between your natal planets have combined to influence your behavior and approach to life.

Finding Planetary Aspects

Finding the aspect between two planets means finding how many degrees they are apart in the zodiac. An easy way to do that is to take the difference between the Sky Position numbers of the two planets (you have recorded the Sky Position numbers on Worksheet I). Two planets in the same Sky Position are 0 degrees apart (within an orb of 10 degrees)—therefore they are in conjunction. Since each Sky Position number represents 10 degrees, two planets *six* Sky Positions apart are 60 degrees apart—they would be in trine.

Worksheet III—Natal Aspects—makes it easy for you to find the aspects between your natal planets by taking the difference in their Sky Positions and then using the following Aspect Key:

Aspect Key

Difference in Sky Positions	Aspect
0	Conjunction
6	Sextile
9	Square
12	Trine
18	Opposition
24	Trine
27	Square
30	Sextile

Figure 5–1 shows a typical worksheet filled in—you will find blank worksheets at the back of the book.

Notice the spaces provided for Sky Position numbers of planets across the top row and down the left column. You should now transfer the natal Sky Position numbers from Worksheet I into the spaces provided for them on Worksheet III. Be sure to write them in the left column as well as across the top row.

I'll show you two ways to find the aspects. The first is for those who enjoy doing arithmetic. The second is for the rest of us—it makes use of a simple look-up table. Here's the arithmetic way.

Once you have entered the Sky Positions for each natal planet on Worksheet III, take the difference between the Sky Positions of pairs of planets and look for differences that correspond with a major aspect. Start with the planet on the first row (Sun) and

NAME: ____________________ DATE: ____________

	SU (25)	MO (27)	ME (27)	VE (22)	MA (35)	JU (27)	SA (22)	UR (35)	NE (14)	PL (11)
SU (25)	--									
MO (27)	--	--	☌			☌				
ME (27)	--	--	--			☌				
VE (22)	--	--	--	--			☌			
MA (35)	--	--	--	--	--			☌		(△)
JU (27)	--	--	--	--	--	--				
SA (22)	--	--	--	--	--	--	--			
UR (35)	--	--	--	--	--	--	--	--		(△)
NE (14)	--	--	--	--	--	--	--	--	--	

CIRCLE THE "CLOSING ASPECTS"

ASPECTS: Take difference between Sky Position numbers of two planets. Find the aspects that correspond with those differences below.

0	CONJUNCTION	☌	18	OPPOSITION	☍
6	SEXTILE	✱	24	TRINE	△
9	SQUARE	□	27	SQUARE	□
12	TRINE	△	30	SEXTILE	✱

Figure 5–1. Typical Worksheet III—Natal Aspects

take the difference between its Sky Position and the Sky Position of all the planets listed across the top row. When you find a difference that corresponds with an aspect, write the symbol for that aspect at the intersection of the two planets involved. (Aspect symbols are shown at the bottom of Worksheet III.) If the differences in Sky Positions are not listed on the Aspect Key, the two planets are not in a major aspect with respect to each other.

After you have taken the differences across the row for the Sun, do the same for the second row for the Moon, and so on for all the remaining rows of planets.

Another way to find the aspects between planets is to use Table 16: Aspect Finder. You can see it at the back of the book. All you do is place a straight edge across the row corresponding with the Sky Position of your row planet on Worksheet III, and then look across to the column corresponding with the Sky Position number of the planets listed in the columns of your Worksheet III. The intersection of your row and column Sky Position numbers will show if those Sky Positions are in aspect with each other, using the same symbols as shown on the bottom of your Worksheet III.

For example, if you look at Table 16, you will see the symbol for a trine at the intersection of the row for Sky Position 35 and the column for Sky Position 11. Of course you would have known that this is a trine by taking the difference between 35 and 11—24—which is a trine in the Aspect Key. However, the Aspect Finder eliminates mental error and mental fatigue in finding aspects for many planets.

The shaded areas on Table 16 show the aspects which are closing ("applying"), while the unshaded areas show where the aspects are opening ("separating"). You may recall from Chapter One that closing aspects intensify their effect, while separating aspects are less intense in their effects. You may also remember that closing or separating aspects are affected by retrograde motions.

A closing aspect on the Aspect Finder may actually be a separating aspect if the faster planet is in retrograde motion, and a separating aspect may actually be closing when the faster planet is retrograde. Conversely, when the slower planet is retrograde, closing aspects close faster, and separating aspects separate

NAME:			DATE:	
PLANETS	RETR	(From WS I & II) SIGN	HOUSE	(From Worksheet III) NATAL ASPECTS
SUN		Sagitt.	12	–
MOON		Sagitt.	1	☌ ME ☌ JU
MERCURY		Sagitt.	1	☌ JU
VENUS		Scorpio	11	☌ SA
MARS		Pisces	4	☌ UR (△) PL
JUPITER		Sagitt.	1	–
SATURN		Scorpio	11	–
URANUS		Scorpio	4	(△) PL
NEPTUNE		Leo	9	–
PLUTO		Cancer	8	–
ASCEND.	Sagitt.		SCOUT PLANET:	Venus / Saturn

Figure 5-2. Typical Worksheet IV—Summary of Natal Planets

faster. Finally, if both planets are retrograde, closing aspects close slower and separating aspects separate more slowly.

The speed of the planets depends on their distance from the earth, with the fastest planet closest to the earth. The order of the planets, from fastest to slowest, is as follows: Moon, Mercury, Venus, Sun, Mars, Jupiter, Saturn, Uranus, Neptune and Pluto.

When you use Table 16 to find your natal aspects, you can identify a closing aspect by drawing a circle around the aspect symbol as shown in Figure 5–1. That circled aspect reminds you that its effects are emphasized in your chart. Conjunctions and oppositions are neither closing nor separating.

After you have written your natal aspects on your Worksheet III, transfer them to Worksheet IV as shown in Figure 5–2. Worksheet IV is your summary sheet for the collection of information about your natal planets.

Interpreting Your Natal Aspects

After you have found your natal aspects and written them on your Worksheet IV, you are ready to see what they mean. The first thing to notice is whether there is a preponderance of one kind of aspect over another. For example, you may find that most of your aspects are conjunctions such as in Figure 5–2. Or that most of your aspects are squares, or trines. A preponderance of one kind of aspect over another signifies the following:

Conjunctions Predominate. You are aggressive in the pursuit of your ambitions. You thrive on hard work and in overcoming difficult obstacles. You need your freedom to act.

Sextiles Predominate. You are an idea person who enjoys the intellectual stimulation of your social relationships. You love to communicate your ideas to anyone who will listen.

Squares Predominate. You have an intense drive to succeed in your career. You find yourself facing one crisis after another—each of which you overcome by hard work.

Oppositions Predominate. You are forever enmeshed in a complex of interpersonal problems—you either look for a good way to resolve them or a safe way to dissolve them.

Trines Predominate. You are an enthusiastic person who finds it easy to get what you want—too easy. Things may slip away unless you make some efforts on your own.

In general you will find a mixture of the different aspects between your natal planets. The significance of these different aspects is summarized in the following brief profiles arranged by all the planets. The profiles for each planet show the significance for three groups of aspects—the neutral aspects (conjunctions), harmonious aspects (sextiles and trines), and the inharmonious aspects (squares and oppositions).

Here's how to use the following listing.

Look at your Worksheet IV to see which planets make aspects with the planets on each row. Let's say that, as in Figure 5–2, your first aspects appear on the second row, where the Moon is conjunct Mercury and also conjunct Jupiter. You would therefore go to the portion of the listing for the Moon to find the section for MOON—Mercury aspects. There you would find the interpretation of the Moon-Mercury conjunction, along with interpretations of the harmonious and inharmonious aspects. After you read that interpretation, you would move along to the MOON—Jupiter section, where you would find the meaning of a Moon-Jupiter conjunction.

After you finish the Moon aspects, move along to the portion of the listing for the next row planet with aspects. In the example shown in Figure 5–2 you would go to the Mercury portion of the listing to find the MERCURY—Jupiter section, where you would find the meaning of the Mercury-Jupiter conjunction.

Continue in this way until you have looked up all the aspects of your natal planets. The aspects are listed with the faster planets shown first (except for Sun—Moon, Sun—Mercury, Sun—Venus). Therefore, to find an aspect between Mars and Venus, you would look up VENUS—Mars. The significance of the aspect between them does not depend on the order in the list.

SUN—Moon

Conjunction: You are too involved in your own needs to notice the needs of others. Don't overtax your health.

Sextile-Trine: You enjoy a healthy and happy life with good friends, good habits, and a good marriage.

Square-Opposition: You are often torn between your thoughts and your feelings. Your personal relationships suffer.

SUN—Mercury

Conjunction: You have a sound mind and enjoy using it in following either scientific or artistic pursuits. (Sun and Mercury do not make sextile, square, etc. aspects.)

SUN—Venus

Conjunction: You are an optimistic lover of life—you make people happy with your gentle approach to relationships. (Sun and Venus do not make sextile, square, etc. aspects.)

SUN—Mars

Conjunction: You are aggressive in your rush to reach the top in your business and your sex life. You usually win.

Sextile-Trine: You are a self-starter with exceptional courage, tact, and leadership ability. You work hard.

Square-Opposition: You are too quick to lash out angrily at anyone who stands in your way. Learn to listen to others.

SUN—Jupiter

Conjunction: Lady Luck always smiles on you. In turn, you always smile on others. Your generosity is legend.

Sextile-Trine: People like you for your positive outlook and natural leadership abilities. You have a spiritual view.

Square-Opposition: You are overextended in your expectation of yourself and in your promises to others. Curb impulses.

SUN—Saturn

Conjunction: You take everything seriously in your endless effort to overcome your difficulties and frustrations.

Sextile-Trine: You are patient and practical in your solemn approaches. Self-discipline wins you success.

Square-Opposition: Everywhere you turn there is an obstacle to be overcome, with no one to help. Fight off self-pity.

SUN—Uranus

Conjunction: You have a quick mind for spotting opportunities in untried areas—and for making important discoveries there.

Sextile-Trine: Your intuitive insights and magnetic personality make you an excellent leader, admired by your followers.

Square-Opposition: Your insistence on having your own way—which often seems eccentric—stresses your relationships.

SUN—Neptune

Conjunction: The reason you have that far-away look is that you actually *are* "far out," on spiritual planes.

Sextile-Trine: You have a well-developed imagination that can win you fame in the creative arts. You are psychic.

Square-Opposition: You have an overworked imagination that deceives you more than it does others. Be more objective.

SUN—Pluto

Conjunction: You often reach deep inside yourself to discover how to improve the way you tick. You're a loner.

Sextile-Trine: You can bounce back after the worst of ordeals. You are fascinated by the occult mysteries.

Square-Opposition: You tend to dominate the people in your life—which is made even worse by your impulsiveness.

MOON—Mercury

Conjunction: Your mind is well aware of the tugs of your heart—and can easily control them. You have a quick wit.

Sextile-Trine: You have a generous supply of common sense supported by an excellent mind and a good memory.

Square-Opposition: You are so bogged down with yesterday's details that you can't seem to rise above trivial concerns.

MOON—Venus

Conjunction: You have a flair for the tasteful decoration of yourself and your home. You have affectionate friends.

Sextile-Trine: Your sensitivity to the opposite sex assures you a happy marriage. Your presence soothes others.

Square-Opposition: Your financial burdens are not eased by your added frustrations with an unresponsive partner.

MOON—Mars

Conjunction: You tend to overreact, with angry outbursts at the slightest emotional frustration. Control yourself!

Sextile-Trine: You have a moneymaking drive, coupled with a need for domestic security. You have good health.

Square-Opposition: You fly off the handle too easily. You lack patience with routine work—and with parents.

MOON—Jupiter

Conjunction: You are concerned about other people, and you help them whenever possible. You must avoid overdoing it.

Sextile-Trine: You have strong ties to your family and home. You always seem to have enough financial resources.

Square-Opposition: Your easy generosity is exploited by those who know that you are indiscriminately extravagant.

MOON—Saturn

Conjunction: You live in the past—feeling too insecure to test yourself against the troubles of today. Very moody.

Sextile-Trine: You are well organized, keeping yourself to a slow-but-sure course in life. You are responsible.

Square-Opposition: You feel that you have been living under a dark cloud. You are uptight from your childhood inhibitions.

MOON—Uranus

Conjunction: Your mood flip-flops, and impulsive behavior keeps everyone uptight. You are looking for unusual kicks.

Sextile-Trine: You are always on the alert for new business or social opportunities—you can sense them coming up.

Square-Opposition: You find your daily life dull and uninteresting. You are wasteful in your search for stimulation.

MOON—Neptune

Conjunction: You are impractical and highly impressionable. You are too heavily dependent on the feelings of others.

Sextile-Trine: You are fully aware of your psychic abilities. Many of your dreams have told you of things that came to pass.

Square-Opposition: You live so much in your fantasy world that you can't tell what is real anymore. Confusion reigns.

MOON—Pluto

Conjunction: Your psychic abilities no longer confuse you. You can make major and dramatic changes in your life.

Sextile-Trine: You are in complete control of your thoughts and feelings, which helps you in your efforts at self-improvement.

Square-Opposition: Your unconscious need to exercise control over your family and friends makes them very uneasy with you.

MERCURY—Venus

Conjunction: You have a golden tongue and a silver pen—you could talk and write yourself to financial success.

Sextile-Trine: Your literary and artistic abilities, coupled with your ability to charm people, make you popular. (Mercury and Venus do not make squares or oppositions.)

MERCURY—Mars

Conjunction: You have a quick mind for technical matters. Your fast talking gets you both into and out of trouble.

Sextile-Trine: You are decisive and practical. When you say something you say it clearly—and you mean what you say.

Square-Opposition: You are quick to take offense at the remarks of others—and to find fault with their actions.

MERCURY—Jupiter

Conjunction: You could convince anyone of almost anything with your gift of gab. You are a born teacher or preacher.

Sextile-Trine: You prefer the challenges of an intellectual career—especially if it requires that you travel a lot.

Square-Opposition: Your expansive ideas are usually beyond the realm of practical implementation. Be more practical.

MERCURY—Saturn

Conjunction: You are skeptical and exacting enough to be an excellent scientist. You plan things well and work hard.

Sextile-Trine: You have an orderly mind and systematic work habits. Your caution seldom leaves anything to chance.

Square-Opposition: You worry too much about too little. You are easily depressed, and you often become jealous of others.

MERCURY—Uranus

Conjunction: You often can see things in a flash. You need your freedom to follow up on your original ideas.

Sextile-Trine: You have learned to trust and follow up on your intuitive hunches. You enjoy study of scientific subjects.

Square-Opposition: You take off on more tangents than you can follow. But you insist on trying to follow them anyway.

MERCURY—Neptune

Conjunction: You have an impressionable mind—you can tune in to nonphysical sensations all around you.

Sextile-Trine: Your sensitive perceptions extend out to include the feelings and thoughts of others—and the future.

Square-Opposition: You have trouble keeping focused in physical reality—you are too busy in your subjective world.

MERCURY—Pluto

Conjunction: You can spot a phony in a minute. You would rather be right than rich. You should stop nagging others.

Sextile-Trine: You can see into the heart of complex scientific subjects. Your mind will rise to any challenge.

Square-Opposition: You can't be accused of being tactful. You think that others have as many secrets as you have.

VENUS—Mars

Conjunction: You love all kinds of emotional excitement, but especially sexual excitement. You're a passionate lover.

Sextile-Trine: You find it easy to be compatible with most people. With you simple affection can become sensuous.

Square-Opposition: You have more than your share of problems with others—usually centered on a sexual conflict.

VENUS—Jupiter

Conjunction: You are known for your optimistic outlook and your generous nature. You need affection from others.

Sextile-Trine: You get along very well with most people. You are popular because of your refined tastes and manners.

Square-Opposition: You posture and pose to impress others with your importance—but you're the only one impressed.

VENUS—Saturn

Conjunction: You have artistic talents and the discipline to make practical use of them. You are looking for status.

Sextile-Trine: Your loyalty and emotional stability assure that you will have a happy marriage. It also helps business.

Square-Opposition: You seem plagued by emotional frustrations that often block you from making lasting relationships.

VENUS—Uranus

Conjunction: Your love life is full of sudden attractions and equally sudden separations. You spread love too widely.

Sextile-Trine: Your popularity stems from your spontaneous, fun-loving approach to life. You add excitement to everything.

Square-Opposition: You can't brag about your emotional stability. However, you do love intensely while it lasts.

VENUS—Neptune

Conjunction: You are extremely sensitive to the feelings of those around you. You must learn to be more realistic.

Sextile-Trine: Your gentle nature makes you attractive to many people—some of whom you meet in very unusual ways.

Square-Opposition: Your past problems seem to come back to haunt you—especially those having something to do with sex.

VENUS—Pluto

Conjunction: Your love life is as intense as it is complicated. You seem to be caught in a revolving door of love.

Sextile-Trine: Your love life brings you to the higher planes of experience. Your marriage was made in heaven.

Square-Opposition: Your sex life skirts the edge of disaster—the intensity of your passions defies restraint.

MARS—Jupiter

Conjunction: You have the self-confidence that most people envy. You can accomplish anything you set out to do.

Sextile-Trine: You are generous to a fault. You seem compelled to help those who are in need—but you do so cheerfully.

Square-Opposition: You seem to get ahead at the expense of other people. Your friendly manner covers an ulterior motive.

MARS—Saturn

Conjunction: You are ambitious, but can't quite make up your mind about your goals. You are too easily imposed upon.

Sextile-Trine: You don't mind starting at the bottom, since you are confident of your ability to reach the very top.

Square-Opposition: Your frustrations often turn into deep resentments—against yourself as well as others blocking you.

MARS—Uranus

Conjunction: Your mind craves excitement and adventure—but you are too high-strung to handle the emotional pressure.

Sextile-Trine: You have the courage to take decisive actions—usually to implement original ideas of a practical nature.

Square-Opposition: Your impulsiveness leads you into angry confrontations. You are enrolled at the School of Hard Knocks.

MARS—Neptune

Conjunction: You have mysterious powers over others which you enjoy using to your own advantage. Keep lofty goals.

Sextile-Trine: You are a behind-the-scenes, action-oriented executive. You can inspire others to do their best work.

Square-Opposition: Your imagination has produced a clutter of unrealistic fears that put you down in your own eyes.

MARS—Pluto

Conjunction: You have the endurance to take on superhuman tasks—and are stubborn enough to finish what you start.

Sextile-Trine: You can easily sense anyone's attempt to deceive you. You are fearless in defending noble causes.

Square-Opposition: You are known for your violent temper. Your use of force costs you more than you can ever gain.

JUPITER—Saturn

Conjunction: You are concerned with maintaining the dignity and morality of the past. You are honest and responsible.

Sextile-Trine: Your common sense and practical approach will assure you of a successful business career. You are diplomatic.

Square-Opposition: You have always had more than your share of hardships. You have to work for everything you get.

JUPITER—Uranus

Conjunction: You make lofty plans based on idealistic goals—and you implement them with an objective detachment.

Sextile-Trine: Your intuitive insights give you an advantage in business. You are interested in self-development.

Square-Opposition: You begin more projects than you can finish. You jump the gun on opportunities—then lose them.

JUPITER—Neptune

Conjunction: You can convert your idealistic goals into money-making ventures—usually through an artistic outlet.

Sextile-Trine: Your intuitions help you to understand the people around you. You have developed a spiritual outlook.

Square-Opposition: You always promise more than you can deliver. That's because you are in the clouds. Come back down to earth.

JUPITER—Pluto

Conjunction: Your intense ambition causes you to dominate others. You can recycle old ideas into new ones that work.

Sextile-Trine: You are eager to understand the mysteries of the ages. You exercise a strong influence on other people.

Square-Opposition: You try to convert others to your own dogmatic beliefs. Your tactless approach leads to resentment.

SATURN—Uranus

Conjunction: You can be very practical in implementing your ideas. You build on older, more solid foundations.

Sextile-Trine: You are an excellent organizer with the will power necessary to run large public organizations.

Square-Opposition: Your insecurities make you very touchy. Your oppressive martyr complex has cost you many friends.

SATURN—Neptune

Conjunction: You have more power over others than you have over yourself. Be on the alert for deceptions.

Sextile-Trine: You work best at planning large operations from behind the scenes—no detail escapes your notice.

Square-Opposition: Your distrust of others has caused irrational fears and phobias—bring them out in the open.

SATURN—Pluto

Conjunction: You are engaged in an endless struggle to discard old habits so that you can gain control of your life.

Sextile-Trine: You have the ability to endure many hardships in your determination to succeed—and you usually do.

Square-Opposition: Your life seems to be an uninterrupted series of major disappointments—never of your own fault.

URANUS—Neptune

Conjunction: Your generation will bring in the new age of spiritual progress, supported by the marvels of science.

Sextile-Trine: Your generation searches for a utopian life style. You all have a respect for mystical messages.

Square-Opposition: You seem to be continually confused by the surrounding turmoil of the times. You are a pioneer.

URANUS—Pluto

Conjunction: You are at the center of reform movements that seek to bring our social system into harmony.

Sextile-Trine: Your generation introduces changes as a group effort to convert occult teachings into a new science.

Square-Opposition: Your life has had its share of disruption and upheaval. Somehow you take it all in stride.

NEPTUNE—Pluto

Conjunction: You feel some uncomfortable shifts in your beliefs—causing you confusion about how to know the truth.

Sextile-Trine: Yours is a generation of mystically oriented individuals—each of you is psychic to some degree.

Square-Opposition: Your life is full of abrupt surprises—some of which are caused by the deceptions of others.

More About Natal Aspects

In addition to these interpretations of the aspects between two planets, there are interpretations for aspects that can arise between three or more planets. You can see such multiple aspects by looking at how the planets fall on your Horoscope Wheel. Some of the more significant of these multiple aspects are the Grand Trine, the T-Square, the Grand Square, and the Stellium. The interpretation of these major multiple aspects is as follows:

Grand Trine. When three planets fall on your chart such that they are 120 degrees from each other, they are in the Grand Trine aspect. This aspect brings great stability into your life and signifies a potential for creative self-expression, along with deep spiritual awareness.

T-Square. When two planets are in opposition to each other, with a third planet square to both of them, you have a T-Square in your chart. This arrangement signifies a life that is faced with obstacles to be overcome—along with the drive needed to overcome them.

Grand Square. When four planets are arranged such that they are 90 degrees from each other like the corners of a square, they form a Grand Square. This multiple aspect signifies a continual round of crises. You barely resolve one crisis before another one arises.

Stellium. If three or more planets fall into the same Sky Position (a conjunction), it is called a Stellium. This aspect signifies that the effects of their common sign and the affairs of their common house are especially important considerations in your life.

In the preface I said that you would soon know what it means when someone says that their Mars is conjunct Venus in Taurus in their Fifth House. Now that you have come this far it should be clear to you how you can do that.

First you would find the meaning of Mars conjunct Venus in this chapter. You would look up Venus—Mars to find that a conjunction signifies "You love all kinds of emotional excitement, but especially sexual excitement. You are a passionate lover."

Then you would go to Chapter Four to look up the meaning of each planet in its sign and house (Taurus and Fifth House). Venus in Taurus shows that "You are a slow starter when it comes to romance. You need someone like yourself who enjoys physical contact and who will reciprocate your fidelity. . . ." Venus in the Fifth House says that "Your activities center on the pursuit of pleasure. Your affectionate nature and sunny disposition lead you into many pleasant love affairs, one of which ends in a happy marriage with lovely, loving children."

So far we see a person who may be slow to start up a romance, but who can go far with it. Let's finish this off by looking up the meaning of Mars in Taurus and Mars in the Fifth House. Mars in Taurus—"You are determined to earn a lot of money. You are able to follow a carefully planned career that depends on your pride of craftsmanship and your perseverance. You would like to get married early in life and enjoy sex." (There it is again!) And now, for Mars in the Fifth House. "Your activities center on the pursuit of love and other pleasures. There is a sense of urgency in finding your sex partner. You are a natural disciplinarian, causing problems with children. Gambler."

Considering that these profiles were not prepared to meet the needs of this example, they describe a rather consistent behavior pattern for someone who has Venus conjunct Mars in Taurus in the Fifth House.

As you study your horoscope, and those of your friends and family, you will find that the behavior profiles fall into such consistent patterns. Where there are major differences between separate profiles, it indicates that the person is indeed being pulled in different directions by the forces of his natal planets.

Now, let's move on to see how you can determine what the astrological forces are doing to you as the planets pass overhead this week, transiting your natal horoscope.

Chapter Six

Your Daily Horoscope

As the planets slowly move along the zodiac each day, they pass through the different houses of your natal horoscope and make different aspects with the positions of your natal planets. These transiting planets energize the latent potentials promised by your natal horoscope, and trigger the behavior and events which then become part of your daily experience.

This chapter shows you how to examine these transiting planets to see what effects they may have on your daily life. In other words, it shows you how to make your own daily horoscope.

Setting Up a Transit Horoscope

The effect of a transiting planet depends on where it is with respect to the planets and houses of your natal horoscope. If you haven't already done so, prepare your natal horoscope as described in Chapter Two. You will need at least Worksheet

II—Planets in Signs and Houses. It would help if you also prepared a Horoscope Wheel as described at the end of Chapter Two (see Figure 2–4). You can decide later if you want to do without the Horoscope Wheel when you prepare your daily horoscope.

When you prepare your Horoscope Wheel be sure to keep your natal planets within the inner circle as shown in Figure 6–1. Also, be sure to check the space in the upper left corner to show that this is a Transit Horoscope.

Once you have your natal horoscope you must then find the positions of all the planets on the date of interest. Suppose you want to know how the planets are affecting you today. You first must find where all the planets are in the zodiac today. You would follow the same steps that you used for finding the planet positions for your natal horoscope—except that you would use today's date instead of your birth date. Use the same Tables 1 through 14 along with a new Worksheet I—in this case don't bother with the Ascendant Sky Position.

After you have found the Sky Positions of all the planets for the date of interest, you can do two things. First, you can place them directly on the outer ring of your Transit Horoscope at their respective Sky Position numbers (see Figure 6–1). Notice that this automatically shows you where each of the transiting planets falls into the houses of the natal horoscope. In the figure you can see that transiting Neptune, which is at Sky Position 26, falls into the natal First House. The transiting Moon at Sky Position 3 is in the natal Fifth House.

You can also see from this Transit Horoscope Wheel that the transiting Neptune is nine Sky Positions from the natal Mars and Uranus (on the inner ring)—showing Neptune to be square to the natal Mars and Uranus. You can use the Aspect Key at the lower left corner of the Horoscope Wheel to help determine the aspects between each of the transiting planets and the natal planets. But before you do that, consider the second way to work out your daily horoscope.

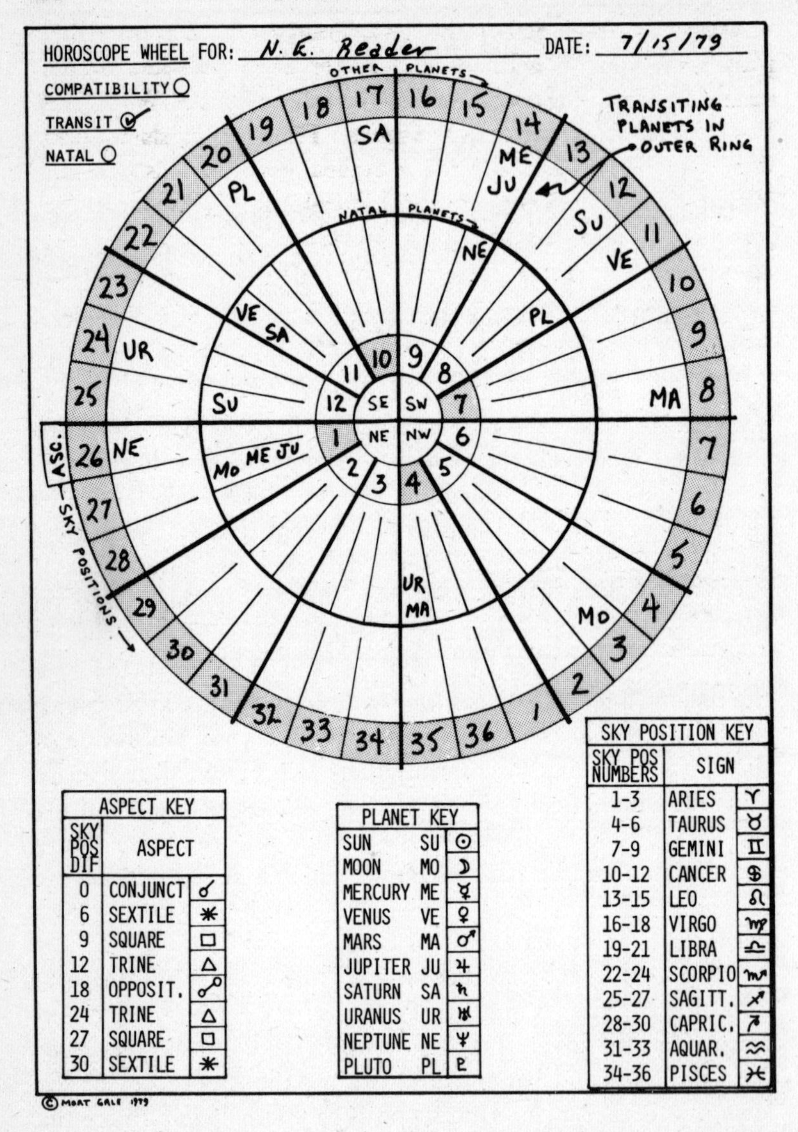

Figure 6–1. Horoscope Wheel with Transiting Planets

After you have found the Sky Positions of the transiting planets on your Worksheet I, transfer those positions to the spaces next to the planets listed in the left column of Worksheet V—Transits or Companion Aspects. Figure 6–2 shows how Worksheet V is filled out for a typical case. In this case the "Other Planet Positions" in the left column are for transiting planets. You will use this same worksheet in Chapter Seven, where the Other Planet Positions will be the natal planets from a companion's horoscope, to determine the astrological compatibility between you and your companion.

In either case, the Sky Positions shown under the planets on the top row are the positions of your natal planets—from your Worksheet II or your Horoscope Wheel. Once you have the transiting and natal Sky Positions on Worksheet V you can find the aspects between them in the same way you found the aspects between your natal planets on Worksheet III (see the beginning of Chapter Five). Either take the difference between Sky Position numbers and use the Aspect Key, or use the Aspect Finder in Table 16. Regardless of how you find them, write the symbols for the aspects between all the planets shown on Worksheet V.

If you take Sky Position differences from the Transit Horoscope Wheel to find the transiting aspects, you can use Worksheet V to keep track of those aspects.

After you have found all the aspects between the transiting planets (left column) and your natal planets (top row), write them on the appropriate rows in the lower portion of Worksheet V. Each row in the lower part corresponds with the same planet row on the upper part of the worksheet. Just read across each row on the upper portion and copy down the aspects in the order in which they appear on that row (see Figure 6–2).

After you have written the transiting aspects on the lower part of Worksheet V you must find the natal houses in which those transiting planets fall. If you have prepared a Transit Horoscope Wheel you can find the house for each transiting planet just by looking at the chart. Each of the transiting planets in the outer

NAME: N.E. Reader — 7/15/79 TRANSIT DATE

COMPANION: -

(OTHER PLANET POSITIONS)	SU (25)	MO (27)	ME (27)	VE (22)	MA (35)	JU (27)	SA (22)	UR (35)	NE (14)	PL (11)
	(YOUR NATAL PLANET SKY POSITIONS)									
SU (12)										
MO (3)		△	△			△				
ME (14)									☌	
VE (11)					△			△		☌
MA (8)					□			□	✱	
JU (14)									☌	
SA (17)					☍			☍		✱
UR (24)										
NE (26)					□			□	△	
PL (20)									✱	□

KEY: 0-☌ 6-✱ 9-■ 12-▲ 18-☍ 24-▲ 27-■ 30-✱

OTHER PLANETS	RET	IN YOUR HOUSE #	OTHER PLANETS MAKE THESE ASPECTS TO YOUR NATAL PLANETS
SUN		8	
MOON		5	△MO △ME △JU
MERCURY	-	9	☌ NE
VENUS	-	8	△ MA △UR ☌PL
MARS	-	7	□ MA □ UR ✱ NE
JUPITER	-	9	☌ NE
SATURN	-	10	☍ MA ☍UR ✱ PL
URANUS	✓	12	
NEPTUNE	✓	1	□ MA □UR △NE
PLUTO	-	11	✱ NE □PL

Figure 6–2. Typical Worksheet V for Transiting Aspects

ring of the chart falls into the house shown by the numbers on the innermost ring of the Horoscope Wheel. For example, you just saw that transiting Neptune fell into the First House in Figure 6–1.

If you do not choose to make up a Transit Horoscope Wheel, you can still find the houses of your transiting planets. You will have to compare Worksheet I for the transiting planets with Worksheet II for your natal horoscope. Look at the Sky Positions of each transiting planet (on Worksheet I) and then find the natal house number corresponding with that Sky Position on your Worksheet II.

After you find the house for each transiting planet (from either the Transit Horoscope Wheel or your Worksheet II), write it in the space next to that planet on the lower part of Worksheet V, in the column headed "In Your House #." When you have done that, you are ready to begin interpreting the effects of those planets on your life on the date you selected.

Interpreting Transits

The effect of a transiting planet on your life depends in part on the significance of the planet in your natal horoscope. You'll recall from Chapter Five that certain planets were more important than others—the Sun, Moon, and the planetary rulers of your Sun sign and your Ascendant. Also, the planets found at the four angles of your natal horoscope (cusps of the first, fourth, seventh, and tenth houses) have stronger influences on your life. You should pay more attention to the interpretation of the transits of these special planets.

The day-to-day changes in your life depend on the transits of the Sun, Moon, Mercury, Venus, and Mars. Their transits through the aspects and houses are measured in days and weeks. The outer planets—Jupiter, Saturn, Uranus, Neptune, and Pluto—are important for the long-term effects on your life, measured in years and decades.

The duration of a transit effect also depends on whether or not the transiting planet is in retrograde motion on your date of interest. (Be sure to transfer the retrograde checks from Worksheet I to the bottom of Worksheet V.) Retrograde planets may remain in retrograde from twenty-one days to five months (for Mercury and Pluto respectively).

The following list shows how long the planets remain in each Sky Position (decan) and in each house of a transit horoscope. The durations are rounded out to useful approximations.

Time Spent by Transiting Planets

Planet	Time in One Sky Position	Time in One Natal House	Time Spent Retrograde
SUN	10 days	1 month	——
MOON	1 day	2½ days	——
MERCURY	2 days	6 days	21 days
VENUS	6 days	3 weeks	1½ months
MARS	19 days	2 months	3 months
JUPITER	4 months	1 year	4 months
SATURN	10 months	2½ years	4½ months
URANUS	2½ years	7 years	5 months
NEPTUNE	4½ years	14 years	5 months
PLUTO	7 years	21 years	5 months

The effects of a planet's transit through a natal house are felt over the duration of its stay in that house. However, the duration of the effect of a transiting aspect may be somewhat shorter than the duration of the planet's stay in each Sky Position. For example, the effect of a transiting Sun is most strongly felt over a three-day period within its ten-day stay in one Sky Position. The effect will be felt to a lesser extent on the other days in that Sky Position. It all depends on how closely the aspect falls within its orb during the time it is in each Sky Position.

The transit interpretations that follow will give you an idea of what to expect when a transiting planet falls into your natal houses and makes aspects with your natal planets. The five major aspects are grouped into three classifications—neutral aspects (conjunctions), harmonious aspects (sextiles and trines) and inharmonious or discordant aspects (squares and oppositions).

As you read the interpretations for all the transiting planets you may find that some contradict others. That is a reflection of the conflict of astrological forces at work—forces that you must learn to cope with. Knowing that they are there makes it easier to deal with them.

The arrangement of these interpretations follows the order of the planets as shown on the bottom of your Worksheet V. Read across each planet row to see its effect in your house, and then its effect as it makes aspects with each of the planets shown on the worksheet.

One more point. The meaning of an aspect does not depend on the order of the planets in the aspect. A transiting Mars in an aspect to your natal Jupiter has the same meaning as a transiting Jupiter in that same aspect to your natal Mars. Except that the transiting Jupiter aspect lasts much longer than the transiting Mars aspect.

If you can't find a listing for a particular planet pair, reverse the order of the planets in the pair and then look up the meaning of the aspects between them. (The list of meanings is arranged with the faster planets shown first.) But remember that the duration of the aspect effect depends on the speed of the transiting planet of the pair.

Transits of the Sun

The Sun is the source of all energies. These energies stimulate the activities of the houses occupied by the transiting Sun, and reinforce or weaken the planetary effects, depending on the

Sun's aspects to the natal planets. When the Sun transits an inner planet, it may trigger a dormant aspect between that inner planet and a slower moving outer planet. If a planet is being transited by another planet when it is transited by the Sun, the effect of the transit is strengthened.

The following brief profiles tell you what you can expect when the Sun transits through the houses of your natal horoscope. The Sun spends about one month in each natal house.

Sun Transits First House. You feel an upsurge in self-confidence. This is the time to impress others. It is also the time to take stock of your self-improvement program.

Sun Transits Second House. During this period you try to improve your financial status—especially since you will be spending money to impress others and to please yourself.

Sun Transits Third House. Things perk up around the house and office as you get more involved with other people. This is a good time to clear the air on earlier misunderstandings.

Sun Transits Fourth House. You feel the need to get back to familiar surroundings. A good time to fix up the house—and to repair sagging family relationships, or go off alone.

Sun Transits Fifth House. You feel like forgetting your troubles and going out for a good time. You have the urge to start up, or renew, romantic relationships (objective—sex!).

Sun Transits Sixth House. It's time to get back to work. Look for new ways to "work smarter, not harder." It's also time to start making compromises that meet the needs of others.

Sun Transits Seventh House. Time to reevaluate how well you hold up your end of partnerships or romantic relationships. You may need help from others to see things objectively.

Sun Transits Eighth House. Time to face up to your hidden feelings—the ones that are behind your compulsive desires. Someone may force you into making a major change.

Sun Transits Ninth House. A good time to back off for a fresh look at your life—or to freshen up the way you live it. Stretch your mind with intellectual interests, like a course.

Sun Transits Tenth House. Here's your chance to show everyone how well you can do your job—it should be a snap. But don't substitute a pretense for your true performance.

Sun Transits Eleventh House. You are interested in getting out with friends, or more involved in the activities of groups. You will find it easier to work with others this month.

Sun Transits Twelfth House. You feel like being alone with your thoughts so you can evaluate your progress over the past year. Time to clean up your act for the next scene.

The following profiles describe the effects of the transiting Sun as it makes aspects with your natal planets.

SUN—Sun

Conjunction: A time of new enthusiasms and fresh starts. You feel happy and optimistic—time to ask for that raise.

Sextile-Trine: Everything's coming up roses—you are getting along with everyone. Anything you do seems to work out.

Square-Opposition: Problems seem to be coming to a head all at once. Failure seems almost imminent—face the challenge.

SUN—Moon (or Moon-Sun)

Conjunction: You seem to be getting it all together—your inner feelings are out in the open. Time to discover yourself.

Sextile-Trine: A good time to visit friends or invite them to your house—you are feeling good about yourself.

Square-Opposition: You feel under pressure—either control your frustration or take the consequences of blowing your top.

SUN—Mercury (or Mercury-Sun)

Conjunction: Here's your chance to let others know what's on your mind. They will understand what you say today.

Sextile-Trine: Your mind is clicking along in high gear—a good time to learn new things or start new ventures.

Square-Opposition: A good time to practice how to listen to others before speaking your piece—better be sure than sorry.

SUN—Venus (or Venus-Sun)

Conjunction: You will put your best foot forward today to attract romantic attention—your chances are very good.

Sextile-Trine: Today you have no enemies. A good day to recharge your friendships, and to clean up financial matters.

Square-Opposition: Today you feel like being with a close friend—someone who lets you do the talking. Let it flow.

SUN—*Mars (or Mars-Sun)*

Conjunction: You feel the urge to start something new on your own. Avoid any impulses that may strain a relationship.

Sextile-Trine: This is a good time to get work done—especially if you can work alone. Clean up your backlogs.

Square-Opposition: You feel that other people are hostile in challenging your position. Don't become aggressive.

SUN—*Jupiter (or Jupiter-Sun)*

Conjunction: Things look very good to you—you want to branch out into new ventures. Be optimistic but careful.

Sextile-Trine: You should feel optimistic and in tune with everything and everyone. Time for a change, or a trip.

Square-Opposition: You have an excess of energy which may lead you to take on more than you can reasonably handle.

SUN—*Saturn (or Saturn-Sun)*

Conjunction: A good time to get organized—even though you don't feel that you have the energy to do so now.

Sextile-Trine: This is the time to take care of those jobs that require self-discipline and attention to details.

Square-Opposition: Unpleasant things keep coming up that need to be resolved. Don't let them overwhelm you now.

SUN—*Uranus (or Uranus-Sun)*

Conjunction: This is a time for surprising changes—mostly because of your need to replace your old routines.

Sextile-Trine: You will find yourself involved with friends in new and exciting experiences—your openness surprises you.

Square-Opposition: Be alert for sudden disruptions in your daily routine. You will feel restless with other people.

SUN—*Neptune (or Neptune-Sun)*

Conjunction: This is one of those times when you want to get away from it all. You are tuned in to spiritual matters.

Sextile-Trine: Everyone seems to be coming to you for some help—you find it rewarding to be able to help them out.
Square-Opposition: Your body is telling you that it's time to take it easy—everything is either confusing or depressing.

SUN—Pluto (or Pluto-Sun)

Conjunction: You won't be able to remain indifferent in what you are doing. Steer clear of unwholesome situations.
Sextile-Trine: This is your chance to make those changes you have been thinking about. A good time to clean up your act.
Square-Opposition: Brace yourself for an eyeball-to-eyeball confrontation with a superior. If you keep cool you can win.

Transits of the Moon

The Moon spends less than a day in each Sky Position, and only two and a half days in a natal house. This means that its effects occur so quickly that you feel them more as unconscious urges and impulses than as conscious reactions to situations.

The effects of the transiting Moon, as it makes aspects with your natal planet positions, are often felt for only a matter of hours. But, regardless of whether or not you are consciously aware of them, you will feel the effects of the Moon as described in the following brief profiles.

Moon Transits First House. You are emotionally tuned in to the feelings of those around you. You will find that it's hard to be objective about anything for a few days.

Moon Transits Second House. You feel especially defensive because of emotional insecurities—you may try to compensate by going on a buying spree you can't afford.

Moon Transits Third House. Things are becoming more serious than usual. You sense a hidden significance in what people say to you. This is a good time to listen quietly.

Moon Transits Fourth House. Give in to that feeling and stay home alone. You need time to sort out past events for their true meaning in your life. Don't fear that loss.

Moon Transits Fifth House. Women become important to you now (regardless of your sex). Don't try to hide your feelings in your relationship. You feel especially protective.

Moon Transits Sixth House. During this period you feel like a martyr. That's because you have repressed your feelings to the point of resentment. It's time to put them in the open.

Moon Transits Seventh House. Beware of jealousies and unreasonable behavior with loved ones—or confrontations with your business partners. Think twice before sounding off.

Moon Transits Eighth House. You may find that you are getting into senseless disputes with people who have a strong influence over you—disputes over joint possessions.

Moon Transits Ninth House. You feel like getting away from it all—at least for a little while. A short trip or a little excitement is all that you really need for now.

Moon Transits Tenth House. Here's your chance to show the boss what you can really do—the stage is set to help you pass the test. But only if you have prepared for it.

Moon Transits Eleventh House. A good time to set things straight between you and a friend. But don't use this as an opportunity to gain the upper hand over that person.

Moon Transits Twelfth House. During this period you need someone to talk to about your fears and concerns. But you will probably end up just pulling back into your shell. Talk.

The following profiles describe the effects of the transiting Moon as it makes aspects with your natal planets.

MOON—Moon

Conjunction: Your need for emotional reassurance is very strong at this time. Don't hide yourself from others.

Sextile-Trine: You feel a strong need to be among close friends in familiar surroundings. Relationships run smoothly.

Square-Opposition: You find it difficult to get along with others now—everyone seems to be quibbling over nothing.

MOON—Mercury (or Mercury-Moon)

Conjunction: Try to put off any important decisions while your head argues with your heart over trivial matters.

Sextile-Trine: Now is the time to make those social contacts, since you won't have any trouble expressing yourself.

Square-Opposition: This isn't the best time to make a rational argument with anyone—your feelings get in the way.

MOON—Venus (or Venus-Moon)

Conjunction: An excellent time to go out socializing—people will find you irresistibly cheerful and charming.

Sextile-Trine: This is the time to throw that party at your house—you will enjoy yourself and everyone else.

Square-Opposition: Your feelings of love grow stronger during this period, and you shower your partner with affection.

MOON—Mars (or Mars-Moon)

Conjunction: A good time to avoid controversial matters—you would find it too difficult to control your temper.

Sextile-Trine: You feel like stepping in and taking over—and the way things are, you could easily carry it off.

Square-Opposition: Now's the time to see how well you can walk on eggs and keep your cool—tension fills the air.

MOON—Jupiter (or Jupiter-Moon)

Conjunction: Everything is right with the world and you are on top of it all. Your generosity flows freely.

Sextile-Trine: A good time to be with other people—they find that you are warm and affectionate now.

Square-Opposition: You feel good about yourself as you look past the petty details of your daily routines.

MOON—Saturn (or Saturn-Moon)

Conjunction: This is one of those times you can't seem to shake off those gloomy feelings of despair. Ease off.

Sextile-Trine: You are more serious about things than you usually are—seek out the company of an older person.

Square-Opposition: Loneliness seems to be the mood of the moment—because you send out "leave me alone" messages.

MOON—Uranus (or Uranus-Moon)

Conjunction: Feelings of impatience come up from nowhere. You can't seem to keep your mind on one thing for very long.

Sextile-Trine: You would like something exciting to happen for a change—but you won't go out to make it happen.

Square-Opposition: You will have to keep a good grip on yourself to avoid making a sudden rash change in your life.

MOON—Neptune (or Neptune-Moon)

Conjunction: You find that you have a special sensitivity to the feelings of others and to the things going on around you.

Sextile-Trine: A fine time to be sharing yourself with some trusted friends—feelings of spirituality flow freely.

Square-Opposition: You seem to run into minor misunderstandings lately as you move into and out of strange moods.

MOON—Pluto (or Pluto-Moon)

Conjunction: You find yourself going through a series of reevaluations as you try to root out annoying obsessions.

Sextile-Trine: Your feelings run very deep now as you search for a meaningful relationship—you need a change.

Square-Opposition: You may be suddenly startled by the release of a pent-up emotion as you confront a companion.

Transits of Mercury

Mercury spends about two days in each Sky Position and a week in each natal house. During that time it affects your mental outlook, communications with others, and urges to take trips. When Mercury is in retrograde motion during its transit it may introduce delays in the affairs under its influence.

The following brief profiles tell you what you might expect when Mercury transits through your natal houses.

Mercury Transits First House. Your mind is sharp today—a good time to take on that difficult project. However, you may have trouble keeping focused on one thing.

Mercury Transits Second House. Your mind is on taking care of your material needs—from trying to improve your financial position to purchasing new things for the house.

Mercury Transits Third House. This is a good time for getting together with other people, especially if it involves intellectual exchanges—you will shine like a star.

Mercury Transits Fourth House. You feel like getting off by yourself so that you can think things out quietly. You seem preoccupied with reviewing past experiences.

Mercury Transits Fifth House. You seem to be more interested in mental amusements than in serious matters. That's a pity, since people would understand anything you tell them now.

Mercury Transits Sixth House. Be careful in dealing with others at work—you are much too critical at this time. You feel anxious about your health—get more rest than usual.

Mercury Transits Seventh House. Now's the time to clear up that intimate problem with your mate, or that difference with a business associate—you can make your point clear now.

Mercury Transits Eighth House. You may find yourself immersed in deep thought about the brevity of life. You may also find yourself involved in problems with property and taxes.

Mercury Transits Ninth House. You may be thinking about taking an advanced course—you feel an urge to expand your mind. You may also develop an urge to take a trip or two.

Mercury Transits Tenth House. This is a good time to review where you stand in your career. Should you take some courses to improve your skills? move up a step? change jobs?

Mercury Transits Eleventh House. You find yourself wondering about your friends and the groups you belong to—should you become more active? drop out? make new friends?

Mercury Transits Twelfth House. You feel you would rather keep your thoughts to yourself than discuss them with anyone else. In fact, you want to be by yourself now.

The following profiles describe the effects of transiting Mercury as it makes aspects with your natal planets.

MERCURY—Mercury

Conjunction: You will make more than your usual number of contacts with others at this time—don't waste any of them.

Sextile-Trine: A good time to plan things out carefully—and to communicate those plans to others. Take a short trip.

Square-Opposition: This is a good time to test your idea on another person—but keep your mind open to his views.

MERCURY—Venus (or Venus-Mercury)

Conjunction: You will find it easier now to express your feelings of affection—it's time to see that special person.

Sextile-Trine: This is a good time to be among old friends or to make new ones—you feel warm and affectionate now.

Square-Opposition: A good time to face up to a minor difficulty in a personal relationship—you can compromise.

MERCURY—Mars (or Mars-Mercury)

Conjunction: You have the mental stamina to work all night or to argue all day. Don't do either—save your energy.

Sextile-Trine: A good time to catch up on that backlog of work—especially if you can get it done by yourself.

Square-Opposition: People get on your nerves as they try to tell you things—avoid the temptation to tell them off.

MERCURY—Jupiter (or Jupiter-Mercury)

Conjunction: You can be more understanding and forgiving now because you see things from a broader perspective.

Sextile-Trine: Your mind seems to be preoccupied with finding new ways to make your life better in the future.

Square-Opposition: You feel that you can do anything you set your mind on—but remember that it takes discipline.

MERCURY—Saturn (or Saturn-Mercury)

Conjunction: You are more careful now about attending to the details that you normally overlook. A friend may leave now.

Sextile-Trine: You need to take stock of things to see what has to be done to improve your life—time to get organized.

Square-Opposition: A good time to dig into those hard jobs that require your full attention—but don't overwork yourself.

MERCURY—Uranus (or Uranus-Mercury)

Conjunction: Your mind is racing along so fast that it gets ahead of itself. You can feel quite creative at this time.

Sextile-Trine: Exciting things fill up your days—new friends, new ideas, and new experiences. Keep yourself open.

Square-Opposition: Ideas come and go so fast that you feel inspired. You won't be able to keep up your daily routine.

MERCURY—Neptune (or Neptune-Mercury)

Conjunction: Your mind seems to be fascinated with some elusive ideas—keep your imagination from running wild.

Sextile-Trine: You are especially sensitive to the moods of people, and to the things going on around you.

Square-Opposition: You can't decide if it's you who are confused, or whether others just don't want to hear what you say.

MERCURY—Pluto (or Pluto-Mercury)

Conjunction: You can get to the bottom of the most difficult problem now—but don't become preoccupied with it.

Sextile-Trine: You may be getting curious about the deeper mysteries of life—or about "whodunit" in a detective story.

Square-Opposition: You may find yourself becoming obsessed with the need to carry out a pet project—keep your cool.

Transits of Venus

Venus spends about one week in each Sky Position and about three weeks in each natal house. Venus is the planet of love and material pleasures, so that its transits bring different degrees of enjoyment. The effects are felt as subjective experiences rather than as urges to action.

Transiting Venus is retrograde for about one and a half months each year. During that time the affairs affected by Venus may be slowed down or delayed.

The following profiles describe how the transits of Venus affect you as they pass through each natal house.

Venus Transits First House. This is an excellent time to be with the people you like. The pleasant warmth and affection you feel for them is quickly sensed and returned.

Venus Transits Second House. The time is ripe for taking advantage of those opportunities for financial gains. You can bring them off quite easily now. Avoid any extravagance.

Venus Transits Third House. Your contacts with family and friends become more pleasant as you turn from serious matters to social pleasantries. You may enjoy a short trip.

Venus Transits Fourth House. A good time for spending a quiet evening at home alone. You feel the urge to redecorate your home to make it seem a little more luxurious than it is.

Venus Transits Fifth House. Get out of your rut and go out with friends for a good time—or go see that special person in your life. You would enjoy doing something creative.

Venus Transits Sixth House. A good time to buckle down to work—you will have to hold off on your desire to have fun. Make sure that arrangements with others are clearly stated.

Venus Transits Seventh House. Now is the time to explore that romantic affair, or to establish that business partnership. Everything you do will turn out to be the right thing for you.

Venus Transits Eighth House. Things seem to come to you through your relationship with a partner, or your mate. It's a good time to go to the bank for a loan—they will give it.

Venus Transits Ninth House. A good time to expose yourself to the higher values in life. Visit museums or take in a concert. Be sure to take your romantic partner with you.

Venus Transits Tenth House. You will find that higher-ups are favorably impressed with you now. Your relations with co-workers are harmonious—they cooperate with you willingly.

Venus Transits Eleventh House. You will enjoy going out to meetings and social affairs now. If you throw a party at your house it will be a smashing success—you exude warmth.

Venus Transits Twelfth House. Somehow, things seem to require that you take care of someone else at this time. Use this opportunity to learn the rewards of unselfish giving.

The following profiles describe the effects of transiting Venus as it makes aspects with your natal planets.

VENUS—Venus

Conjunction: This is an excellent time to make new friends and to get together with old ones—you take the initiative.

Sextile-Trine: Your relaxed attitude and feeling of contentment set you up for pleasant contacts and events.

Square-Opposition: You find yourself in situations where it is better to make a compromise than to make an issue.

VENUS—Mars (or Mars-Venus)

Conjunction: Your sexual urges are aroused. You must find a partner, or sublimate your energies into physical activities.

Sextile-Trine: A good time to get together with others—you can meet your physical needs while also serving their needs.

Square-Opposition: Your need for sexual contact may be too intense for you to control—don't offend your partner now.

VENUS—Jupiter (or Jupiter-Venus)

Conjunction: This may be your lucky day—lucky for love, and lucky for money. It's a great time to have a wedding.

Sextile-Trine: Nothing can bother you now—you feel too good to notice anything unpleasant. A good time for a vacation.

Square-Opposition: Here's where you have to be careful about indulging yourself in careless extravagances (what diet?).

VENUS—Saturn (or Saturn-Venus)

Conjunction: You find it difficult to express how you feel about others at this time—especially about the one you love.

Sextile-Trine: A good time to clear things up between you and someone you care about. An older person becomes important.

Square-Opposition: You are torn between your feelings of affection for someone, and your annoyance at his or her minor misdeed.

VENUS—Uranus (or Uranus-Venus)

Conjunction: You should expect an unexpected turn of events in your romantic affairs—but you will welcome the surprise.

Sextile-Trine: Now's the time to take that wild fling—you are ready for the excitement of meeting new people.

Square-Opposition: Don't attach too much importance to a romantic episode at this time—no one else does.

VENUS—Neptune (or Neptune-Venus)

Conjunction: You find that your mind is drifting off into romantic fantasies—you see yourself as pure as driven snow.

Sextile-Trine: It's not likely that you will get much done now—your mind is off into romantic daydreams and fantasies.

Square-Opposition: You are probably upset with a romantic partner now—that's because of your unreasonable expectation.

VENUS—Pluto (or Pluto-Venus)

Conjunction: Your romantic urges are more intense than usual at this time—it can make you jealous or make you wander.

Sextile-Trine: Your friendships become more important now, as you seek to share your affections more actively with others.

Square-Opposition: The intensification of your emotions makes you critical of slight changes in your partner's responses.

Transits of Mars

Mars spends about three weeks in each Sky Position and about two months in each natal house. Mars provides you with the energies needed to assert yourself in the pursuit of your needs and desires.

Transiting Mars is retrograde for about three months each year. During that time you may experience reversals or delays in the affairs affected by Mars at that time.

The following profiles describe how the transits of Mars may affect you as they pass through each of your natal houses.

Mars Transits First House. This is your time to shine. You have the enthusiasm and energy to take on the most difficult tasks, and to show others you mean business. But don't overdo it.

Mars Transits Second House. You may become especially sensitive about your own value—tending to identify yourself with the things you own. Avoid foolish purchases for self-esteem.

Mars Transits Third House. Be especially careful about flying off the handle over some minor difference of opinion. You make others feel that you have a chip on your shoulder.

Mars Transits Fourth House. Problems come up around the home—things that seem to have their roots in past conflicts which you can neither remember nor ever resolve.

Mars Transits Fifth House. Juices are flowing that make you want to go out to have physical fun—either with outdoor sports or bedroom sports. Be careful not to neglect your job.

Mars Transits Sixth House. You can't seem to find enough work to throw your energies into. Conflicts may arise over who should get the credit for the work you are engaged in.

Mars Transits Seventh House. You find it much easier to work along with others now. In fact, cooperation seems to be the order of the day—except with those you call "enemies."

Mars Transits Eighth House. You feel the need to face up to a nagging problem, to resolve it once and for all. It may have to do with the financial management of joint resources.

Mars Transits Ninth House. You feel the need to take a broader look at life, and your role in it. Your need for an expanded view may give you the urge to take a long trip abroad.

Mars Transits Tenth House. You have a renewed interest in becoming successful in your chosen career. Your drive to succeed puts you in conflict with those above you on the ladder.

Mars Transits Eleventh House. A good time to join forces with others trying to achieve the same goals. But you find it hard to become a team player—this is an excellent time to learn.

Mars Transits Twelfth House. It frustrates you that you are coming across in the wrong light, no matter how hard you try to create a good impression. Better stop trying for a little while.

The following profiles describe the effects of transiting Mars as it makes aspects with your natal planets.

MARS—Mars

Conjunction: A good time to take care of a backlog of back-breaking physical chores—or to undertake new ones.

Sextile-Trine: Your feeling of self-confidence is at its peak—you can impress anyone with your abilities and potential.

Square-Opposition: You can get a lot done now if you control impulsive behavior that provokes other people.

MARS—Jupiter (or Jupiter-Mars)

Conjunction: You feel so great now that you run the risk of overextending yourself—both physically and financially.

Sextile-Trine: Anything you start now has an excellent chance for success, based on your own efforts and on your luck.

Square-Opposition: Now is the time to think twice before you strike out on a new venture. Consider the risks involved.

MARS—Saturn (or Saturn-Mars)

Conjunction: Everything you try to do seems to be blocked in some way—better stick to your routine for a little while.

Sextile-Trine: This is the time to take care of those difficult details that you kept putting off for another time.

Square-Opposition: You are frustrated now because things are not working out the way you want—other people stop you.

MARS—Uranus (or Uranus-Mars)

Conjunction: If there ever was a time to expect surprises, this is it. You may upset your own plans by an impulsive move.

Sextile-Trine: You want to break away from your routine now—you are looking for excitement in new and unusual experiences.

Square-Opposition: You will have to control yourself now—your restlessness may erupt in angry outbursts at a friend.

MARS—Neptune (or Neptune-Mars)

Conjunction: Don't bet on yourself at this time—you can't be sure of accomplishing anything in this irritable state.

Sextile-Trine: This would be a good time to do something for someone else—either that or go off alone for a while.

Square-Opposition: You can't seem to shake off those feelings of self-doubt and hopelessness. Try to conserve your energy.

MARS—Pluto (or Pluto-Mars)

Conjunction: You feel a surge of enthusiasm that can fire up dormant ambitions—just don't run over people in your way.

Sextile-Trine: This is the time to make those planned changes in your life. Try to consider the needs of other people.
Square-Opposition: This is a time of confrontation and power struggles—success depends on how hard you have worked.

Transits of the Slower Planets

Earlier you saw that the day-to-day changes in your life are affected by the fast-moving personal planets—the Sun, Moon, Mercury, Venus, and Mars. You just saw how these personal planets affect your life as they transit through your houses and make aspects with your natal planet positions each day.

The slower outer planets—Jupiter, Saturn, Uranus, Neptune, and Pluto—also produce important effects as they transit through your horoscope. But these effects are felt over years and decades—hardly something to be considered in a daily horoscope. Still, these effects are important and should be understood.

The following brief summaries describe the influence of the outer planets as they transit through your horoscope. In each case, the influence will be felt in the affairs of the house occupied by the planet at that time. If the transiting planet is in retrograde motion, you may experience delays or reversals in the affairs affected by the planet.

Transiting Jupiter opens you up to expansive feelings and triggers new opportunities to enlarge the scope of your life. It is in each house for about one year, and becomes retrograde for about four months each year.

Transiting Saturn brings opportunities to learn self-discipline and how to face responsibilities in the areas of life it touches in each house. The difficulties that arise during a Saturn transit offer you the best opportunities to grow wiser as you grow older.

Saturn is in each house for about two and a half years, and is retrograde for about four and a half months.

Transiting Uranus brings major changes in your life—it breaks up the rigid past and challenges you to put the pieces together into a more viable pattern for living in the present. Uranus is in each natal house for about seven years and is retrograde for about five months each year.

Transiting Neptune brings opportunities for discovery and use of your creative abilities in the areas affected by the house it occupies. Unfortunately it also blurs your ability to distinguish between reality and illusion in those same areas—perhaps because it energizes your sixth sense, or psychic abilities. Neptune is in each house for about fourteen years, and is retrograde for about five months each year.

Transiting Pluto brings down the established order in the affairs of the house it occupies, and then creates the conditions from which new beginnings can emerge. You will experience major transformations in the areas affected by the house occupied by transiting Pluto. Pluto spends about twenty years in each natal house, and is in retrograde motion for about five months each year.

Transits and Your Health

The state of your health is influenced by the transiting planets—especially as they move through your Sixth House. The specific influence depends on the planets involved, and on your susceptibility to different illnesses. The part of you that is susceptible, and the nature of any afflictions, depends on your Sun sign and your rising sign as shown in the following list.

Aries (head, face, eyes)
Exhaustion; accident-proneness; hypertension in late life

Taurus (neck, ears, throat, thyroid)
Diseases of ear, nose, and throat; metabolism; varicose veins
Gemini (arms, shoulders, lungs, bronchi, thymus)
Bronchial and chest ailments; psychosomatic (emotional) illness
Cancer (stomach, breasts, chest, armpits, pancreas)
Digestive disorders; anemia; obesity; fatigue
Leo (heart, back, spine)
Heart and blood problems; back and intestines; obesity
Virgo (intestines, alimentary canal, spleen)
Stomach ailments; nervous upsets; duodenal problems
Libra (kidneys, ovaries, adrenals, appendix, skin)
Abdominal ailments (bladder, liver); diabetes; hernia
Scorpio (generative organs, prostate, colon, rectum)
Urinary and rectal ailments; indigestion; duodenal problems
Sagittarius (hips, thighs, lower spine, sciatic nerve)
Rheumatic and arthritic problems; nervous exhaustion
Capricorn (knee, hair, skin, joints, bones)
Nervous stomach; skin, hair, and nail problems; hernia
Aquarius (legs, calves, ankles, teeth, blood)
Blood-circulation problems; lymphatic problems; exhaustion
Pisces (feet, toes, generative organs, lungs)
Nerve and blood problems; bronchial problems

Once you become aware of your susceptibilities to specific illnesses, you can exercise the care necessary to avoid them—by avoiding the conditions that bring them about. You can tell when conditions are especially stressful by keeping an eye on the transiting planets. The following brief profiles tell you what to expect during the transits of each of the planets.

Sun in Sixth House (thirty days). You are especially prone to colds and fevers, allergy outbreaks, or other illnesses which can bring you the sympathy and attention you need at this time. Heart patients should exercise more caution during this period.

Moon in Sixth House (two and a half days). Female disorders erupt, along with functional irregularities. Emotional depressions can deepen into despondency, impairing your ability to function normally. Glands may swell, and the body take up excess fluids.

Mercury in Sixth House (two days). The accumulating effects of excessive excitement, overwork, and stress can now strike with a debilitating headache, breathing problems, or sluggish elimination. Siphon your jittery nervous tension into pleasant diversions.

Venus in Sixth House (one week). If you were sick, Venus's entry in the Sixth House signals the beginning of your recovery. If you were not sick, Venus will stimulate you into an overindulgence in food and drink. Try to resist these urges.

Mars in Sixth House (two months). During this transit your angry outbursts may trigger acute illnesses. However, you will have the energy to recover quickly. You may also become accident-prone during this period because of your great impatience.

Jupiter in Sixth House (one year). Like Venus, Jupiter in your Sixth House starts you on the road to recovery from an illness. It's a good time to check up on those health warnings your body has been giving you about your overindulgences.

Saturn in Sixth House (two and a half years). Illnesses which have been dormant for a long time may erupt during this transit. Unresolved emotional stresses and nutritional insults to your body will begin to emerge as ailments and complaints at this time.

Uranus in Sixth House (seven years). During this transit you may become vulnerable to freak accidents or sudden and unusual illnesses, such as hives and rashes. The risk is greatest when Uranus is in conjunction with Mars or Mercury in the Sixth House.

Neptune in Sixth House (fourteen years). This is a period of increased susceptibility to latent psychosomatic illnesses based on deep-rooted, unresolved emotional hurts. The risk is greatest when Neptune is conjuncted by the Sun or the Moon.

Pluto in Sixth House (twenty-one years). Pluto's entry into your Sixth House may trigger ailments stemming from chronic acidosis, or from precipitated minerals—arthritis or arteriosclerosis. New drugs or hypnosis can often bring sudden cures during this transit.

Now that you have seen how to examine the effects of the daily motions of the planets, it's time to see how the positions of the planets in the natal horoscope of a companion can tell you something about how well each of you might get along with the other.

Chapter Seven

Astrological Compatibility

When two people meet, their chances for a compatible relationship depend on how their basic needs and personality traits will mesh in the give and take of social or business interactions. You already know enough astrology to make a good guess about whether or not two people might hit it off well. For example, when you meet someone of interest to you, you can prepare her—or his—natal horoscope (if you can get her birth date somehow). Then all you have to do is look up the behavior profiles for the natal horoscope in Chapters Three, Four, and Five. You will soon know if this is the kind of person you want to get to know better.

But you can do more than that.

You can compare your companion's natal horoscope with your own—see how his planets fall among your houses and check for important aspects between specific planets that affect your compatibility. This chapter shows you how to do that.

Setting Up a Compatibility Horoscope

A compatibility horoscope shows where your companion's natal planets fall on *your* natal horoscope. Therefore, you must first prepare your own natal horoscope as described in Chapter Two. This time you will need to prepare a horoscope wheel such as the one shown in Figure 2–4 in Chapter Two.

After you have your natal horoscope wheel, fill out Worksheets I and II for your companion's birth date. That tells you the Sky Positions of his or her natal planets—and how those planets are distributed among the signs of the zodiac.

Now place your companion's natal planets around the outer circle of *your* horoscope wheel as shown in Figure 7–1. Notice that when you place your companion's planets in their Sky Positions on your horoscope wheel, it shows where they fall among your natal houses. For example, the companion's Saturn (in outer circle) at Sky Position 25 falls into the Twelfth House in Figure 7–1. Earlier, you saw the same thing happen when you placed the transiting planets around your natal horoscope wheel in Chapter Six.

In the same way that the significance of the transiting planets depended upon where they fell among your houses, so too does the significance of your companion's planets depend on where they fall in your natal houses. You will find the significance of each planet in each house later in this chapter.

Again, just as there was significance attached to the *aspects* between transiting and natal planets, so too is there significance attached to the aspects between your companion's natal planets and your natal planets. One way to find these aspects is by counting the difference between the planet's Sky Positions and then using the Aspect Key shown on the horoscope wheel. However, it's easier to use the Aspect Finder (Table 16), along with Worksheet V—Transits (or Companion) Aspects.

Follow the same steps that you learned in Chapter Six for setting up the transit horoscope. In this case, the planet positions on

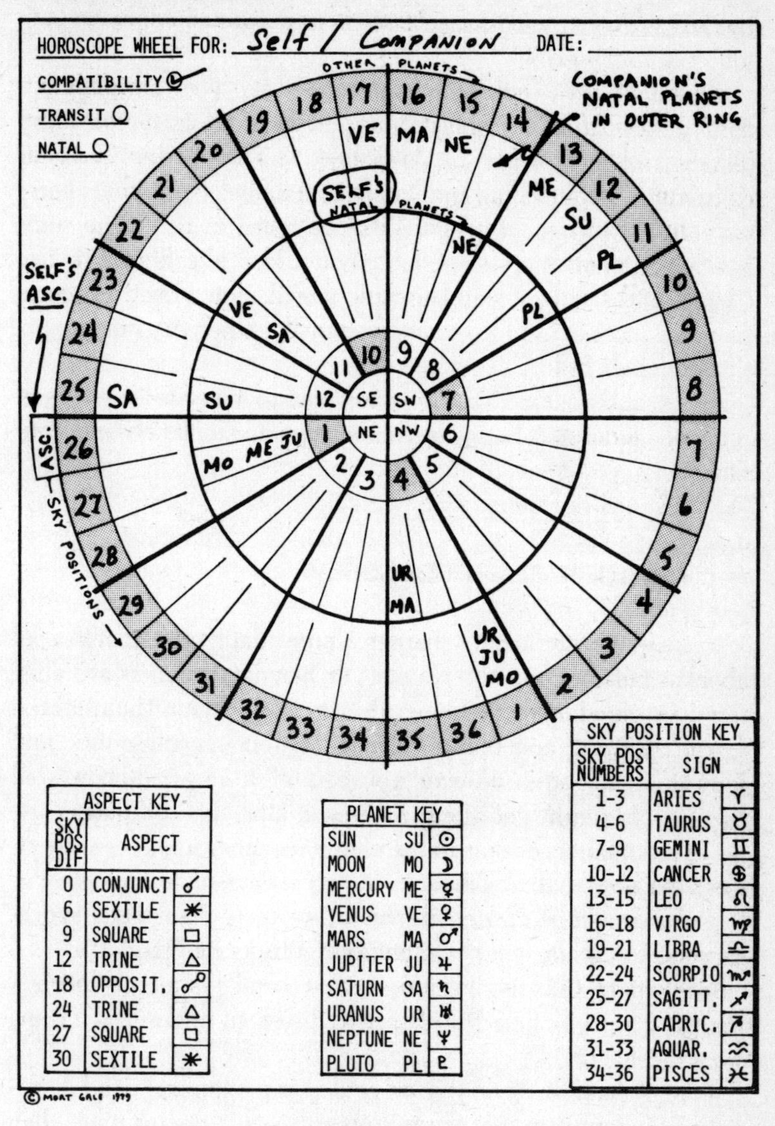

ASPECT KEY		
SKY POS DIF	ASPECT	
0	CONJUNCT	☌
6	SEXTILE	✳
9	SQUARE	□
12	TRINE	△
18	OPPOSIT.	☍
24	TRINE	△
27	SQUARE	□
30	SEXTILE	✳

PLANET KEY		
SUN	SU	☉
MOON	MO	☽
MERCURY	ME	☿
VENUS	VE	♀
MARS	MA	♂
JUPITER	JU	♃
SATURN	SA	♄
URANUS	UR	♅
NEPTUNE	NE	♆
PLUTO	PL	♇

SKY POSITION KEY		
SKY POS NUMBERS	SIGN	
1-3	ARIES	♈
4-6	TAURUS	♉
7-9	GEMINI	♊
10-12	CANCER	♋
13-15	LEO	♌
16-18	VIRGO	♍
19-21	LIBRA	♎
22-24	SCORPIO	♏
25-27	SAGITT.	♐
28-30	CAPRIC.	♑
31-33	AQUAR.	♒
34-36	PISCES	♓

Figure 7-1. Horoscope Wheel for Compatibility Analysis

the left side of the worksheet are the positions of your companion's natal planets.

After you have found the aspects between your companion's natal planets and your natal planets, write them in the summary section in the lower part of Worksheet V. Then find where your companion's planets fall into your natal houses (from your compatibility horoscope wheel) and write them in this same summary section of Worksheet V. It should look like Figure 6–2 in Chapter Six—except that this time it will show how your companion's planets fall into your horoscope, rather than how transiting planets fall in.

You will see later in this chapter how to examine for the significance of aspects between your companion's planets and your planets.

A First Look at Compatibility

You remember from Chapter Three that you can tell a lot about a person from the way his or her natal planets are clustered in the elements (fire, earth, air, and water), the qualities (cardinal, fixed, and mutable), and the genders (masculine and feminine). In the same way, you can tell a lot about how well two people might get along with each other by comparing the way their planets cluster in the elements, qualities, and genders. Let's see how that works.

Comparison of Planets in the Elements. Place your Worksheet II alongside your companion's Worksheet II so that you can compare the distribution of your natal planets in the elements. You will find the elements listed in Section C of the worksheet.

First notice whether you or your companion has a predominance of planets in one of the elements—that means more than four planets in one element. A predominance of planets in one element tells you something about what that person brings to the relationship. For example:

- A person with a predominance of *fire signs* brings an impulsive enthusiasm to the relationship.
- A person with a predominance of *earth signs* introduces a stabilizing influence on the relationship.
- A person with a predominance of *air signs* puts the relationship on an intellectual level.
- A person with a predominance of *water signs* will flood the relationship with deep emotional actions and reactions.

In general, people are more likely to be compatible with each other when their natal planets fall into compatible elements. The compatible elements are fire with air, and earth with water. That means that if you have a predominance of natal planets in the fire signs, you are more likely to have a compatible relationship with someone who has a predominance of natal planets in the air signs. If your companion's planets are mostly in the earth or water signs, you can expect assorted difficulties, depending on which elements are involved.

Here are the likely relationships between people with a predominance of natal planets in the different elements:

Fire-Fire: This combination of two fire-people is highly combustible. Unless their enthusiasms are directed toward the same objectives, they can easily burn each other up.

Fire-Earth: The enthusiastic fire-person will feel stifled by the cautious earth-person. However, the earth-person can provide the much needed balance to stabilize the relationship.

Fire-Air: The enthusiastic fire-person is fed by the intellectual idealism of the air-person—which makes them an exciting pair who, unfortunately, become oblivious to reality.

Fire-Water: The fire-person's enthusiasm for stimulating activity will too often be doused by the water-person's emotional timidity and desire to avoid stressful situations.

Earth-Earth: These two are so practical about everything that they will find little to disagree about. In fact, they may have to seek other partners for some stimulation.

Earth-Air: The earth-person may not be too thrilled about the air-person's intellectualization over matters which must be obvious to any other person with some common sense.

Earth-Water: Both the earth-person and the water-person are likely to sit and wait for the other person to make the first move in the relationship—but that's the way they like it.

Air-Air: These two spend so much time airing their brilliant ideas to each other they never seem to notice that neither of them has bought the groceries, paid the bills, or taken out the trash.

Air-Water: The logical arguments of the air-person will threaten the emotional security of the water-person—and neither one will understand the "logic" of the other one.

Water-Water: This is a partnership of two highly sensitive people who can almost read each other's minds. It may work out if each one can make some allowance for the other's moods.

Comparison of Planets in the Qualities. Now look at Section C of Worksheet II to see where your planets and your companion's planets fall among the cardinal, fixed, and mutable signs. A predominance of planets in one quality (i.e., five or more planets in a cardinal, fixed, or mutable sign) tells you how someone is likely to act in a relationship. For example:

- A person with a predominance of *cardinal signs* is anxious to see things get started.
- A person with a predominance of *fixed signs* is more likely to be stubborn and unyielding in a relationship.

- A person with a predominance of *mutable signs* will be adaptable and willing to make most of the compromises.

Here are the probable relationships between people with a preponderance of their natal planets in the different qualities.

Cardinal-Cardinal: This twosome can really make things happen—provided that both partners can ever agree on what it is that they would like to have happen.

Cardinal-Fixed: The cardinal-person's need for action may be frustrated by the fixed-person's need for maintaining the status quo indefinitely. A test of their ability to compromise.

Cardinal-Mutable: The mutable-person's willingness to adapt and to follow the lead of the cardinal-person puts the relationship directly in the hands of the cardinal-person.

Fixed-Fixed: With these two people both set on keeping things just the way they are, there is a good chance that their relationship will last a long time, if it ever gets started.

Fixed-Mutable: The mutable-person may find it difficult to satisfy his or her need for variety with the fixed-person's passion to keep things just the way they are.

Mutable-Mutable: These two people are each looking for someone to take the lead in their joint activities. They should limit themselves to activities of the mind alone.

Comparison of Planets in the Genders. Look at Section D of Worksheet II to see how your planets, and your companion's planets, are distributed among the masculine and feminine signs. Most people have an even balance of five-to-five, or six-to-four, between masculine and feminine signs. If you and your companion each have these normal ratios of planets, you should have no trouble getting along with each other. You can work things out even when one of you has a gender ratio of seven-to-three (i.e., seven planets in masculine signs and three planets in feminine signs) while the other has a ratio of four-to-six (four masculine signs and six feminine signs).

In other words, if there is a difference of one or two planets in masculine (or feminine) signs between you and your companion, you should have no trouble establishing a compatible relationship. If there is a difference of three planets, you can still work things out. However, if there are more than three planets between you and your companion in one gender, you will both have to work very hard to maintain a relationship. The reason is that the dominantly masculine person's aggressive behavior will threaten and harass the reserved, security-motivated feminine person (again, sorry about the sexist astrological terms!).

If both people are dominated by the same gender (either masculine or feminine), they share the same viewpoint and approach to life. Initially, this can give them a strong feeling of compatibility. However, they will soon feel a need for the kind of stimulation that comes from defending mildly different points of view. They will have to turn to someone else to meet that need.

Someone with eight or more planets in a single gender may find it difficult to find comfortable companionship.

Companion's Planets in Your Natal Houses

You already know from Chapter Four that your natal planets affect you in different ways, depending on which house they occupy in your natal horoscope. Astrologers have also found that your companion's natal planets (which determine his or her basic traits) will affect your relationship in different ways, depending on which house they occupy in *your* natal horoscope.

If you have prepared your Worksheet V—Transits (or Companion) Aspects as requested at the beginning of this chapter, you already have a listing of your companion's planets showing where they fall into your natal houses. It's in the summary section at the bottom of the worksheet—see the example in Figure 6–2 in Chapter Six. If you haven't prepared Worksheet V, you can see where your companion's natal planets fall into your natal houses on your compatibility horoscope (see Figure 7–1).

The following brief profiles describe the relationship that would prevail between you and a companion whose natal planets fall into your natal houses. They are listed for your companion's planets in your houses. In the interest of clarity, profiles refer to you as female and your companion as male. However, the relationships described would be the same regardless of the sexes of you or your companion.

His Sun in Your First House. Your companion's character traits match those that you would like to project for yourself. This leads you into a mutual admiration society with each other.

His Sun in Your Second House. Your companion can be a loyal friend whose efforts may support you as you search for new ways to accumulate material wealth. Avoid unintentional manipulation.

His Sun in Your Third House. You enjoy the mental stimulation of your partner's conversation. He enjoys the opportunities to help you express your own point of view and your beliefs.

His Sun in Your Fourth House. Your companion encourages you just as a parent encourages a child. Yet you accept his guidance because it seems to bring out the best in you.

His Sun in Your Fifth House. Your partner stimulates your creative urges by his enthusiastic support and encouragement. He can arouse your affections easily—making you glad he's near.

His Sun in Your Sixth House. This relationship, while it is gratifying to each of you, is based on the sharing of mutual services to each other rather than on emotional involvement.

His Sun in Your Seventh House. This person is an excellent partner for you since his strengths make up for your areas of weakness. You can easily work out your minor differences.

His Sun in Your Eighth House. This companion makes you feel uncomfortable because of his well-intentioned criticism, which somehow always focuses attention on your shortcomings.

His Sun in Your Ninth House. Your companion plays the role of teacher in your life—helping you to expand your mental horizons. It will take special efforts to avoid misunderstandings.

His Sun in Your Tenth House. Your companion can help you in your career—first by smoothing your path, and then by giving you the encouragement to improve your skills and abilities.

His Sun in Your Eleventh House. Your companion can help you toward a broader view of life by introducing you to more interesting social circles, and to unusual study groups.

His Sun in Your Twelfth House. Your companion can give you that inspirational uplift that lets you see yourself from a spiritual viewpoint—from which you can see your best qualities.

His Moon in Your First House. This combination appears very often in the horoscopes of marriage partners. It indicates that you and your companion feel very much at home with each other.

His Moon in Your Second House. Your companion feels the need to help you to improve your financial position. Be sure to let him know that you appreciate his sincere generosity.

His Moon in Your Third House. Your companion is fascinated by the swiftness and depth of your thoughts. He can help you to sharpen your mind and to improve your communications abilities.

His Moon in Your Fourth House. Your companion always makes you feel right at home—he anticipates your every need. Unfortunately, he often slips into the role of smother-mother.

His Moon in Your Fifth House. Your companion is attracted by your talents and your love of fun. He enjoys the challenge of helping you to develop and display your creative abilities.

His Moon in Your Sixth House. Your companion is always ready to offer you whatever help you need—and he has an uncanny way of knowing what you need and when you need it.

His Moon in Your Seventh House. This pattern often occurs in the horoscopes of married couples. It shows that you and your companion can share yourselves equally in a partnership.

His Moon in Your Eighth House. You either adore or despise this person—there's little chance that you two will ever find the happy middle ground of a compatible relationship.

His Moon in Your Ninth House. Believe it or not, your companion is attracted by your philosophical view of the world. At least he is charmed by the way you look at life.

His Moon in Your Tenth House. Your companion seems to know what you must do to become more successful in your career. And he stands ready to help you do whatever needs to be done.

His Moon in Your Eleventh House. Your companion is attracted by the way you express your individuality as you cooperate with others on your common humanitarian objectives.

His Moon in Your Twelfth House. Your companion has an intuitive awareness of your inner concerns and anxieties. So he carefully protects your vulnerabilities as he offers help.

His Mercury in Your First House. You are fascinated by your companion's ability to think so swiftly and to communicate his ideas so clearly. He is always suggesting a short trip to take.

His Mercury in Your Second House. This friend is full of ideas for you on how you can improve your financial status. He has a knack for spotting those things you always do wrong.

His Mercury in Your Third House. Your companion keeps you mentally stimulated with new ideas and with a continuous stream of news about what's going on with friends and neighbors.

His Mercury in Your Fourth House. Your companion will either focus your attention on things that have to be done at home, or else turn your mind to thoughts of other places to visit.

His Mercury in Your Fifth House. Your companion turns your mind to all the creative things you want to do—that is, when you're not both engaged in planning your pursuit of pleasures.

His Mercury in Your Sixth House. Your companion seems to be a storehouse of valuable ideas on how you can do your work in a more efficient manner. He even knows better ways to diet.

His Mercury in Your Seventh House. Your companion can fill in the gaps in your thoughts on important matters—he would make an excellent partner in a business that depends on brains.

His Mercury in Your Eighth House. Your companion may unknowingly unnerve you with his unconscious awareness of your innermost needs and concerns. You must keep up your guard.

His Mercury in Your Ninth House. You may have met this person on one of your trips—he also travels a lot. You have a lot to say to each other, but the topics are usually trivial.

His Mercury in Your Tenth House. Your companion understands your career goals and your approach to meeting them. He can tout your abilities to others in an effort to help you along.

His Mercury in Your Eleventh House. Your companion may have charmed you out of the trees with his talk of a utopian future—but he keeps you in touch with others of similar interests.

His Mercury in Your Twelfth House. You suspect that your companion can see right through you—down to the core of your concerns. He can. But he can also offer you helpful advice.

His Venus in Your First House. Your companion is as much impressed with your personality as you are with his charm. This astrological alignment often favors marriage partners.

His Venus in Your Second House. Your companion has a sense of values which makes him especially appreciative of your good qualities. You both enjoy sharing emotional experiences.

His Venus in Your Third House. You find it easy to establish a mental rapport with your companion. Conversations with him help you contact your own feelings and express them better.

His Venus in Your Fourth House. You knew you would like this person when you first met him. He makes you remember and relive all those warm feelings that go with a comfortable home life.

His Venus in Your Fifth House. Your companion brings you a great deal of joy by his desire to please you, and by his sincere appreciation of your efforts to please him in return.

His Venus in Your Sixth House. You probably met your companion at work, where he took great pleasure in showing you how to make your job easier. He would now like you to show interest in him.

His Venus in Your Seventh House. You and your partner should be able to maintain a compatible relationship—once someone picks up the ball to get it moving. Makings of a good marriage.

His Venus in Your Eighth House. Your companion can't quite understand his strong sexual desires for you—any more than you can explain those deep emotional responses he evokes from you.

His Venus in Your Ninth House. You feel that your companion is a good influence on you. He makes you want to understand more about the world and more about yourself. He's like a teacher.

His Venus in Your Tenth House. Your companion's generosity can become a temptation for you. You can easily take advantage of him—especially where he can help in your career.

His Venus in Your Eleventh House. Your companion shares your far-out views on how to make this a far better world to live in. But he seems more interested in living with you in this world.

His Venus in Your Twelfth House. You can depend on your friend to come up with the right answers and support when you need sympathetic understanding during those difficult situations.

His Mars in Your First House. Your companion never lets you rest—he's always pushing you to put your best foot forward. That may be because he's so proud of the woman he loves.

His Mars in Your Second House. Your companion is not bashful about prodding you into better ways to handle your financial affairs. But you have to be careful about following his advice.

His Mars in Your Third House. Your companion likes nothing better than to have those open discussions about private matters—he feels that clear thinking can clear up any problem.

His Mars in Your Fourth House. Your companion apparently likes you for what you really are—this can be a problem for you if you are living under a delusion. You may not be his ideal.

His Mars in Your Fifth House. Your companion brings out your urge to be creative and aggressive in expressing your needs and desires. He can also bring out your hidden passionate impulses.

His Mars in Your Sixth House. Your companion sometimes seems more interested in how you work than in anything else. He would enjoy working alongside you in some service to others.

His Mars in Your Seventh House. You respect your companion's ambition and drive, which nicely compensate for your timidity. Unfortunately, your opposite traits can also lead to conflicts.

His Mars in Your Eighth House. Sometimes your companion acts as though he's fully aware of your dark secrets—especially when he tries to be helpful by probing into your anxieties.

His Mars in Your Ninth House. Your companion seems to expect you to have profound and well-informed opinions about major questions on the meaning of life. But he always stimulates you.

His Mars in Your Tenth House. Your companion somehow brings out your best efforts, which then serve to convince others of your ability to move farther along in your chosen career.

His Mars in Your Eleventh House. Your companion serves as a motivator for you—getting you to take actions toward implementing those impossible dreams. His friends can help you, too.

His Mars in Your Twelfth House. Your companion brings you pain, unintentionally, as he makes you confront your secret weaknesses. But he can help you repair those weaknesses if you can trust him.

His Jupiter in Your First House. There's something about you that makes your companion go all out in your behalf. It's as though he needed you as an excuse for his open generosity.

His Jupiter in Your Second House. Your companion can be a very important asset to you in matters relating to your financial security. He can be a link to a sound investment.

His Jupiter in Your Third House. It seems that all your companion wants to do is talk, talk, and talk. That's because he's trying to expand your mind to include his whole world.

His Jupiter in Your Fourth House. Your companion can make you feel like an overpampered child as he goes about helping you improve your home setting with his own ideas of comfort.

His Jupiter in Your Fifth House. Your companion often seeks new ways to help you expand upon your creative abilities and interests. He probably wants you to go into the performing arts.

His Jupiter in Your Sixth House. Your companion can help you become more effective at work. He encourages you to do work in the service of others. He also has tips for good health.

His Jupiter in Your Seventh House. Your companion is most generous in his arrangements involving business partnerships—and equally generous with you in your social relationships.

His Jupiter in Your Eighth House. Your companion may frighten you by the way he expands your awareness of faults you would rather forget. Yet he can help you correct them, if you let him.

His Jupiter in Your Ninth House. Your companion tries to expand your understanding of the higher things in life—at least what he considers higher. You share a bond of trust.

His Jupiter in Your Tenth House. Your companion offers you a steady stream of encouragement in your efforts to improve your career. He may also open some doors to help it along.

His Jupiter in Your Eleventh House. Your companion is the one that forces you out to meet those more interesting people—people who will work with you toward those high-minded goals.

His Jupiter in Your Twelfth House. Your companion is always there with that friendly smile and calm advice when you need him the most—right after your bouts with "fear-of-failure."

His Saturn in Your First House. Your companion sees something in you that makes him feel safe—he uses you like a security blanket. You find that role too much of a responsibility.

His Saturn in Your Second House. Your companion becomes impatient with anything he considers to be frivolous about your financial affairs. He is full of advice on how to reduce risks.

His Saturn in Your Third House. Your companion has set himself the task of bringing order into your muddled way of thinking. He can also give you all the reasons for not taking that trip.

His Saturn in Your Fourth House. Your companion comes on strong in an apparent need to run your life. You sometimes wonder who elected him to become your domineering father figure.

His Saturn in Your Fifth House. You find it hard to get your companion interested in any of your pet projects. It seems that he lacks any confidence in your creative abilities.

His Saturn in Your Sixth House. Your companion is likely

to be critical of the way you do things. He even goes out of his way to test you—just to prove his point. Trust yourself.

His Saturn in Your Seventh House. Your companion makes difficult demands on your relationship—he has to be sure about everything. Once made, this relationship will last long.

His Saturn in Your Eighth House. Your companion always seems to be holding out for a little more time before committing himself to the relationship. He seems to be checking you out.

His Saturn in Your Ninth House. Your companion is especially anxious that you accept his personal views on the deeper issues of life. The intensity of his insistence turns you off.

His Saturn in Your Tenth House. Your companion places you in the position of having to justify yourself for not pushing harder in your efforts to succeed. He acts more like a parent.

His Saturn in Your Eleventh House. Your companion gets you into situations with others where you have to make commitments in his behalf rather than your own. But he often helps you out.

His Saturn in Your Twelfth House. Your companion seems to be blind to your signals to avoid certain areas of sensitivity in your life. He, or the sensitivity, will soon fade from your life.

His Uranus in Your First House. There's something unusual about your companion that you can't quite understand—but that only heightens the fascination you feel for him.

His Uranus in Your Second House. Your companion has a happy-go-lucky attitude about your money matters—which may be all well and good until you find yourself paying his bills.

His Uranus in Your Third House. Your companion's unusual ideas keep your mind racing along in high gear—but keep your seat belt fastened for those sudden changes of gear!

His Uranus in Your Fourth House. Your companion can bring about an unsettling influence in your home life, and on the way you do things. He could even cause a rift with your parents.

His Uranus in Your Fifth House. Your companion is full of

unusual ideas for how you can revive your creative abilities. He can also stimulate your dormant desire for pleasure in life.

His Uranus in Your Sixth House. Your companion can show you interesting new ways to do your job more efficiently. He also has many ideas on how you can keep yourself healthy, naturally.

His Uranus in Your Seventh House. Your companion is often the cause of some change in your relationship with others. He may show up in your life overnight—and leave just as abruptly.

His Uranus in Your Eighth House. Your companion's ideas may cause you to reevaluate your life to the extent that you decide to make a major overhaul—avoid those "culty" easy solutions.

His Uranus in Your Ninth House. Conversations with your companion have opened you up to an entirely new way of looking at life. Puzzles are still puzzling, but now you know why.

His Uranus in Your Tenth House. A relationship with this person may be the cause of a sudden change in your career. He will fling open the door to an unexpected opportunity.

His Uranus in Your Eleventh House. Your companion will give you the understanding you need to join him in new groups with unusual goals in life. If you try it, you might like it.

His Uranus in Your Twelfth House. Your companion's unusual behavior makes you feel nervous. No matter how much you try to understand his point of view, you can't become sympathetic.

His Neptune in Your First House. Your companion's influence over you is through his appeal to your charitable instincts—he makes you feel like giving. Guard against misunderstandings.

His Neptune in Your Second House. Your companion may be generous with his ideas on how you should handle your money. Often these are only new ways for you to demonstrate generosity.

His Neptune in Your Third House. You seem to be more

intuitive and more imaginative when your companion is near you. He gives you the impression that he knows what you are thinking about.

His Neptune in Your Fourth House. Contacts with your companion have the effect of loosening your connections to your familiar family values and traditions. Learn to keep a tight grip.

His Neptune in Your Fifth House. Your companion inspires you to become more relaxed in the way you express yourself. You find that you are spending more time in romantic fantasies.

His Neptune in Your Sixth House. For some reason, you become confused in what you are doing when your companion is near. And yet his presence often feels like a soothing caress.

His Neptune in Your Seventh House. You feel that this person would make an ideal partner—especially in marriage. Reserve your judgment until you can be sure of longtime reliability.

His Neptune in Your Eighth House. You are not as comfortable as you would like to be with this companion. Somehow he gives you the feeling that you could use a course in self-improvement.

His Neptune in Your Ninth House. Your experiences with your companion seem to open you up to more expansive views of the world. You have to protect yourself from being swept away.

His Neptune in Your Tenth House. Your companion makes it clear that he has higher expectations for you than you ever had for yourself. It will be hard to meet his expectations.

His Neptune in Your Eleventh House. Your companion appeals to you because he seems to be the one who can meet your highest expectations. However, as the relationship ripens, it gets rotten.

His Neptune in Your Twelfth House. Your companion encourages you to let up on your heavy guilt feelings—perhaps too much. You can't solve your problems by pretending they don't exist.

His Pluto in Your First House. For some reason, your companion makes you see yourself as you would really like to be. But you don't have to become indebted to him just for that.

His Pluto in Your Second House. Your companion takes a special interest in offering you a better understanding of your finances. That's no reason to let him use your checkbook.

His Pluto in Your Third House. Your companion certainly has new ideas about almost everything! You will find most of them interesting. Is that because he finds you so interesting?

His Pluto in Your Fourth House. Your companion sometimes says or does something that triggers a forgotten feeling from the past—something that makes you feel you should be punished.

His Pluto in Your Fifth House. Your companion makes you well aware of your creative abilities—as well as his strong emotional feelings for you. He has interesting ideas of fun.

His Pluto in Your Sixth House. Your companion makes you feel that he is testing you to see how well you can do things his way. Your extended contacts with him leave you exhausted.

His Pluto in Your Seventh House. Your relationship with this person seems to be a test of your ability to get along with someone under the most trying conditions. You can try, or fly.

His Pluto in Your Eighth House. Your companion encourages you to take part in self-improvement programs to regenerate yourself. No problem—as long as you decide on what programs to follow.

His Pluto in Your Ninth House. Your companion brings you face to face with your religious and spiritual beliefs. You may want to revise or renew some of them as you go along in life.

His Pluto in Your Tenth House. Your companion may play an important role in the direction to be taken by your career—by showing you a new way to look at it, and at yourself.

His Pluto in Your Eleventh House. Your companion may introduce you to unusual social arrangements that will cause you to reexamine your attitudes about group relations.

His Pluto in Your Twelfth House. Your experiences with this companion bring you dangerously close to facing yourself in areas you would rather keep closed. Face them by yourself.

If some of these profiles do not seem to fit in your case, it may be because of stressful aspects between your natal planets and the natal planets of your companion. Let's take a closer look at that.

Planetary Aspects and Compatibility

Earlier in this chapter you were asked to find the planetary aspects between your companion's natal planets and your own, and to write them in the lower section of Worksheet V—Transits (or Companion) Aspects. Check that section now to see how many aspects there are between your natal planets and his natal planets—these are called "cross-aspects." See whether most of them are harmonious (sextiles and trines) or inharmonious (squares and oppositions).

There should be at least a dozen or more cross-aspects between two people for there to be a substantial relationship. It is not necessary that all these cross-aspects be harmonious—in fact, it can become a dull relationship if they are. A few squares and oppositions go a long way to spruce up a relationship by introducing stresses that have to be worked out. Squares indicate difficulties to be overcome, while oppositions help you become aware of differences to be respected.

The interpretations of cross-aspects are based on recognizing the influence represented by each planet, and then the effect produced by each aspect on those planetary influences. The planetary influences and the aspect-effects were described in Chapter One. For example, Mars represents initiative while

Venus represents affection; conjunctions intensify planetary influences, while oppositions introduce tensions between them.

You can find the cross-aspects between your natal planets and those of your companion by looking at Worksheet V. Each of the rows on the worksheet represents your companion's natal planets. As you look across a row you can see the cross-aspects between any one of his natal planets and each of your natal planets (your planets are shown in the columns). If you want to see the cross-aspects between any one of your planets and his natal planets, just look down the column representing your natal planet.

Not all the cross-aspects on your worksheet are equally important for showing how compatible you may be with your partner. When you examine your cross-aspects, here are some of the more important things to look for:

Sun and Moon Cross-Aspects. Look at the intersections where the Sun and Moon rows meet the Sun and Moon columns on Worksheet V (your companion's Sun and Moon, and your natal Sun and Moon, respectively) to see if there are any cross-aspects between them. If there are conjunctions, sextiles, or trines, it indicates that you can enjoy the compatibility that is often found among couples who enjoy a happily married life together. A very favorable relationship occurs when one person's Sun is in conjunction with the other person's Moon. On the other hand, squares and oppositions between their Suns and Moons (in any combination) indicate stressful relationships.

Venus and Mars Cross-Aspects. Cross-aspects between Venus and Mars on your Worksheet V shows that there is a strong sexual attraction between you and your companion. The way you express or experience that feeling (harmoniously or inharmoniously) depends on the kind of cross-aspects you find (sextile and trine or square and opposition).

Planets Favoring Emotional Compatibility. You are more likely to enjoy a harmonious emotional relationship with someone when there are favorable cross-aspects between the following planets in your horoscopes:

Sun—Jupiter	Mercury—Uranus	Venus—Jupiter
Moon—Mercury	Mercury—Pluto	Venus—Saturn
Moon—Jupiter	Venus—Mars	Mars—Uranus

Aspects to Planets in First, Fifth, and Seventh Houses. Check your horoscope to see which of your natal planets fall into your First, Fifth, and Seventh Houses. Jot them down. Now look at Worksheet V to see which of your companion's planets make cross-aspects to these planets. Do that by looking down the columns representing your natal planets until you see an aspect symbol on one of the rows. The planet on that row is your companion's planet that makes a cross-aspect to your planet in the First, Fifth, or Seventh house of your chart.

When these cross-aspects are harmonious, it signifies that your relationship is the kind that often leads to a successful marriage. (Caution: Men with a retrograde Venus or women with a retrograde Mars in their natal charts may be less likely to enter into marriage.)

Aspects Between Planets in Natal Houses. Each house in your horoscope represents a different area of activity. Your natal planets in your houses determine how you act in those different areas. The same holds true of your companion's natal planets in his houses. You can tell something about the relationship between you and a companion by examining the cross-aspects between the natal planets found in similar houses on your separate charts. You simply look for cross-aspects between the planets in houses relating to the area of activity of interest.

For example, if you expect to deal with someone in matters of personal finance, check for cross-aspects between your planets in your Second House and his natal planets in his Second House. If these cross-aspects are mostly harmonious, your relationship in personal finance will be favorable. You can check out other relationships by looking at the planets in the houses corresponding with the activities of those other activities. Chapter One shows you what activities are covered by each of the houses.

Aspects Between Rulers of Specific Houses. You can make other interesting examinations of cross-aspects—this time between the *ruling planets* of specific houses. The cusp of each house is at a Sky Position that tells you which sign of the zodiac it falls in. You can find the house cusps on Section A of Worksheet II. Once you know the sign of the zodiac on your house cusp, you can find its planetary ruler from the following list:

Aries—Mars
Taurus—Venus
Gemini—Mercury
Cancer—Moon
Leo—Sun
Virgo—Mercury
Libra—Venus
Scorpio—Pluto
Sagittarius—Jupiter
Capricorn—Saturn
Aquarius—Uranus
Pisces—Neptune

Let's say that you want to see what sort of partnership you might have with a particular companion. The Seventh House is the house of partnerships. Find the ruler of your Seventh House and then find the ruler of your companion's Seventh House. Once you find these two planetary rulers, check your Worksheet V to see what kind of aspects, if any, are made between them. If the cross-aspects between the Seventh House rulers in your charts are harmonious, your partnership will be favorable.

These are only some of the ways to check on the way in which your relationship with a companion may turn out. The references in the Bibliography will tell you others.

Chapter Eight

Loose Ends and New Leads

In the earlier chapters I mentioned that you could find out more about a particular item by referring to this chapter. Things such as how to use the Planet Path notations on the Sky Position tables. You will find those items here, along with some other comments that I felt may be of interest to you—but which would have been distracting had I brought them up earlier.

Let me get some of the detailed items out of the way first.

Using the Sky Position Tables

If you look across the rows of your Sky Position tables you will notice that the numbers do not change evenly from one space to the next. Sometimes the same numbers appear in several adjacent spaces, while other times there is a gap between two adjacent numbers (say, from 32 to 29). What does this mean?

When the numbers remain the same over several spaces, it means that the planet is moving very slowly in the skies at that time. Conversely, when there is a gap between adjacent numbers, it means that the planet is moving rapidly at that time. You can see that happen in Tables 7 and 9, for Mercury and Venus respectively, especially near the shaded areas that represent retrograde motion of the planets.

When your Sky Positions fall in these rapidly changing areas, you may have to consider using a different Sky Position from the one you find under your Key Number. For example, in Table 9 (Venus—Sky Positions), you will see Sky Position 29 under Key Number 11 for the date Jan 1–10 (top row). If you look to the left of Sky Position 29, you will see Sky Position number 32. This means that Venus is moving retrograde very quickly from Sky Position 32 (Aquarius) into Sky Position 29 (Capricorn) over a period of a few days. That means that your Venus could be either in Capricorn or Aquarius.

When you check your horoscope interpretations for Venus in its Sky Position at Capricorn, you may find that it does not fit you. In that case, Venus was probably in Aquarius—so you should check that interpretation, too. If it fits you better, change the Sky Position number of Venus on your worksheet from its Capricorn value to an Aquarius value.

Using the Planet Path Notations

You will notice that each Sky Position table has a notation similar to the following one for Mercury: "Five Sky Positions to Right for Each Row Down." The purpose of these notations is to help you see how the planet will move with respect to the retrograde areas on the table, starting from a position of interest to you.

Suppose that you have found the Sky Position for a planet for today's date—you are preparing a transit horoscope to see what's coming up for you. You know the planet's position for today—but will the planet move into a retrograde area next week, causing things to slow down or be reversed? Here's how to tell.

Place your finger on the Sky Position table on the planet's position for today's date. Now move your finger to the right, and then down, for the number of spaces shown on the Planet Path key at the top of that table. If you now draw a light pencil line between your starting position and that final position, it shows the path that the planet will follow during the upcoming period of time. If that path takes you into (or out of) a retrograde area, you can tell the date of that occurrence by referring to the dates at the left of that table.

Extending the Dates of Some Tables

You can extend the range of some tables for finding planet positions into earlier or later years than those shown on the tables. Here's what you have to do.

You must add multiples of a particular number (a list is given below) to your year of interest until the total becomes one of the years shown on the table of Row Letters. For example, to find the position of Mercury in 1895, you must add the number 46 to 1895, which then gives the total 1941. You then proceed to find the Row Letter for Mercury for your month for the year 1941. If your date of interest was 1812, you would add 46 twice, until the total falls into the range of the table (in this case, 1904).

If, instead, you want to know Mercury's position in 1998, subtract 46 from 1998 for the total 1952. Proceed to look up Mercury's position for your date in 1952—that's where it will be again on that date in 1998.

The particular numbers to use on the Row Letter tables for the planets are:

Moon—19 Mars—47
Mercury—46 Jupiter—83

The Ascendant Table

Some of you may be wondering how you can find your Ascendant from Table 15 without considering the longitude of your birthplace—it's required when you use a Table of Houses to find your Ascendant.

The Table of Houses tells you what signs of the zodiac are coming up over the eastern horizon at Greenwich, England, at any time. You then need your longitude to tell the difference in time between your birth location and Greenwich. That difference in time is then used to determine what sign of the zodiac is rising over your eastern horizon at your local time.

Table 15, "Your Ascendant Sky Position," is based on the following considerations. We know where the Sun is in the zodiac for any date. We also know what time the Sun comes up over the eastern horizon on any date. The Ascendant at sunrise is the same as the Sun sign on that date. The Ascendant at any other time that day can be found if you know the difference between sunrise time and birth time, and that the earth's horizon moves through 15 degrees of the zodiac every hour. Table 15 was prepared on that basis.

You may notice in Table 15 that the Ascendant's Sky Position does not change evenly throughout the day, but that it hurries through the eastern signs (Capricorn through Gemini). You can see that by how the numbers across the rows make jumps as they pass through those signs.

If your Ascendant falls in these signs, check the table closely to see whether you want to consider an adjacent sign as your Ascendant—especially if you find that the readings for your planets in the houses don't seem to fit you at all.

A Word About the Key Number Tables

Some of you may have suspected that there is some useful information contained in the Key Number tables that I failed to call to your attention. You're right. The Key Numbers (except those for the Moon) tell you the positions of the planets in the zodiac as they would be seen from the Sun—their heliocentric positions. There has been a recent rise in interest in heliocentric astrology. Traditional astrology is based on the geocentric positions of the planets—where they seem to be as seen from the earth. The Sky Position tables show the geocentric positions of the planets.

Recent scientific discoveries show that events on earth are influenced by the changing positions of the planets with respect to the Sun. For example, John H. Nelson, formerly an R.C.A. propagation analyst, predicted electromagnetic disturbances by examining the aspects between planets. Harmonious aspects between the planets favored radio communications—inharmonious aspects (squares and oppositions) caused a rapid deterioration in communications. These effects were later correlated with the sunspot activity that rises and falls in step with the occurrence of heliocentric aspects between the planets.

Some of you may want to keep track of personal events in your life in terms of heliocentric aspects between planets. You can do that by using the Key Number tables, which tell you the heliocentric positions of the planets for any date. Careful records may then show you which planetary patterns bring you difficulties and which are more favorable for you.

Other Points on Your Horoscope

The earlier chapters considered the effects of planets in the signs and houses, and aspects between them. Other points on the horoscope are also considered significant when making more complete interpretations. You saw that the cusps of the First, Fourth, Seventh, and Tenth Houses were important—the planets found there have more influence than some others. Also, planetary aspects to these cusps can be interpreted for their special significance.

Then there are the "nodes." These are points along the zodiac at which a planet's path crosses the ecliptic either going up (a north node) or going back down (a south node). The Moon's nodes are especially useful—those of the other planets are also used by some astrologers. In the same category of imaginary points, although on a different basis, are the "Arabian Parts." The most commonly used Arabian Part is the Part of Fortune.

The Part of Fortune is an imaginary point whose Sky Position stands in the same relation to your Ascendant (Sky Position 1) as your Moon's Sky Position stands to your Sun's Sky Position. The Sky Position of your Part of Fortune can be found by subtracting your Sun's Sky Position from the Sky Position of your natal Moon. If that difference is a negative number, subtract the value of that difference from thirty-seven to find the Sky Position of your Part of Fortune in the zodiac.

Your Part of Fortune indicates the success you will find as a result of your own efforts in life. The specific ways in which you will gain that success depend upon which sign and house it falls into on your horoscope. Further interpretations are based on the aspects made between your Part of Fortune and your natal planets.

Doing Astrology

The purpose of this book was to introduce you to astrology and to give you some tools so that you could prepare your own horoscopes and interpret them. If you followed each of the steps in the book you should be able to do the following things:

- Find the positions of all the planets for any date.
- Find your Ascendant (or rising sign).
- Find where your planets fall into the different signs and houses.
- Interpret the significance of your planets in the different sign groups (elements, qualities, gender).

- Interpret the significance of your planets in the four hemispheres of your natal houses.
- Find and interpret the significance of the aspects made between your natal planets.
- Prepare a daily horoscope by finding where transiting planets fall with respect to your natal planets and houses.
- Compare your horoscope with someone else's to see what kind of relationship you may expect.

No single book can tell you all there is to know about the planets, signs, houses, aspects, transits, and compatibility comparisons. You will find references in the bibliography that will help you to learn more about the many facets of this fascinating subject.

But practice is the key to doing astrology.

Prepare horoscopes for friends and family and become familiar with how the planets fall in the horoscopes of the different personality types. Do the horoscopes of friends who fall into the different Sun signs—keep them in mind as you interpret the distribution of planets in the signs and houses. Compare these distributions with those you find for friends of opposite personality traits. Soon you will "feel" the significance of a planetary pattern by identifying that pattern with the behavior of people you know.

Once you have become familiar with the basics described in this book, you may want to move on to more detailed horoscopes. You don't have to worry about the mathematical difficulties of erecting a horoscope or finding the aspects. Inexpensive computer services are now available to provide a completed horoscope for a few dollars—check with your popular astrology magazines for those services.

As you become more familiar with it, astrology can become a useful tool in your life. It helps you to realize that you play a role in a larger scheme of things—and that you are here to learn that role.

Bibliography

The following references will provide you with more information about astrology—how to do it and how to understand what you are doing.

ANDERSEN, J. *Sun Signs/Moon Signs: An Astrological Guide to Your Secret Self*. New York: Dell, 1978.

ARROYO, STEPHEN. *Astrology, Psychology, and the Four Elements: An Energy Approach to Astrology and Its Use in the Counseling Arts*. Davis, Calif.: CRCS Pubns., 1975.

DAVISON, RONALD. *Synastry*. New York: ASI Pubs., 1977.

DEAN, GEOFFREY, and ARTHUR MATHER. *Recent Advances in Natal Astrology*. Rockport, Mass.: Para Research, 1977.

DE VORE, NICHOLAS. *Encyclopedia of Astrology*. Totowa, N.J.: Littlefield, Adams, 1976.

HALL, MANLY. *Astrological Keywords*. Totowa, N.J.: Littlefield, Adams, 1975.

HAND, ROBERT. *Planets in Transit*. Rockport, Mass.: Para Research, 1976.

HOLMES, TIFFANY. *Woman's Astrology*. New York: E. P. Dutton, 1977.

JONES, MARC EDMUND. *How to Learn Astrology*. New York: Dolphin, 1969.

LEWI, GRANT. *Astrology for the Millions*. New York: Bantam, 1978.

———. *Heaven Knows What*. New York: Bantam, 1978.

LEWIS, URSULA. *Chart Your Own Horoscope*. New York: Grosset & Dunlap, 1976.

OKEN, ALAN. *As Above, So Below*. New York: Bantam, 1973.

———. *The Horoscope, the Road and Its Travelers*. New York: Bantam, 1974.

PALMER, LYNNE. *Astrological Compatibility*. Tempe, Ariz.: American Federation of Astrologers, 1976.

QUIGLEY, JOAN. *Astrology for Adults*. New York: Warner Books, 1976.

RUDHYAR, DANE. *The Astrology of Personality*. New York: Doubleday, 1970.

SAKOIAN, FRANCES, and LOUIS S. ACKER. *The Astrologer's Handbook*. New York: Harper & Row, 1973.

———. *Predictive Astrology*. New York: Harper & Row, 1977.

TOWNLEY, JOHN. *Astrological Cycles and the Life Crisis Periods*. New York: Weiser, 1977.

TABLE 1—SUN—SKY POSITIONS

LIST OF TABLES

SUN - SKY POSITIONS

TABLE 1
SUN

DATE	SKY POS	DEG	ZODIAC SIGN
JAN 1 - 10	29	15°	CAPRICORN ♑
JAN 11 - 20	30	25°	
JAN 21 - 30	31	5°	AQUARIUS ♒
JAN 31 - FEB 9	32	15°	
FEB 10 - 19	33	25°	
FEB 20 - MAR 1	34	5°	PISCES ♓
MAR 2 - 11	35	15°	
MAR 12 - 21	36	25°	
MAR 22 - 31	1	5°	ARIES ♈
APR 1 - 10	2	15°	
APR 11 - 20	3	25°	
APR 21 - 30	4	5°	TAURUS ♉
MAY 1 - 11	5	15°	
MAY 12 - 21	6	25°	
MAY 22 - JUN 1	7	5°	GEMINI ♊
JUN 2 - 11	8	15°	
JUN 12 - 21	9	25°	
JUN 22 - JUL 2	10	5°	CANCER ♋
JUL 3 - 12	11	15°	
JUL 13 - 23	12	25°	
JUL 24 - AUG 2	13	5°	LEO ♌
AUG 3 - 13	14	15°	
AUG 14 - 23	15	25°	
AUG 24 - SEP 3	16	5°	VIRGO ♍
SEP 4 - 13	17	15°	
SEP 14 - 23	18	25°	
SEP 24 - OCT 3	19	5°	LIBRA ♎
OCT 4 - 13	20	15°	
OCT 14 - 23	21	25°	
OCT 24 - NOV 3	22	5°	SCORPIO ♏
NOV 4 - 12	23	15°	
NOV 13 - 22	24	25°	
NOV 23 - DEC 2	25	5°	SAGITTARIUS ♐
DEC 3 - 12	26	15°	
DEC 13 - 22	27	25°	
DEC 23 - 31	28	5°	CAPRICORN

TABLE 2—MOON ROW LETTERS

YEAR OF INTEREST					MONTH OF INTEREST											
					JAN	FEB	MAR	APR	MAY	JUN	JUL	AUG	SEP	OCT	NOV	DEC
1900	1919	1938	1957	1976	P	N	O	N	M	L	K	J	H	H	F	F
1901	1920	1939	1958	1977	E	C	D	C	B	A	DD	CC	AA	AA	Y	Y
1902	1921	1940	1959	1978	X	V	W	V	U	T	S	R	P	P	N	N
1903	1922	1941	1960	1979	M	K	L	K	J	I	H	G	E	E	C	C
1904	1923	1942	1961	1980	B	DD	A	DD	CC	BB	AA	Z	X	X	V	V
1905	1924	1943	1962	1981	U	S	T	S	R	Q	P	O	M	M	K	K
1906	1925	1944	1963	1982	J	H	I	H	G	F	E	D	B	B	DD	DD
1907	1926	1945	1964	1983	CC	AA	BB	AA	Z	Y	X	W	U	U	S	S
1908	1927	1946	1965	1984	R	P	Q	P	O	N	M	L	J	J	H	H
1909	1928	1947	1966	1985	G	E	F	E	D	C	B	A	CC	CC	AA	AA
1910	1929	1948	1967	1986	Z	X	Y	X	W	V	U	T	R	R	P	P
1911	1930	1949	1968	1987	O	M	N	M	L	K	J	I	G	G	E	E
1912	1931	1950	1969	1988	D	B	C	B	A	DD	CC	BB	Z	Z	X	X
1913	1932	1951	1970	1989	W	U	V	U	T	S	R	Q	O	O	M	M
1914	1933	1952	1971	1990	L	J	K	J	I	H	G	F	D	D	B	B
1915	1934	1953	1972	1991	A	CC	DD	CC	BB	AA	Z	Y	W	W	U	U
1916	1935	1954	1973	1992	T	R	S	R	Q	P	O	N	L	L	J	J
1917	1936	1955	1974	1993	I	G	H	G	F	E	D	C	A	A	CC	CC
1918	1937	1956	1975	1994	BB	Z	AA	Z	Y	X	W	V	T	T	R	R

TABLE 3—MOON KEY NUMBERS

DAY OF THE MONTH

	1	2	3	4	5	6	7	8	9	10	11	12	13	14	15	16	17	18	19	20	21	22	23	24	25	26	27	28	29	30	31	
A	15	16	17	18	19	20	21	22	23	24	25	26	27	28	29	0	1	2	3	4	5	6	7	8	9	10	11	12	13	14	15	A
B	14	15	16	17	18	19	20	21	22	23	24	25	26	27	28	29	0	1	2	3	4	5	6	7	8	9	10	11	12	13	14	B
C	13	14	15	16	17	18	19	20	21	22	23	24	25	26	27	28	29	0	1	2	3	4	5	6	7	8	9	10	11	12	13	C
D	12	13	14	15	16	17	18	19	20	21	22	23	24	25	26	27	28	29	0	1	2	3	4	5	6	7	8	9	10	11	12	D
E	11	12	13	14	15	16	17	18	19	20	21	22	23	24	25	26	27	28	29	0	1	2	3	4	5	6	7	8	9	10	11	E
F	10	11	12	13	14	15	16	17	18	19	20	21	22	23	24	25	26	27	28	29	0	1	2	3	4	5	6	7	8	9	10	F
G	9	10	11	12	13	14	15	16	17	18	19	20	21	22	23	24	25	26	27	28	29	0	1	2	3	4	5	6	7	8	9	G
H	8	9	10	11	12	13	14	15	16	17	18	19	20	21	22	23	24	25	26	27	28	29	0	1	2	3	4	5	6	7	8	H
I	7	8	9	10	11	12	13	14	15	16	17	18	19	20	21	22	23	24	25	26	27	28	29	0	1	2	3	4	5	6	7	I
J	6	7	8	9	10	11	12	13	14	15	16	17	18	19	20	21	22	23	24	25	26	27	28	29	0	1	2	3	4	5	6	J
K	5	6	7	8	9	10	11	12	13	14	15	16	17	18	19	20	21	22	23	24	25	26	27	28	29	0	1	2	3	4	5	K
L	4	5	6	7	8	9	10	11	12	13	14	15	16	17	18	19	20	21	22	23	24	25	26	27	28	29	0	1	2	3	4	L
M	3	4	5	6	7	8	9	10	11	12	13	14	15	16	17	18	19	20	21	22	23	24	25	26	27	28	29	0	1	2	3	M
N	2	3	4	5	6	7	8	9	10	11	12	13	14	15	16	17	18	19	20	21	22	23	24	25	26	27	28	29	0	1	2	N
O	1	2	3	4	5	6	7	8	9	10	11	12	13	14	15	16	17	18	19	20	21	22	23	24	25	26	27	28	29	0	1	O
P	0	1	2	3	4	5	6	7	8	9	10	11	12	13	14	15	16	17	18	19	20	21	22	23	24	25	26	27	28	29	0	P
Q	29	0	1	2	3	4	5	6	7	8	9	10	11	12	13	14	15	16	17	18	19	20	21	22	23	24	25	26	27	28	29	Q
R	28	29	0	1	2	3	4	5	6	7	8	9	10	11	12	13	14	15	16	17	18	19	20	21	22	23	24	25	26	27	28	R
S	27	28	29	0	1	2	3	4	5	6	7	8	9	10	11	12	13	14	15	16	17	18	19	20	21	22	23	24	25	26	27	S
T	26	27	28	29	0	1	2	3	4	5	6	7	8	9	10	11	12	13	14	15	16	17	18	19	20	21	22	23	24	25	26	T
U	25	26	27	28	29	0	1	2	3	4	5	6	7	8	9	10	11	12	13	14	15	16	17	18	19	20	21	22	23	24	25	U
V	24	25	26	27	28	29	0	1	2	3	4	5	6	7	8	9	10	11	12	13	14	15	16	17	18	19	20	21	22	23	24	V
W	23	24	25	26	27	28	29	0	1	2	3	4	5	6	7	8	9	10	11	12	13	14	15	16	17	18	19	20	21	22	23	W
X	22	23	24	25	26	27	28	29	0	1	2	3	4	5	6	7	8	9	10	11	12	13	14	15	16	17	18	19	20	21	22	X
Y	21	22	23	24	25	26	27	28	29	0	1	2	3	4	5	6	7	8	9	10	11	12	13	14	15	16	17	18	19	20	21	Y
Z	20	21	22	23	24	25	26	27	28	29	0	1	2	3	4	5	6	7	8	9	10	11	12	13	14	15	16	17	18	19	20	Z
AA	19	20	21	22	23	24	25	26	27	28	29	0	1	2	3	4	5	6	7	8	9	10	11	12	13	14	15	16	17	18	19	AA
BB	18	19	20	21	22	23	24	25	26	27	28	29	0	1	2	3	4	5	6	7	8	9	10	11	12	13	14	15	16	17	18	BB
CC	17	18	19	20	21	22	23	24	25	26	27	28	29	0	1	2	3	4	5	6	7	8	9	10	11	12	13	14	15	16	17	CC
DD	16	17	18	19	20	21	22	23	24	25	26	27	28	29	0	1	2	3	4	5	6	7	8	9	10	11	12	13	14	15	16	DD
	1	2	3	4	5	6	7	8	9	10	11	12	13	14	15	16	17	18	19	20	21	22	23	24	25	26	27	28	29	30	31	

TABLE 4—MOON—SKY POSITIONS

MOON PATH: TEN SKY POSITIONS TO RIGHT FOR EACH ROW DOWN

KEY NUMBER →		0	1	2	3	4	5	6	7	8	9	10	11	12	13	14	15	16	17	18	19	20	21	22	23	24	25	26	27	28	29
JAN 1-10	♑	29	31	32	33	34	35	1	2	3	4	6	7	8	9	10	12	13	14	15	16	18	19	20	21	22	24	25	26	27	28
JAN 11-20	♑	30	32	33	34	35	1	2	3	4	5	7	8	9	10	11	13	14	15	16	17	19	20	21	22	23	25	26	27	28	29
JAN 21-30	♒	31	33	34	35	36	2	3	4	5	6	8	9	10	11	12	14	15	16	17	18	20	21	22	23	24	26	27	28	29	30
JAN 31-FEB 9	♒	32	34	35	36	1	3	4	5	6	7	9	10	11	12	13	15	16	17	18	19	21	22	23	24	25	27	28	29	30	31
FEB 10-19	♒	33	35	36	1	2	4	5	6	7	8	10	11	12	13	14	16	17	18	19	20	22	23	24	25	26	28	29	30	31	32
FEB 20-MAR 1	♓	34	36	1	2	3	5	6	7	8	9	11	12	13	14	15	17	18	19	20	21	23	24	25	26	27	29	30	31	32	33
MAR 2-11	♓	35	1	2	3	4	6	7	8	9	10	12	13	14	15	16	18	19	20	21	22	24	25	26	27	28	30	31	32	33	34
MAR 12-21	♓	36	2	3	4	5	7	8	9	10	11	13	14	15	16	17	19	20	21	22	23	25	26	27	28	29	31	32	33	34	35
MAR 22-31	♈	1	3	4	5	6	8	9	10	11	12	14	15	16	17	18	20	21	22	23	24	26	27	28	29	30	32	33	34	35	36
APR 1-10	♈	2	4	5	6	7	9	10	11	12	13	15	16	17	18	19	21	22	23	24	25	27	28	29	30	31	33	34	35	36	1
APR 11-20	♈	3	5	6	7	8	10	11	12	13	14	16	17	18	19	20	22	23	24	25	26	28	29	30	31	32	34	35	36	1	2
APR 21-30	♉	4	6	7	8	9	11	12	13	14	15	17	18	19	20	21	23	24	25	26	27	29	30	31	32	33	35	36	1	2	3
MAY 1-11	♉	5	7	8	9	10	12	13	14	15	16	18	19	20	21	22	24	25	26	27	28	30	31	32	33	34	36	1	2	3	4
MAY 12-21	♉	6	8	9	10	11	13	14	15	16	17	19	20	21	22	23	25	26	27	28	29	31	32	33	34	35	1	2	3	4	5
MAY 22-JUN 1	♊	7	9	10	11	12	14	15	16	17	18	20	21	22	23	24	26	27	28	29	30	32	33	34	35	36	2	3	4	5	6
JUN 2-11	♊	8	10	11	12	13	15	16	17	18	19	21	22	23	24	25	27	28	29	30	31	33	34	35	36	1	3	4	5	6	7
JUN 12-21	♊	9	11	12	13	14	16	17	18	19	20	22	23	24	25	26	28	29	30	31	32	34	35	36	1	2	4	5	6	7	8
JUN 22-JUL 2	♋	10	12	13	14	15	17	18	19	20	21	23	24	25	26	27	29	30	31	32	33	35	36	1	2	3	5	6	7	8	9
JUL 3-12	♋	11	13	14	15	16	18	19	20	21	22	24	25	26	27	28	30	31	32	33	34	36	1	2	3	4	6	7	8	9	10
JUL 13-23	♋	12	14	15	15	17	19	20	21	22	23	25	26	27	28	29	31	32	33	34	35	1	2	3	4	5	7	8	9	10	11
JUL 24-AUG 2	♌	13	15	16	17	18	20	21	22	23	24	26	27	28	29	30	32	33	34	35	36	2	3	4	5	6	8	9	10	11	12
AUG 3-13	♌	14	16	17	18	19	21	22	23	24	25	27	28	29	30	31	33	34	35	36	1	3	4	5	6	7	9	10	11	12	13
AUG 14-23	♌	15	17	18	19	20	22	23	24	25	26	28	29	30	31	32	34	35	36	1	2	4	5	6	7	8	10	11	12	13	14
AUG 24-SEP 3	♍	16	18	19	20	21	23	24	25	26	27	29	30	31	32	33	35	36	1	2	3	5	6	7	8	9	11	12	13	14	15
SEP 4-13	♍	17	19	20	21	22	24	25	26	27	28	30	31	32	33	34	36	1	2	3	4	6	7	8	9	10	12	13	14	15	16
SEP 14-23	♍	18	20	21	22	23	25	26	27	28	29	31	32	33	34	35	1	2	3	4	5	7	8	9	10	11	13	14	15	16	17
SEP 24-OCT 3	♎	19	21	22	23	24	26	27	28	29	30	32	33	34	35	36	2	3	4	5	6	8	9	10	11	12	14	15	16	17	18
OCT 4-13	♎	20	22	23	24	25	27	28	29	30	31	33	34	35	36	1	3	4	5	6	7	9	10	11	12	13	15	16	17	18	19
OCT 14-23	♎	21	23	24	25	26	28	29	30	31	32	34	35	36	1	2	4	5	6	7	8	10	11	12	13	14	16	17	18	19	20
OCT 24-NOV 3	♏	22	24	25	26	27	29	30	31	32	33	35	36	1	2	3	5	6	7	8	9	11	12	13	14	15	17	18	19	20	21
NOV 4-12	♏	23	25	26	27	28	30	31	32	33	34	36	1	2	3	4	6	7	8	9	10	12	13	14	15	16	18	19	20	21	22
NOV 13-22	♏	24	26	27	28	29	31	32	33	34	35	1	2	3	4	5	7	8	9	10	11	13	14	15	16	17	19	20	21	22	23
NOV 23-DEC 2	♐	25	27	28	29	30	32	33	34	35	36	2	3	4	5	6	8	9	10	11	12	14	15	16	17	18	20	21	22	23	24
DEC 3-12	♐	26	28	29	30	31	33	34	35	36	1	3	4	5	6	7	9	10	11	12	13	15	16	17	18	19	21	22	23	24	25
DEC 13-22	♐	27	29	30	31	32	34	35	36	1	2	4	5	6	7	8	10	11	12	13	14	16	17	18	19	20	22	23	24	25	26
DEC 23-31	♑	28	30	31	32	33	35	36	1	2	3	5	6	7	8	9	11	12	13	14	15	17	18	19	20	21	23	24	25	26	27
		0	1	2	3	4	5	6	7	8	9	10	11	12	13	14	15	16	17	18	19	20	21	22	23	24	25	26	27	28	29

TABLE 5—MERCURY ROW LETTERS

YEAR		JAN	FEB	MAR	APR	MAY	JUN	JUL	AUG	SEP	OCT	NOV	DEC
1900	1946	L	BB	PP	M	BB	RR	O	DD	B	Q	FF	C
1901	1947	S	II	E	T	II	G	V	KK	I	X	MM	J
1902	1948	Z	OO	K	AA	PP	M	BB	RR	O	DD	B	Q
1903	1949	FF	D	R	GG	D	T	II	F	V	KK	H	W
1904	1950	MM	K	Y	NN	K	AA	PP	M	CC	RR	O	DD
1905	1951	B	Q	EE	C	R	GG	D	T	II	F	V	KK
1906	1952	I	X	LL	J	Y	NN	K	AA	PP	M	CC	RR
1907	1953	O	EE	A	P	EE	C	R	GG	E	T	II	F
1908	1954	V	LL	H	W	LL	J	Y	NN	L	AA	PP	M
1909	1955	CC	RR	N	DD	A	P	EE	C	R	GG	E	T
1910	1956	II	G	U	JJ	G	W	LL	I	Y	NN	K	Z
1911	1957	PP	N	BB	QQ	N	DD	A	P	FF	C	R	GG
1912	1958	E	T	HH	F	U	JJ	G	W	LL	I	Y	NN
1913	1959	K	AA	OO	L	AA	QQ	N	CC	A	P	EE	B
1914	1960	R	HH	D	S	HH	F	U	JJ	H	W	LL	I
1915	1961	Y	NN	J	Z	OO	L	AA	QQ	N	CC	A	P
1916	1962	FF	C	Q	GG	D	S	HH	F	U	JJ	H	W
1917	1963	LL	J	X	MM	J	Z	OO	L	BB	QQ	N	CC
1918	1964	A	P	DD	B	Q	FF	C	S	HH	E	U	JJ
1919	1965	H	W	KK	I	X	MM	J	Z	OO	L	BB	QQ
1920	1966	N	DD	RR	O	DD	B	Q	FF	D	S	HH	E
1921	1967	U	KK	G	V	KK	I	X	MM	K	Z	OO	L
1922	1968	BB	QQ	M	CC	RR	O	DD	B	Q	FF	D	S
1923	1969	HH	F	T	II	F	V	KK	H	X	MM	J	Y
1924	1970	OO	M	AA	PP	M	CC	RR	O	EE	B	Q	FF
1925	1971	D	S	GG	E	T	II	F	V	KK	H	X	MM
1926	1972	J	Z	NN	K	Z	PP	M	BB	RR	O	DD	A
1927	1973	Q	GG	C	R	GG	E	T	II	G	V	KK	H
1928	1974	X	MM	I	Y	NN	K	Z	PP	M	BB	RR	O
1929	1975	EE	B	P	FF	C	R	GG	E	T	II	G	V
1930	1976	KK	I	W	LL	I	Y	NN	K	AA	PP	M	BB
1931	1977	RR	O	CC	A	P	EE	B	R	GG	D	T	II
1932	1978	G	V	JJ	H	W	LL	I	Y	NN	K	AA	PP
1933	1979	M	CC	QQ	N	CC	A	P	EE	C	R	GG	D
1934	1980	T	JJ	F	U	JJ	H	W	LL	J	Y	NN	K
1935	1981	AA	PP	L	BB	QQ	N	CC	A	P	EE	C	R
1936	1982	GG	E	S	HH	E	U	JJ	G	W	LL	I	X
1937	1983	NN	L	Z	OO	L	BB	QQ	N	DD	A	P	EE
1938	1984	C	R	FF	D	S	HH	E	U	JJ	G	W	LL
1939	1985	I	Y	MM	J	Y	OO	L	AA	QQ	N	CC	RR
1940	1986	P	FF	B	Q	FF	D	S	HH	F	U	JJ	G
1941	1987	W	LL	H	X	MM	J	Y	OO	L	AA	QQ	N
1942	1988	DD	A	O	EE	B	Q	FF	D	S	HH	F	U
1943	1989	JJ	H	V	KK	H	X	MM	J	Z	OO	L	AA
1944	1990	QQ	N	BB	RR	O	DD	A	Q	FF	C	S	HH
1945	1991	F	U	II	G	V	KK	H	X	MM	J	Z	OO

TABLE 6—MERCURY KEY NUMBERS

DAY OF MONTH

	1 2	3 4	5 6	7 8	9 10	11 12	13 14	15 16	17 18	19 20	21 22	23 24	25 26	27 28	29 30	31
A	9	10	12	13	14	15	16	17	18	19	19	20	21	21	22	22
B	10	12	13	14	15	16	17	18	19	19	20	21	21	22	22	23
C	12	13	14	15	16	17	18	19	19	20	21	21	22	22	23	24
D	13	14	15	16	17	18	19	19	20	21	21	22	22	23	24	25
E	14	15	16	17	18	19	19	20	21	21	22	22	23	24	25	25
F	15	16	17	18	19	19	20	21	21	22	22	23	24	25	25	26
G	16	17	18	19	19	20	21	21	22	22	23	24	25	25	26	26
H	17	18	19	19	20	21	21	22	22	23	24	25	25	26	26	27
I	18	19	19	20	21	21	22	22	23	24	25	25	26	26	27	27
J	19	19	20	21	21	22	22	23	24	25	25	26	26	27	27	28
K	19	20	21	21	22	22	23	24	25	25	26	26	27	27	28	28
L	20	21	21	22	22	23	24	25	25	26	26	27	27	28	28	29
M	21	21	22	22	23	24	25	25	26	26	27	27	28	28	29	29
N	21	22	22	23	24	25	25	26	26	27	27	28	28	29	29	30
O	22	22	23	24	25	25	26	26	27	27	28	28	29	29	30	30
P	22	23	24	25	25	26	26	27	27	28	28	29	29	30	30	31
Q	23	24	25	25	26	26	27	27	28	28	29	29	30	30	31	32
R	24	25	25	26	26	27	27	28	28	29	29	30	30	31	32	33
S	25	25	26	26	27	27	28	28	29	29	30	30	31	32	33	34
T	25	26	26	27	27	28	28	29	29	30	30	31	32	33	34	34
U	26	26	27	27	28	28	29	29	30	30	31	32	33	34	34	35
V	26	27	27	28	28	29	29	30	30	31	32	33	34	34	35	36
W	27	27	28	28	29	29	30	30	31	32	33	34	34	35	36	1
X	27	28	28	29	29	30	30	31	32	33	34	34	35	36	1	2
Y	28	28	29	29	30	30	31	32	33	34	34	35	36	1	2	3
Z	28	29	29	30	30	31	32	33	34	34	35	36	1	2	3	4
AA	29	29	30	30	31	32	33	34	34	35	36	1	2	3	4	5
BB	29	30	30	31	32	33	34	34	35	36	1	2	3	4	5	7
CC	30	30	31	32	33	34	34	35	36	1	2	3	4	5	7	8
DD	30	31	32	33	34	34	35	36	1	2	3	4	5	7	8	9
EE	31	32	33	34	34	35	36	1	2	3	4	5	7	8	9	10
FF	32	33	34	34	35	36	1	2	3	4	5	7	8	9	10	12
GG	33	34	34	35	36	1	2	3	4	5	7	8	9	10	12	13
HH	34	34	35	36	1	2	3	4	5	7	8	9	10	12	13	14
II	34	35	36	1	2	3	4	5	7	8	9	10	12	13	14	15
JJ	35	36	1	2	3	4	5	7	8	9	10	12	13	14	15	16
KK	36	1	2	3	4	5	7	8	9	10	12	13	14	15	16	17
LL	1	2	3	4	5	7	8	9	10	12	13	14	15	16	17	18
MM	2	3	4	5	7	8	9	10	12	13	14	15	16	17	18	19
NN	3	4	5	7	8	9	10	12	13	14	15	16	17	18	19	19
OO	4	5	7	8	9	10	12	13	14	15	16	17	18	19	19	20
PP	5	7	8	9	10	12	13	14	15	16	17	18	19	19	20	21
QQ	7	8	9	10	12	13	14	15	16	17	18	19	19	20	21	21
RR	8	9	10	12	13	14	15	16	17	18	19	19	20	21	21	22

TABLE 7—MERCURY—SKY POSITIONS

DARK AREAS COVER RETROGRADE MOTION

MERCURY PATH: FIVE SKY POSITIONS TO RIGHT FOR EACH ROW DOWN

KEY NUMBER →	1	2	3	4	5	6	7	8	9	10	11	12	13	14	15	16	17	18	19	20	21	22	23	24	25	26	27	28	29	30	31	32	33	34	35	36
JAN 1-10	31	32	32	32	32	32	31	31	31	30	29	29	28	28	28	27	27	27	27	27	27	28	28	28	28	29	29	29	30	30	30	31	31	31	31	31
JAN 11-20	32	32	33	33	33	33	33	32	32	32	31	30	30	29	29	29	28	28	28	28	28	28	29	29	29	29	30	30	30	30	31	31	31	32	32	32
JAN 21-30	33	33	33	34	34	34	34	34	33	33	33	32	31	31	30	30	30	29	29	29	29	29	29	30	30	30	30	31	31	31	31	32	32	32	33	33
JAN 31-FEB 9	34	34	34	34	35	35	35	35	35	34	34	34	33	32	32	31	31	31	30	30	30	30	30	30	31	31	31	31	32	32	32	32	33	33	33	34
FEB 10-19	35	35	35	35	35	36	36	36	36	36	35	35	35	34	33	33	32	32	32	31	31	31	31	31	31	32	32	32	32	33	33	33	33	34	34	34
FEB 20-MAR 1	35	36	36	36	36	36	1	1	1	1	1	36	36	36	35	34	34	33	33	33	32	32	32	32	32	32	33	33	33	33	34	34	34	34	35	35
MAR 2-11	36	36	1	1	1	1	1	2	2	2	2	2	1	1	1	36	35	35	34	34	34	33	33	33	33	33	33	34	34	34	34	35	35	35	35	36
MAR 12-21	1	1	1	2	2	2	2	2	3	3	3	3	3	2	2	2	1	36	36	35	35	35	34	34	34	34	34	34	35	35	35	35	36	36	36	36
MAR 22-31	1	2	2	2	3	3	3	3	3	4	4	4	4	4	3	3	3	2	1	1	36	36	36	35	35	35	35	35	35	36	36	36	36	1	1	1
APR 1-10	2	2	3	3	3	4	4	4	4	4	5	5	5	5	5	4	4	4	3	2	2	1	1	1	36	36	36	36	36	36	1	1	1	1	2	2
APR 11-20	3	3	3	4	4	4	5	5	5	5	5	6	6	6	6	6	5	5	5	4	3	3	2	2	2	1	1	1	1	1	1	2	2	2	2	3
APR 21-30	4	4	4	4	5	5	5	6	6	6	6	6	7	7	7	7	7	6	6	6	5	4	4	3	3	3	2	2	2	2	2	2	3	3	3	3
MAY 1-11	4	5	5	5	5	6	6	6	7	7	7	7	7	8	8	8	8	8	7	7	7	6	5	5	4	4	4	3	3	3	3	3	3	4	4	4
MAY 12-21	5	5	6	6	6	6	7	7	7	8	8	8	8	8	9	9	9	9	9	8	8	8	7	6	6	5	5	5	4	4	4	4	4	4	5	5
MAY 22-JUN 1	6	6	6	7	7	7	7	8	8	8	9	9	9	9	9	10	10	10	10	10	9	9	9	8	7	7	6	6	6	5	5	5	5	5	5	6
JUN 2-11	7	7	7	7	8	8	8	8	9	9	9	10	10	10	10	10	11	11	11	11	11	10	10	10	9	8	8	7	7	7	6	6	6	6	6	6
JUN 12-21	7	8	8	8	8	9	9	9	9	10	10	10	11	11	11	11	11	12	12	12	12	12	11	11	11	10	9	9	8	8	8	7	7	7	7	7
JUN 22-JUL 2	8	8	9	9	9	9	10	10	10	10	11	11	11	12	12	12	12	12	13	13	13	13	13	12	12	12	11	10	10	9	9	9	8	8	8	8
JUL 3-12	9	9	9	10	10	10	10	11	11	11	11	12	12	12	13	13	13	13	13	14	14	14	14	14	13	13	13	12	11	11	10	10	10	9	9	9
JUL 13-23	10	10	10	10	11	11	11	11	12	12	12	12	13	13	13	14	14	14	14	14	15	15	15	15	15	14	14	14	13	12	12	11	11	11	10	10
JUL 24-AUG 2	11	11	11	11	11	12	12	12	12	13	13	13	13	14	14	14	15	15	15	15	15	16	16	16	16	16	15	15	15	14	13	13	12	12	12	11
AUG 3-13	12	12	12	12	12	12	13	13	13	13	14	14	14	14	15	15	15	16	16	16	16	16	17	17	17	17	17	16	16	16	15	14	14	13	13	13
AUG 14-23	14	13	13	13	13	13	13	14	14	14	14	15	15	15	15	16	16	16	17	17	17	17	17	18	18	18	18	18	17	17	17	16	15	15	14	14
AUG 24-SEP 3	15	15	14	14	14	14	14	14	15	15	15	15	16	16	16	16	17	17	17	18	18	18	18	18	19	19	19	19	19	18	18	18	17	16	16	15
SEP 4-13	16	16	16	15	15	15	15	15	15	16	16	16	16	17	17	17	17	18	18	18	19	19	19	19	19	20	20	20	20	20	19	19	19	18	17	17
SEP 14-23	18	17	17	17	16	16	16	16	16	16	17	17	17	17	18	18	18	18	19	19	19	20	20	20	20	20	21	21	21	21	21	20	20	20	19	18
SEP 24-OCT 3	19	19	18	18	18	17	17	17	17	17	17	18	18	18	18	19	19	19	19	20	20	20	21	21	21	21	21	22	22	22	22	22	21	21	21	20
OCT 4-13	21	20	20	19	19	19	18	18	18	18	18	18	19	19	19	19	20	20	20	20	21	21	21	22	22	22	22	22	23	23	23	23	23	22	22	22
OCT 14-23	23	22	21	21	20	20	20	19	19	19	19	19	19	20	20	20	20	21	21	21	21	22	22	22	23	23	23	23	23	24	24	24	24	24	23	23
OCT 24-NOV 3	24	24	23	22	22	21	21	21	20	20	20	20	20	20	21	21	21	21	22	22	22	22	23	23	23	24	24	24	24	24	25	25	25	25	25	24
NOV 4-12	25	25	25	24	24	23	23	22	22	21	21	21	21	21	21	21	22	22	22	23	23	23	23	24	24	24	25	25	25	25	25	26	26	26	26	26
NOV 13-22	27	26	26	26	25	24	24	23	23	23	22	22	22	22	22	22	23	23	23	23	24	24	24	24	25	25	25	26	26	26	26	26	27	27	27	27
NOV 23-DEC 2	28	28	27	27	27	26	25	25	24	24	24	23	23	23	23	23	23	24	24	24	24	25	25	25	25	26	26	26	27	27	27	27	27	28	28	28
DEC 3-12	29	29	29	28	28	28	27	26	26	25	25	25	24	24	24	24	24	24	25	25	25	25	26	26	26	26	27	27	27	28	28	28	28	28	29	29
DEC 13-22	30	30	30	30	29	29	29	28	27	27	26	26	26	25	25	25	25	25	25	26	26	26	26	27	27	27	27	28	28	28	29	29	29	29	29	30
DEC 23-31	31	31	31	31	31	30	30	30	29	28	28	27	27	27	26	26	26	26	26	26	27	27	27	27	28	28	28	28	29	29	29	30	30	30	30	30

TABLE 8—VENUS ROW LETTERS AND KEY NUMBERS

ROW LETTERS

Years				JAN	FEB	MAR	APR	MAY	JUN	JUL	AUG	SEP	OCT	NOV	DEC
1900 to 1931															
1900	1908	1916	1924	II	D	I	M	R	W	BB	GG	B	G	L	Q
1901	1909	1917	1925	V	AA	EE	JJ	E	J	O	T	Y	CC	HH	C
1902	1910	1918	1926	H	M	R	W	BB	FF	A	F	K	P	U	Z
1903	1911	1919	1927	EE	JJ	D	I	N	S	X	CC	HH	B	G	L
1904	1912	1920	1928	Q	V	AA	FF	JJ	E	J	O	T	Y	DD	II
1905	1913	1921	1929	D	I	M	R	W	BB	GG	B	G	K	P	U
1906	1914	1922	1930	Z	EE	JJ	E	I	N	S	X	CC	HH	C	H
1907	1915	1923	1931	M	R	V	AA	FF	A	F	K	P	T	Y	DD
1932 to 1963															
1932	1940	1948	1956	JJ	E	I	N	S	X	CC	HH	C	G	L	Q
1933	1941	1949	1957	V	AA	FF	A	E	J	O	T	Y	DD	II	D
1934	1942	1950	1958	I	N	R	W	BB	GG	B	G	L	P	U	Z
1935	1943	1951	1959	EE	JJ	E	J	N	S	X	CC	HH	C	H	M
1936	1944	1952	1960	R	W	AA	FF	A	F	K	P	U	Y	DD	II
1937	1945	1953	1961	D	I	N	S	X	BB	GG	B	G	L	Q	V
1938	1946	1954	1962	AA	FF	JJ	E	J	O	T	Y	DD	HH	C	H
1939	1947	1955	1963	M	R	W	BB	FF	A	F	K	P	U	Z	EE
1964 to 1995															
1964	1972	1980	1988	JJ	E	J	O	T	X	CC	HH	C	H	M	R
1965	1973	1981	1989	W	BB	FF	A	F	K	P	U	Z	EE	JJ	D
1966	1974	1982	1990	I	N	S	X	CC	GG	B	G	L	Q	V	AA
1967	1975	1983	1991	FF	A	E	J	O	T	Y	DD	II	D	I	M
1968	1976	1984	1992	R	W	BB	GG	B	G	K	P	U	Z	EE	JJ
1969	1977	1985	1993	E	J	N	S	X	CC	HH	C	H	M	R	W
1970	1978	1986	1994	AA	FF	A	F	K	P	T	Y	DD	II	D	I
1971	1979	1987	1995	N	S	X	BB	GG	B	G	L	Q	V	AA	EE

KEY NUMBERS

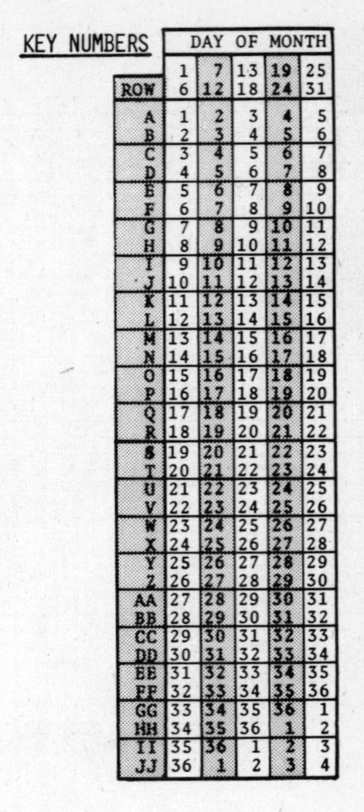

ROW	DAY OF MONTH 1–6	7–12	13–18	19–24	25–31
A	1	2	3	4	5
B	2	3	4	5	6
C	3	4	5	6	7
D	4	5	6	7	8
E	5	6	7	8	9
F	6	7	8	9	10
G	7	8	9	10	11
H	8	9	10	11	12
I	9	10	11	12	13
J	10	11	12	13	14
K	11	12	13	14	15
L	12	13	14	15	16
M	13	14	15	16	17
N	14	15	16	17	18
O	15	16	17	18	19
P	16	17	18	19	20
Q	17	18	19	20	21
R	18	19	20	21	22
S	19	20	21	22	23
T	20	21	22	23	24
U	21	22	23	24	25
V	22	23	24	25	26
W	23	24	25	26	27
X	24	25	26	27	28
Y	25	26	27	28	29
Z	26	27	28	29	30
AA	27	28	29	30	31
BB	28	29	30	31	32
CC	29	30	31	32	33
DD	30	31	32	33	34
EE	31	32	33	34	35
FF	32	33	34	35	36
GG	33	34	35	36	1
HH	34	35	36	1	2
II	35	36	1	2	3
JJ	36	1	2	3	4

TABLE 9—VENUS SKY POSITIONS

DARK AREAS COVER RETROGRADE MOTION

VENUS PATH: FIVE SKY POSITIONS TO RIGHT FOR EACH THREE ROWS DOWN

KEY NUMBERS→	1	2	3	4	5	6	7	8	9	10	11	12	13	14	15	16	17	18	19	20	21	22	23	24	25	26	27	28	29	30	31	32	33	34	35	36
JAN 1-10	33	33	33	34	34	34	34	34	33	32	29	27	26	25	25	25	25	25	26	26	26	27	27	27	28	28	29	29	29	30	30	31	31	32	32	32
JAN 11-20	33	34	34	35	35	35	35	35	35	34	33	30	28	27	26	26	26	26	26	27	27	27	28	28	28	29	29	30	30	30	31	31	32	32	33	33
JAN 21-30	34	34	35	35	36	36	36	36	36	36	35	34	31	29	28	27	27	27	27	27	28	28	28	29	29	29	30	30	31	31	31	32	32	33	33	34
JAN 31-FEB 9	35	35	35	36	36	1	1	1	1	1	1	36	35	32	30	29	28	28	28	28	28	29	29	29	30	30	30	31	31	32	32	32	33	33	34	34
FEB 10-19	35	36	36	36	1	1	2	2	2	2	2	2	1	36	33	31	30	29	29	29	29	29	30	30	30	31	31	31	32	32	33	33	33	34	34	35
FEB 20-MAR 1	36	36	1	1	1	2	2	3	3	3	3	3	3	2	1	34	32	31	30	30	30	30	30	31	31	31	32	32	32	32	32	34	34	34	35	35
MAR 2-11	36	1	1	2	2	2	3	3	4	4	4	4	4	4	3	2	35	33	32	31	31	31	31	31	32	32	32	33	33	33	34	34	35	35	35	36
MAR 12-21	1	1	2	2	3	3	3	4	4	5	5	5	5	5	5	4	3	36	34	33	32	32	32	32	32	33	33	33	34	34	34	35	35	36	36	36
MAR 22-31	1	2	2	3	3	4	4	4	5	5	6	6	6	6	6	6	5	4	1	35	34	33	33	33	33	33	34	34	34	35	35	35	36	36	1	1
APR 1-10	2	2	3	3	4	4	5	5	5	6	6	7	7	7	7	7	7	6	5	2	36	35	34	34	34	34	34	35	35	35	36	36	36	1	1	2
APR 11-20	3	3	3	4	4	5	5	6	6	6	7	7	8	8	8	8	8	8	7	6	3	1	36	35	35	35	35	35	36	36	36	1	1	1	2	2
APR 21-30	3	4	4	4	5	5	6	6	7	7	7	8	8	9	9	9	9	9	9	8	7	4	2	1	36	36	36	36	36	1	1	1	2	2	2	3
MAY 1-11	4	4	5	5	6	6	6	7	7	8	8	8	9	9	10	10	10	10	10	10	9	8	5	3	2	1	1	1	1	1	2	2	2	3	3	3
MAY 12-21	4	5	5	6	6	7	7	7	8	8	9	9	9	10	10	11	11	11	11	11	11	10	9	6	4	3	2	2	2	2	2	3	3	3	4	4
MAY 22-JUN 1	5	5	6	6	7	7	8	8	8	9	9	10	10	10	11	11	12	12	12	12	12	12	11	10	7	5	4	3	3	3	3	3	4	4	4	5
JUN 2-11	6	6	6	7	7	8	8	9	9	9	10	10	11	11	11	12	12	13	13	13	13	13	13	12	11	8	6	5	4	4	4	4	4	5	5	5
JUN 12-21	6	7	7	7	8	8	9	9	10	10	10	11	11	12	12	12	13	13	14	14	14	14	14	14	13	12	9	7	6	5	5	5	5	5	6	6
JUN 22-JUL 2	7	7	8	8	8	9	9	10	10	11	11	11	12	12	13	13	13	14	14	15	15	15	15	15	15	14	13	10	8	7	6	6	6	6	6	7
JUL 3-12	8	8	8	9	9	9	10	10	11	11	12	12	12	13	13	14	14	14	15	15	16	16	16	16	16	16	15	14	11	9	8	7	7	7	7	7
JUL 13-23	8	9	9	9	10	10	10	11	11	12	12	13	13	13	14	14	15	15	15	16	16	17	17	17	17	17	17	16	15	12	10	9	8	8	8	8
JUL 24-AUG 2	9	9	10	10	10	11	11	11	12	12	13	13	14	14	14	15	15	16	16	16	17	17	18	18	18	18	18	18	17	16	13	11	10	9	9	9
AUG 3-13	10	10	10	11	11	11	12	12	12	13	13	14	14	15	15	15	16	16	17	17	17	18	18	19	19	19	19	19	19	18	17	14	12	11	10	10
AUG 14-23	11	11	11	11	12	12	12	13	13	13	14	14	15	15	16	16	16	17	17	18	18	18	19	19	20	20	20	20	20	20	19	18	15	13	12	11
AUG 24-SEP 3	12	12	12	12	12	13	13	13	14	14	14	15	15	16	16	17	17	17	18	18	19	19	19	20	20	21	21	21	21	21	21	20	19	16	14	13
SEP 4-13	14	13	13	13	13	13	14	14	14	15	15	15	16	16	17	17	18	18	18	19	19	20	20	20	21	21	22	22	22	22	22	22	21	20	17	15
SEP 14-23	16	15	14	14	14	14	14	15	15	15	16	16	16	17	17	18	18	19	19	19	20	20	21	21	21	22	22	23	23	23	23	23	23	22	21	18
SEP 24-OCT 3	19	17	16	15	15	15	15	15	16	16	16	17	17	17	18	18	19	19	20	20	20	21	21	22	22	22	23	23	24	24	24	24	24	24	23	22
OCT 4-13	23	20	18	17	16	16	16	16	16	17	17	17	18	18	18	19	19	20	20	21	21	21	22	22	23	23	23	24	24	25	25	25	25	25	25	24
OCT 14-23	25	24	21	19	18	17	17	17	17	17	18	18	18	19	19	19	20	20	21	21	22	22	22	23	23	24	24	24	25	25	26	26	26	26	26	26
OCT 24-NOV 3	27	26	25	22	20	19	18	18	18	18	18	19	19	19	20	20	20	21	21	22	22	23	23	23	24	24	25	25	25	26	26	27	27	27	27	27
NOV 4-12	28	28	27	26	23	21	20	19	19	19	19	19	20	20	20	21	21	21	22	22	23	23	24	24	24	25	25	26	26	26	27	27	28	28	28	28
NOV 13-22	29	29	29	28	27	24	22	21	20	20	20	20	20	21	21	21	22	22	22	23	23	24	24	25	25	25	26	26	27	27	27	28	28	29	29	29
NOV 23-DEC 2	30	30	30	30	29	28	25	23	22	21	21	21	21	21	22	22	22	23	23	23	24	24	25	25	26	26	26	27	27	28	28	28	29	29	30	30
DEC 3-12	31	31	31	31	31	30	29	26	24	23	22	22	22	22	22	23	23	23	24	24	24	25	25	26	26	27	27	27	28	28	29	29	29	30	30	31
DEC 13-22	31	32	32	32	32	32	31	30	27	25	24	23	23	23	23	23	24	24	24	25	25	25	26	26	27	27	28	28	28	29	29	30	30	30	31	31
DEC 23-31	32	32	33	33	33	33	33	32	31	28	26	25	24	24	24	24	24	25	25	25	26	26	26	27	27	28	28	29	29	29	30	30	31	31	31	32

TABLE 10—MARS ROW LETTERS AND KEY NUMBERS

	JAN		FEB		MAR		APR		MAY		JUN		JUL		AUG		SEP		OCT		NOV		DEC	
	1 15	16 31	1 15	16 29	1 15	16 31	1 15	16 30	1 15	16 31	1 15	16 30	1 15	16 31	1 15	16 31	1 15	16 30	1 15	16 31	1 15	16 30	1 15	16 31
A	29	30	31	32	33	34	35	36	1	2	3	4	4	5	6	7	8	9	9	10	11	12	12	13
B	14	14	15	16	16	17	18	18	19	20	20	21	22	22	23	24	25	26	26	27	28	28	30	31
C	32	33	34	35	36	1	1	2	3	4	5	6	7	8	9	9	10	11	11	12	13	14	14	15
D	16	16	17	18	18	19	20	20	21	22	22	23	24	25	25	26	27	28	29	30	31	32	33	34
E	35	35	36	1	2	3	4	5	6	7	8	8	9	10	11	11	12	13	14	14	15	16	16	17
F	18	18	19	20	20	21	22	22	23	24	25	25	26	27	28	29	30	31	32	33	34	35	35	36
G	1	2	3	4	5	6	7	7	8	9	10	11	11	12	13	13	14	15	15	16	17	17	18	19
H	19	20	21	22	22	23	24	25	25	26	27	28	29	30	31	32	33	34	34	35	36	1	2	3
I	4	5	6	7	7	8	9	10	10	11	12	13	13	14	15	15	16	17	17	18	19	19	20	21
J	21	22	23	24	24	25	26	27	28	29	30	30	31	32	33	34	35	36	1	2	3	4	5	6
K	6	7	8	9	10	10	11	12	13	13	14	15	15	16	17	17	18	19	19	20	21	21	22	23
L	24	24	25	26	27	28	28	29	30	31	32	33	34	35	36	1	2	3	4	5	5	6	7	8
M	9	10	10	11	12	12	13	14	14	15	16	17	17	18	18	19	20	21	21	22	23	23	24	25
N	26	27	28	28	29	30	31	32	33	34	35	36	1	2	3	4	4	5	6	7	8	9	9	10
O	11	12	12	13	14	14	15	16	16	17	18	18	19	20	20	21	22	23	23	24	25	26	27	27
P	28	29	30	31	32	33	34	35	36	1	1	2	3	4	5	6	7	8	8	9	10	11	11	12
Q	13	14	14	15	16	16	17	18	18	19	20	21	21	22	22	23	24	25	26	26	27	28	29	30
R	31	32	33	34	35	35	36	1	2	3	4	5	6	7	8	8	9	10	11	11	12	13	14	14
S	15	16	16	17	18	18	19	20	20	21	22	22	23	24	25	25	26	27	28	29	30	31	32	33
T	34	35	36	36	1	2	3	4	5	6	7	7	8	9	10	11	11	12	13	13	14	15	15	16
U	17	17	18	19	19	20	21	22	22	23	24	25	25	26	27	28	29	30	31	32	33	34	34	35
V	36	1	2	3	4	5	6	6	7	8	9	10	10	11	12	13	13	14	15	15	16	17	17	18
W	19	19	20	21	21	22	23	24	24	25	26	27	28	29	30	30	31	32	33	34	35	36	1	2
X	3	4	5	6	6	7	8	9	10	10	11	12	13	13	14	15	15	16	17	17	18	19	19	20
Y	21	21	22	23	24	24	25	26	27	28	29	29	30	31	32	33	34	35	36	1	2	3	4	5
Z	5	6	7	8	9	9	10	11	12	12	13	14	14	15	16	17	17	18	18	19	20	21	21	22
AA	23	23	24	25	26	27	28	28	29	30	31	32	33	34	35	36	1	2	3	4	5	5	6	7
BB	8	9	10	10	11	12	12	13	14	14	15	16	16	17	18	18	19	20	20	21	22	23	23	24
CC	25	26	27	27	28	29	30	31	32	33	34	35	36	1	2	3	4	4	5	6	7	8	9	9
DD	10	11	12	12	13	14	14	15	16	16	17	18	18	19	20	20	21	22	22	23	24	25	26	26
EE	27	28	29	30	31	32	33	34	35	36	1	1	2	3	4	5	6	7	8	8	9	10	11	11
FF	12	13	14	14	15	15	16	17	17	18	19	19	20	21	22	22	23	24	25	25	26	27	28	29
GG	30	31	32	33	34	35	35	36	1	2	3	4	5	6	7	7	8	9	10	11	11	12	13	13
HH	14	15	15	16	17	17	18	19	19	20	21	21	22	23	24	25	25	26	27	28	29	30	31	31
II	32	33	34	35	36	1	2	3	4	5	6	6	7	8	9	10	10	11	12	13	13	14	15	15
JJ	16	17	17	18	19	19	20	21	21	22	23	24	24	25	26	27	28	29	30	30	31	32	33	34
KK	35	36	1	2	3	4	5	6	6	7	8	9	10	10	11	12	13	13	14	15	15	16	17	17
LL	18	19	19	20	21	21	22	23	23	24	25	26	27	28	28	29	30	31	32	33	34	35	36	1
MM	2	3	4	5	5	6	7	8	9	9	10	11	12	12	13	14	14	15	16	17	17	18	18	19
NN	20	21	21	22	23	23	24	25	26	27	27	28	29	30	31	32	33	34	35	35	1	2	3	4
OO	4	5	6	7	8	9	9	10	11	12	12	13	14	14	15	16	17	17	18	18	19	20	20	21
PP	22	23	23	24	25	26	26	27	28	29	30	31	32	33	34	35	36	1	1	2	3	4	5	6
QQ	7	8	9	9	10	11	11	12	13	14	14	15	16	16	17	18	18	19	20	20	21	22	22	23
RR	24	25	26	26	27	28	29	30	31	32	33	34	35	35	36	1	2	3	4	5	6	7	8	8
SS	9	10	11	11	12	13	14	14	15	16	16	17	18	18	19	20	20	21	22	22	23	24	25	25
TT	26	27	28	29	30	31	32	33	34	34	35	36	1	2	3	4	5	6	7	7	8	9	10	11
UU	11	12	13	13	14	15	15	16	17	17	18	19	19	20	21	21	22	23	24	25	25	26	27	28

MARS ROW LETTERS			
1900	A	1945	TT
1901	B	1946	UU
1902	C	1947	A
1903	D	1948	B
1904	E	1949	C
1905	F	1950	D
1906	G	1951	E
1907	H	1952	F
1908	I	1953	G
1909	J	1954	H
1910	K	1955	I
1911	L	1956	J
1912	M	1957	K
1913	N	1958	L
1914	O	1959	M
1915	P	1960	N
1916	Q	1961	O
1917	R	1962	P
1918	S	1963	Q
1919	T	1964	R
1920	U	1965	S
1921	V	1966	T
1922	W	1967	U
1923	X	1968	V
1924	Y	1969	W
1925	Z	1970	X
1926	AA	1971	Y
1927	BB	1972	Z
1928	CC	1973	AA
1929	DD	1974	BB
1930	EE	1975	CC
1931	FF	1976	DD
1932	GG	1977	EE
1933	HH	1978	FF
1934	II	1979	GG
1935	JJ	1980	HH
1936	KK	1981	II
1937	LL	1982	JJ
1938	MM	1983	KK
1939	NN	1984	LL
1940	OO	1985	MM
1941	PP	1986	NN
1942	QQ	1987	OO
1943	RR	1988	PP
1944	SS	1989	QQ

TABLE 11—MARS SKY POSITIONS

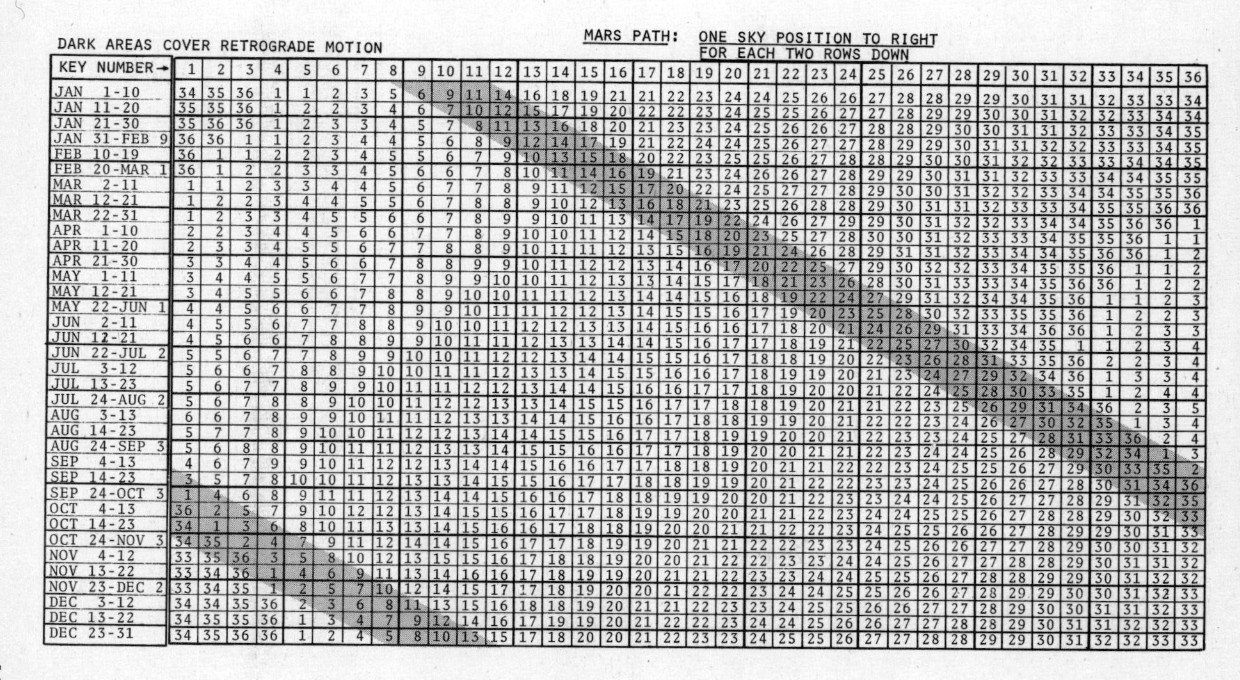

DARK AREAS COVER RETROGRADE MOTION

MARS PATH: ONE SKY POSITION TO RIGHT FOR EACH TWO ROWS DOWN

KEY NUMBER→	1	2	3	4	5	6	7	8	9	10	11	12	13	14	15	16	17	18	19	20	21	22	23	24	25	26	27	28	29	30	31	32	33	34	35	36
JAN 1-10	34	35	36	1	1	2	3	5	6	9	11	14	16	18	19	21	21	22	23	24	24	25	26	26	27	28	28	29	29	30	31	31	32	33	33	34
JAN 11-20	35	35	36	1	2	2	3	4	6	7	10	12	15	17	19	20	22	22	23	24	25	25	26	27	27	28	29	29	30	30	31	32	32	33	34	34
JAN 21-30	35	36	36	1	2	3	3	4	5	7	8	11	13	16	18	20	21	23	23	24	25	26	26	27	28	28	29	30	30	31	31	32	33	33	34	35
JAN 31-FEB 9	36	36	1	1	2	3	4	4	5	6	8	9	12	14	17	19	21	22	24	24	25	26	27	27	28	29	29	30	31	31	32	32	33	33	34	35
FEB 10-19	36	1	1	2	2	3	4	5	5	6	7	9	10	13	15	18	20	22	23	25	25	26	27	28	28	29	30	30	31	32	32	33	33	34	34	35
FEB 20-MAR 1	36	1	2	2	3	3	4	5	6	6	7	8	10	11	14	16	19	21	23	24	26	26	27	28	29	29	30	31	31	32	33	33	34	34	35	35
MAR 2-11	1	1	2	3	3	4	4	5	6	7	7	8	9	11	12	15	17	20	22	24	25	27	27	28	29	30	30	31	32	32	33	34	34	35	35	36
MAR 12-21	1	2	2	3	4	4	5	5	6	7	8	8	9	10	12	13	16	18	21	23	25	26	28	28	29	30	31	31	32	33	33	34	35	35	36	36
MAR 22-31	1	2	3	3	4	5	5	6	6	7	8	9	9	10	11	13	14	17	19	22	24	26	27	29	29	30	31	32	32	33	34	34	35	36	36	1
APR 1-10	2	2	3	4	4	5	6	6	7	7	8	9	10	10	11	12	14	15	18	20	23	25	27	28	30	30	31	32	33	33	34	35	35	36	1	1
APR 11-20	2	3	3	4	5	5	6	7	7	8	8	9	10	11	11	12	13	15	16	19	21	24	26	28	29	31	31	32	33	34	34	35	36	36	1	2
APR 21-30	3	3	4	4	5	6	6	7	8	8	9	9	10	11	12	12	13	14	16	17	20	22	25	27	29	30	32	32	33	34	35	35	36	1	1	2
MAY 1-11	3	4	4	5	5	6	7	7	8	9	9	10	10	11	12	13	13	14	15	17	18	21	23	26	28	30	31	33	33	34	35	36	36	1	2	2
MAY 12-21	3	4	5	5	6	6	7	8	8	9	10	10	11	11	12	13	14	14	15	16	18	19	22	24	27	29	31	32	34	34	35	36	1	1	2	3
MAY 22-JUN 1	4	4	5	6	6	7	7	8	9	9	10	11	11	12	12	13	14	15	15	16	17	19	20	23	25	28	30	32	33	35	35	36	1	2	2	3
JUN 2-11	4	5	5	6	7	7	8	8	9	10	10	11	12	12	13	13	14	15	16	16	17	18	20	21	24	26	29	31	33	34	36	36	1	2	3	3
JUN 12-21	4	5	6	6	7	8	8	9	9	10	11	11	12	13	13	14	14	15	16	17	17	18	19	21	22	25	27	30	32	34	35	1	1	2	3	4
JUN 22-JUL 2	5	5	6	7	7	8	9	9	10	10	11	12	12	13	14	14	15	15	16	17	18	18	19	20	22	23	26	28	31	33	35	36	2	2	3	4
JUL 3-12	5	6	6	7	8	8	9	10	10	11	11	12	13	13	14	15	15	16	16	17	18	19	19	20	21	23	24	27	29	32	34	36	1	3	3	4
JUL 13-23	5	6	7	7	8	9	9	10	11	11	12	12	13	14	14	15	16	16	17	17	18	19	20	20	21	22	24	25	28	30	33	35	1	2	4	4
JUL 24-AUG 2	5	6	7	8	8	9	10	10	11	12	12	13	13	14	15	15	16	17	17	18	18	19	20	21	21	22	23	25	26	29	31	34	36	2	3	5
AUG 3-13	6	6	7	8	9	9	10	11	11	12	13	13	14	14	15	16	16	17	18	18	19	19	20	21	22	22	23	24	26	27	30	32	35	1	3	4
AUG 14-23	5	7	7	8	9	10	10	11	12	12	13	14	14	15	15	16	17	17	18	19	19	20	20	21	22	23	23	24	25	27	28	31	33	36	2	4
AUG 24-SEP 3	5	6	8	8	9	10	11	11	12	13	13	14	15	15	16	16	17	17	18	19	20	20	21	21	22	23	24	24	25	26	28	29	32	34	1	3
SEP 4-13	4	6	7	9	9	10	11	12	12	13	14	14	15	16	16	17	17	18	18	19	20	21	21	22	22	23	24	25	25	26	27	29	30	33	35	2
SEP 14-23	3	5	7	8	10	10	11	12	13	13	14	15	15	16	17	17	18	18	19	19	20	21	22	22	23	23	24	25	26	26	27	28	30	31	34	36
SEP 24-OCT 3	1	4	6	8	9	11	11	12	13	14	14	15	16	16	17	18	18	19	19	20	20	21	22	23	23	24	24	25	26	27	27	28	29	31	32	35
OCT 4-13	36	2	5	7	9	10	12	12	13	14	15	15	16	17	17	18	19	19	20	20	21	21	22	23	24	24	25	25	26	27	28	28	29	30	32	33
OCT 14-23	34	1	3	6	8	10	11	13	13	14	15	16	16	17	18	18	19	20	20	21	21	22	22	23	24	25	25	26	26	27	28	29	29	30	31	33
OCT 24-NOV 3	34	35	2	4	7	9	11	12	14	14	15	16	17	17	18	19	19	20	21	21	22	22	23	23	24	25	26	26	27	27	28	29	30	30	31	32
NOV 4-12	33	35	36	3	5	8	10	12	13	15	15	16	17	18	18	19	20	20	21	22	22	23	23	24	24	25	26	27	27	28	28	29	30	31	31	32
NOV 13-22	33	34	36	1	4	6	9	11	13	14	16	16	17	18	19	19	20	21	21	22	23	23	24	24	25	25	26	27	28	28	29	29	30	31	32	32
NOV 23-DEC 2	33	34	35	1	2	5	7	10	12	14	15	17	17	18	19	20	20	21	22	22	23	24	24	25	25	26	26	27	28	29	29	30	30	31	32	33
DEC 3-12	34	34	35	36	2	3	6	8	11	13	15	16	18	18	19	20	21	21	22	23	23	24	25	25	26	26	27	27	28	29	30	30	31	31	32	33
DEC 13-22	34	35	35	36	1	3	4	7	9	12	14	16	17	19	19	20	21	22	22	23	24	24	25	26	26	27	27	28	28	29	30	31	31	32	32	33
DEC 23-31	34	35	36	36	1	2	4	5	8	10	13	15	17	18	20	20	21	22	23	23	24	25	25	26	27	27	28	28	29	29	30	31	32	32	33	33

TABLE 12—JUPITER KEY NUMBERS

	JAN FEB MAR	APR MAY JUN	JUL AUG SEP	OCT NOV DEC
1900	24	25	26	26
1901	27	28	29	29
1902	30	31	32	32
1903	33	34	35	36
1904	1	1	2	3
1905	4	5	6	6
1906	7	8	9	10
1907	10	11	12	13
1908	13	14	15	16
1909	16	17	18	18
1910	19	20	20	21
1911	22	22	23	24
1912	25	25	26	27
1913	28	28	29	30
1914	31	31	32	33
1915	34	35	35	36
1916	1	2	3	4
1917	4	5	6	7
1918	8	8	9	10
1919	11	12	12	13
1920	14	14	15	16
1921	17	17	18	19
1922	19	20	21	22
1923	22	23	24	24

	JAN FEB MAR	APR MAY JUN	JUL AUG SEP	OCT NOV DEC
1924	25	26	26	27
1925	28	29	29	30
1926	31	32	33	33
1927	34	35	36	1
1928	2	2	3	4
1929	5	6	7	7
1930	8	9	10	10
1931	11	12	13	13
1932	14	15	16	16
1933	17	18	18	19
1934	20	20	21	22
1935	23	23	24	25
1936	25	26	27	28
1937	28	29	30	31
1938	31	32	33	34
1939	35	35	36	1
1940	2	3	4	5
1941	5	6	7	8
1942	9	9	10	11
1943	12	12	13	14
1944	15	15	16	17
1945	17	18	19	19
1946	20	21	22	22
1947	23	24	24	25

	JAN FEB MAR	APR MAY JUN	JUL AUG SEP	OCT NOV DEC
1948	26	27	27	28
1949	29	30	30	31
1950	32	33	34	34
1951	35	36	1	2
1952	2	3	4	5
1953	6	7	7	8
1954	9	10	11	11
1955	12	13	14	14
1956	15	16	16	17
1957	18	19	19	20
1958	21	21	22	23
1959	23	24	25	25
1960	26	27	28	28
1961	29	30	31	32
1962	32	33	34	35
1963	36	1	1	2
1964	3	4	5	5
1965	6	7	8	9
1966	10	10	11	12
1967	13	13	14	15
1968	15	16	17	18
1969	18	19	20	20
1970	21	22	22	23
1971	24	25	25	26

	JAN FEB MAR	APR MAY JUN	JUL AUG SEP	OCT NOV DEC
1972	27	27	28	29
1973	30	31	31	32
1974	33	34	34	35
1975	36	1	2	3
1976	4	4	5	6
1977	7	8	8	9
1978	10	11	11	12
1979	13	14	14	15
1980	16	17	17	18
1981	19	19	20	21
1982	21	22	23	23
1983	24	25	26	26
1984	27	28	29	29
1985	30	31	32	32
1986	33	34	35	36
1987	1	1	2	3
1988	4	5	6	6
1989	7	8	9	10
1990	10	11	12	13
1991	13	14	15	16
1992	16	17	18	18
1993	19	20	20	21
1994	22	22	23	24
1995	25	25	26	27

TABLE 13—JUPITER SKY POSITIONS

DARK AREAS COVER RETROGRADE MOTION

JUPITER PATH: ONE SKY POSITION TO RIGHT FOR EACH TWELVE ROWS DOWN

KEY NUMBER →	1	2	3	4	5	6	7	8	9	10	11	12	13	14	15	16	17	18	19	20	21	22	23	24	25	26	27	28	29	30	31	32	33	34	35	36
JAN 1-10	1	1	2	3	4	6	7	8	9	10	11	13	14	15	16	17	18	20	21	22	22	23	24	25	26	27	28	29	29	30	31	32	33	34	35	36
JAN 11-20	1	2	2	3	4	5	7	8	9	10	11	12	14	15	16	17	18	19	21	22	23	23	24	25	26	27	28	29	30	30	31	32	33	34	35	36
JAN 21-30	1	2	3	3	4	5	6	8	9	10	11	12	13	15	16	17	18	19	20	22	23	24	24	25	26	27	28	29	30	31	31	32	33	34	35	36
JAN 31-FEB 9	1	2	3	4	4	5	6	7	9	10	11	12	13	14	16	17	18	19	20	21	23	24	25	25	26	27	28	29	30	31	32	32	33	34	35	36
FEB 10-19	1	2	3	4	5	5	6	7	8	10	11	12	13	14	15	17	18	19	20	21	22	24	25	26	26	27	28	29	30	31	32	33	33	34	35	36
FEB 20-MAR 1	1	2	3	4	5	6	6	7	8	9	11	12	13	14	15	16	18	19	20	21	22	23	25	26	27	27	28	29	30	31	32	33	34	34	35	36
MAR 2-11	1	2	3	4	5	6	7	7	8	9	10	12	13	14	15	16	17	19	20	21	22	23	24	26	27	28	28	29	30	31	32	33	34	35	35	36
MAR 12-21	1	2	3	4	5	6	7	8	8	9	10	11	13	14	15	16	17	18	20	21	22	23	24	25	27	28	29	29	30	31	32	33	34	35	36	36
MAR 22-31	1	2	3	4	5	6	7	8	9	9	10	11	12	14	15	16	17	18	19	21	22	23	24	25	26	28	29	30	30	31	32	33	34	35	36	1
APR 1-10	2	2	3	4	5	6	7	8	9	10	10	11	12	13	15	16	17	18	19	20	22	23	24	25	26	27	29	30	31	31	32	33	34	35	36	1
APR 11-20	2	3	3	4	5	6	7	8	9	10	11	11	12	13	14	16	17	18	19	20	21	23	24	25	26	27	28	30	31	32	32	33	34	35	36	1
APR 21-30	2	3	4	4	5	6	7	8	9	10	11	12	12	13	14	15	17	18	19	20	21	22	24	25	26	27	28	29	31	32	33	33	34	35	36	1
MAY 1-11	2	3	4	5	5	6	7	8	9	10	11	12	13	13	14	15	16	18	19	20	21	22	23	25	26	27	28	29	30	32	33	34	34	35	36	1
MAY 12-21	2	3	4	5	6	6	7	8	9	10	11	12	13	14	14	15	16	17	19	20	21	22	23	24	26	27	28	29	30	31	33	34	35	36	36	1
MAY 22-JUN 1	2	3	4	5	6	7	7	8	9	10	11	12	13	14	15	15	16	17	18	20	21	22	23	24	25	27	28	29	30	31	32	34	35	36	36	1
JUN 2-11	2	3	4	5	6	7	8	8	9	10	11	12	13	14	15	16	16	17	18	19	21	22	23	24	25	26	28	29	30	31	32	33	35	36	1	1
JUN 12-21	2	3	4	5	6	7	8	9	9	10	11	12	13	14	15	16	17	17	18	19	20	22	23	24	25	26	27	29	30	31	32	33	34	36	1	2
JUN 22-JUL 2	3	3	4	5	6	7	8	9	10	10	11	12	13	14	15	16	17	18	18	19	20	21	23	24	25	26	27	28	30	31	32	33	34	35	1	2
JUL 3-12	3	4	4	5	6	7	8	9	10	11	11	12	13	14	15	16	17	18	19	19	20	21	22	24	25	26	27	28	29	31	32	33	34	35	36	2
JUL 13-23	3	4	5	5	6	7	8	9	10	11	12	12	13	14	15	16	17	18	19	20	20	21	22	23	25	26	27	28	29	30	32	33	34	35	36	1
JUL 24-AUG 2	2	4	5	6	6	7	8	9	10	11	12	13	13	14	15	16	17	18	19	20	21	21	22	23	24	26	27	28	29	30	31	33	34	35	36	1
AUG 3-13	2	3	5	6	7	7	8	9	10	11	12	13	14	14	15	16	17	18	19	20	21	22	22	23	24	25	27	28	29	30	31	32	34	35	36	1
AUG 14-23	2	3	4	6	7	8	8	9	10	11	12	13	14	15	15	16	17	18	19	20	21	22	23	23	24	25	26	28	29	30	31	32	33	35	36	1
AUG 24-SEP 3	2	3	4	5	7	8	9	9	10	11	12	13	14	15	16	16	17	18	19	20	21	22	23	24	24	25	26	27	29	30	31	32	33	34	36	1
SEP 4- 13	2	3	4	5	6	8	9	10	10	11	12	13	14	15	16	17	17	18	19	20	21	22	23	24	25	25	26	27	28	30	31	32	33	34	35	1
SEP 14-23	2	3	4	5	6	7	8	10	11	11	12	13	14	15	16	17	18	18	19	20	21	22	23	24	25	26	26	27	28	29	31	32	33	34	35	36
SEP 24-OCT 3	1	3	4	5	6	7	8	9	11	12	12	13	14	15	16	17	18	19	19	20	21	22	23	24	25	26	27	27	28	29	30	32	33	34	35	36
OCT 4-13	1	2	4	5	6	7	8	9	11	12	13	13	14	15	16	17	18	19	20	20	21	22	23	24	25	26	27	28	28	29	30	31	33	34	35	36
OCT 14-23	1	2	3	5	6	7	8	9	10	12	13	14	14	15	16	17	18	19	20	21	21	22	23	24	25	26	27	28	29	29	30	31	32	34	35	36
OCT 24-NOV 3	1	2	3	4	6	7	8	9	10	11	13	14	15	15	16	17	18	19	20	21	22	22	23	24	25	26	27	28	29	30	30	31	32	33	35	36
NOV 4-12	1	2	3	4	5	7	8	9	10	11	12	14	15	16	16	17	18	19	20	21	22	23	23	24	25	26	27	28	29	30	31	31	32	33	34	36
NOV 13-22	1	2	3	4	5	6	8	9	10	11	12	13	15	16	17	17	18	19	20	21	22	23	24	24	25	26	27	28	29	30	31	32	32	33	34	35
NOV 23-DEC 2	36	2	3	4	5	6	7	9	10	11	12	13	14	16	17	18	18	19	20	21	22	23	24	25	25	26	27	28	29	30	31	32	33	33	34	35
DEC 3-12	36	1	3	4	5	6	7	8	10	11	12	13	14	15	17	18	19	19	20	21	22	23	24	25	26	26	27	28	29	30	31	32	33	34	34	35
DEC 13-22	36	1	2	4	5	6	7	8	9	11	12	13	14	15	16	18	19	20	20	21	22	23	24	25	26	27	27	28	29	30	31	32	33	34	35	35
DEC 23-31	36	1	2	3	5	6	7	8	9	10	12	13	14	15	16	17	19	20	21	21	22	23	24	25	26	27	28	28	29	30	31	32	33	34	35	36

TABLE 14—SATURN/URANUS/NEPTUNE/PLUTO SKY POSITIONS

	SAT	URN	NEP	PLU
1900	28	25	9	8
1901	29	26	9	8
1902	30	26	10	8
1903	31	27	10	8
1904	32	27	10	8
1905	33	28	10	9
1906	34	28	10	9
1907	36	29	11	9
1908	1	29	11	9
1909	2	29	11	9
1910	3	30	11	9
1911	5	30	12	9
1912	6	31	12	9
1913	7	31	12	9
1914	9	31	12	10
1915	10	32	13	10
1916	11	32	13	10
1917	13	33	13	10
1918	14	33	13	10
1919	15	33	13	10

	SAT	URN	NEP	PLU
1920	17	34	14	10
1921	18	34	14	10
1922	19	35	14	10
1923	21	35	14	11
1924	22	35	14	11
1925	23	36	15	11
1926	24	36	15	11
1927	25	1	15	11
1928	26	1	15	11
1929	27	1	16	11
1930	28	2	16	11
1931	29	2	16	11
1932	30	2	16	12
1933	32	3	16	12
1934	33	3	17	12
1935	34	4	17	12
1936	35	4	17	12
1937	36	5	17	12
1938	2	5	18	12
1939	3	5	18	13

	SAT	URN	NEP	PLU
1940	4	6	18	13
1941	6	6	18	13
1942	7	7	18	13
1943	8	7	19	13
1944	9	7	19	13
1945	11	8	19	13
1946	12	8	19	14
1947	13	9	19	14
1948	15	9	20	14
1949	16	10	20	14
1950	17	10	20	14
1951	19	11	20	14
1952	20	11	21	15
1953	21	11	21	15
1954	22	12	21	15
1955	24	12	21	15
1956	25	13	22	15
1957	26	13	22	16
1958	27	14	22	16
1959	28	14	22	16

	SAT	URN	NEP	PLU
1960	29	15	22	16
1961	30	15	23	16
1962	31	16	23	16
1963	32	16	23	17
1964	34	17	23	17
1965	35	17	23	17
1966	36	17	24	17
1967	1	18	24	17
1968	2	18	24	18
1969	4	19	24	18
1970	5	19	25	18
1971	6	20	25	18
1972	8	20	25	19
1973	9	21	25	19
1974	10	21	25	19
1975	12	22	26	19
1976	13	22	26	20
1977	14	23	26	20
1978	16	23	26	20
1979	17	24	26	20

	SAT	URN	NEP	PLU
1980	18	24	27	21
1981	20	24	27	21
1982	21	25	27	21
1983	22	25	27	21
1984	23	26	28	22
1985	22	28	26	24
1986	25	27	28	22
1987	26	27	28	22
1988	27	27	28	23
1989	29	28	29	23
1990	30	28	29	23
1991	31	29	29	23
1992	32	29	29	24
1993	33	30	29	24
1994	34	30	30	24
1995	35	30	30	24
1996	36	31	30	25
1997	2	31	30	25
1998	3	32	31	25
1999	4	32	31	25

PERIODS OF RETROGRADE MOTION (DARKER AREAS)

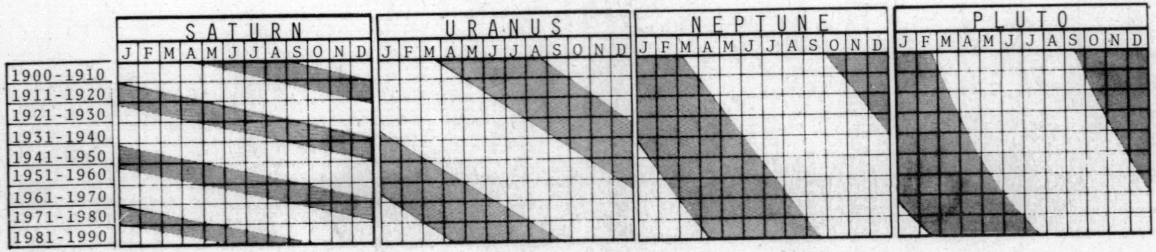
SATURN
URANUS
NEPTUNE
PLUTO
J F M A M J J A S O N D
1900-1910
1911-1920
1921-1930
1931-1940
1941-1950
1951-1960
1961-1970
1971-1980
1981-1990

TABLE 15—YOUR ASCENDANT SKY POSITION

	MORNING HOURS →										NOON	← AFTERNOON HOURS											
	1	2	3	4	5	6	7	8	9	10	11	12	1	2	3	4	5	6	7	8	9	10	11	12
JAN 1-10	21	22	23	24	26	27	28	30	32	34	36	3	5	7	9	10	11	13	14	15	16	17	19	20
JAN 11-20	22	23	24	25	26	28	29	31	33	35	2	4	7	8	10	11	12	13	14	16	17	18	19	20
JAN 21-30	22	24	25	26	27	28	30	32	35	1	4	6	8	9	10	12	13	14	15	16	18	19	20	21
JAN 31-FEB 9	23	24	25	27	28	30	32	34	36	3	5	7	9	10	11	13	14	15	16	17	18	20	21	22
FEB 10-19	24	25	26	28	29	31	33	35	2	4	7	8	10	11	12	13	14	16	17	18	19	20	22	23
FEB 20-MAR 1	25	26	27	29	30	32	35	1	4	6	8	9	10	12	13	14	15	16	18	19	20	21	22	23
MAR 2-11	25	27	28	30	32	34	36	3	5	7	9	10	11	13	14	15	16	17	18	20	21	22	23	24
MAR 12-21	26	28	29	31	33	35	2	4	6	8	10	11	12	13	15	16	17	18	19	20	22	23	24	25
MAR 22-31	27	29	30	32	34	1	4	6	8	9	10	12	13	14	15	16	18	19	20	21	22	23	25	26
APR 1-10	28	30	31	34	36	3	5	7	9	10	11	12	14	15	16	17	18	20	21	22	23	24	25	27
APR 11-20	29	31	33	35	2	4	6	8	10	11	12	13	14	16	17	18	19	20	22	23	24	25	26	28
APR 21-30	30	32	34	1	4	6	7	9	10	12	13	14	15	16	17	19	20	21	22	23	25	26	27	29
MAY 1-11	31	34	36	3	5	7	8	10	11	12	14	15	16	17	18	19	21	22	23	24	25	27	28	30
MAY 12-21	33	35	2	4	6	8	10	11	12	13	14	16	17	18	19	20	22	23	24	25	26	28	29	31
MAY 22-JUN 1	34	1	4	6	8	9	10	12	13	14	15	16	18	19	20	21	22	23	25	26	27	29	30	32
JUN 2-11	36	3	5	7	9	10	11	13	14	15	16	17	18	20	21	22	23	24	26	27	28	30	32	34
JUN 12-21	2	4	7	9	10	11	12	13	14	16	17	18	19	20	22	23	24	25	26	28	29	31	33	35
JUN 22-JUL 2	4	6	8	9	10	12	13	14	15	16	18	19	20	21	22	23	25	26	27	29	30	32	35	1
JUL 3-12	5	7	9	10	11	13	14	15	16	17	19	20	21	22	23	24	25	27	28	30	31	34	36	3
JUL 13-23	7	8	10	11	12	13	14	16	17	18	19	20	22	23	24	25	26	28	29	31	33	36	2	5
JUL 24-AUG 2	8	9	11	12	13	14	15	17	18	19	20	21	22	24	25	26	27	29	30	32	35	1	4	6
AUG 3-13	9	10	11	13	14	15	16	17	19	20	21	22	23	24	26	27	28	30	32	34	1	3	5	7
AUG 14-23	10	11	12	13	15	16	17	18	19	21	22	23	24	25	27	28	29	31	33	36	2	5	7	8
AUG 24-SEP 3	11	12	13	14	15	17	18	19	20	21	23	24	25	26	27	29	31	33	35	2	4	6	8	9
SEP 4-13	12	13	14	15	16	17	19	20	21	22	23	25	26	27	28	30	32	34	1	3	5	7	9	10
SEP 14-23	12	13	15	16	17	18	19	21	22	23	24	25	27	28	29	31	33	36	2	5	7	8	10	11
SEP 24-OCT 3	13	14	16	17	18	19	20	21	23	24	25	26	28	29	31	33	35	2	4	6	8	9	11	12
OCT 4-13	14	15	16	17	18	20	21	22	23	25	26	27	28	30	32	34	1	3	5	7	9	10	11	13
OCT 14-23	15	16	17	18	19	21	22	23	24	25	27	28	29	31	33	36	1	5	7	8	10	11	12	13
OCT 24-NOV 3	15	17	18	19	20	21	23	24	25	26	27	29	31	33	35	2	4	6	8	9	11	12	13	14
NOV 4-12	16	17	19	20	21	22	23	25	26	27	28	30	32	34	1	3	5	7	9	10	12	13	14	15
NOV 13-22	17	18	19	21	22	23	24	25	27	28	29	31	33	36	2	5	7	8	10	11	12	13	15	16
NOV 23-DEC 2	18	19	20	21	22	24	25	26	27	29	30	32	35	1	4	6	8	9	11	12	13	14	15	17
DEC 3-12	19	20	21	22	23	24	26	27	28	30	32	34	1	3	5	7	9	10	11	13	14	15	16	17
DEC 13-22	19	20	22	23	24	25	26	28	29	31	33	36	2	5	7	8	10	11	12	13	15	16	17	18
DEC 23-31	20	21	22	24	25	26	27	29	30	32	35	1	4	6	8	9	11	12	13	14	15	17	18	19

IF YOU WERE BORN DURING DAYLIGHT SAVINGS TIME:
LOOK UP ONE HOUR EARLIER THAN YOUR ACTUAL BIRTH TIME.

TABLE 16—ASPECT FINDER

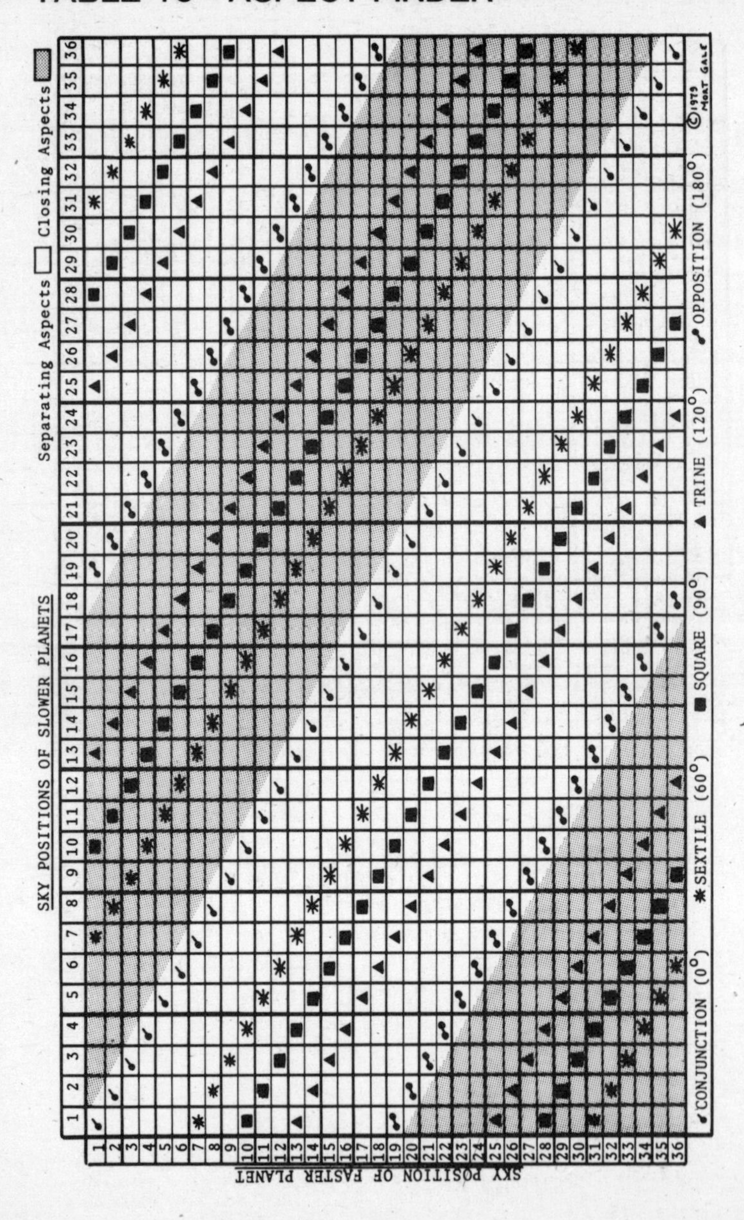

WORKSHEET I—PLANET POSITIONS

NAME: ____________________

DATE: ______________ TIME: ________ ☐ DAYLIGHT SAVING

PLANET	ROW LETTER	KEY NUMBER	SKY POSITION		RETRO. (✓)
SUN			(1)	(SU) ____	
MOON	(2) ____	(3) ____	(4)	(MO) ____	
MERCURY	(5) ____	(6) ____	(7)	(ME) ____	____
VENUS	(8) ____	(8) ____	(9)	(VE) ____	____
MARS	(10) ____	(10) ____	(11)	(MA) ____	____
JUPITER		(12) ____	(13)	(JU) ____	____
SATURN			(14)	(SA) ____	____
URANUS			(14)	(UR) ____	____
NEPTUNE			(14)	(NE) ____	____
PLUTO			(14)	(PL) ____	____
ASCENDANT			(15)	(AS) ____	

WORKSHEET I—PLANET POSITIONS

NAME: ____________________

DATE: ____________ TIME: ________ ☐DAYLIGHT SAVING

PLANET	ROW LETTER	KEY NUMBER	SKY POSITION		RETRO. (✓)
SUN			(1)	(SU) ____	
MOON	(2) ____	(3) ____	(4)	(MO) ____	
MERCURY	(5) ____	(6) ____	(7)	(ME) ____	____
VENUS	(8) ____	(8) ____	(9)	(VE) ____	____
MARS	(10) ____	(10) ____	(11)	(MA) ____	____
JUPITER		(12) ____	(13)	(JU) ____	____
SATURN			(14)	(SA) ____	____
URANUS			(14)	(UR) ____	____
NEPTUNE			(14)	(NE) ____	____
PLUTO			(14)	(PL) ____	____
ASCENDANT			(15)	(AS) ____	

WORKSHEET I—PLANET POSITIONS

NAME: ______________________

DATE: ______________ TIME: ________ ☐ DAYLIGHT SAVING

PLANET	ROW LETTER	KEY NUMBER	SKY POSITION		RETRO. (✓)
SUN			(1)	(SU) ____	
MOON	(2) ____	(3) ____	(4)	(MO) ____	
MERCURY	(5) ____	(6) ____	(7)	(ME) ____	____
VENUS	(8) ____	(8) ____	(9)	(VE) ____	____
MARS	(10) ____	(10) ____	(11)	(MA) ____	____
JUPITER		(12) ____	(13)	(JU) ____	____
SATURN			(14)	(SA) ____	____
URANUS			(14)	(UR) ____	____
NEPTUNE			(14)	(NE) ____	____
PLUTO			(14)	(PL) ____	____
ASCENDANT			(15)	(AS) ____	

WORKSHEET I—PLANET POSITIONS

NAME: ______________________

DATE: ____________ TIME: ________ ☐ DAYLIGHT SAVING

PLANET	ROW LETTER	KEY NUMBER	SKY POSITION		RETRO. (✓)
SUN			(1)	(SU) ____	
MOON	(2) ____	(3) ____	(4)	(MO) ____	
MERCURY	(5) ____	(6) ____	(7)	(ME) ____	____
VENUS	(8) ____	(8) ____	(9)	(VE) ____	____
MARS	(10) ____	(10) ____	(11)	(MA) ____	____
JUPITER		(12) ____	(13)	(JU) ____	____
SATURN			(14)	(SA) ____	____
URANUS			(14)	(UR) ____	____
NEPTUNE			(14)	(NE) ____	____
PLUTO			(14)	(PL) ____	____
ASCENDANT			(15)	(AS) ____	

WORKSHEET I—PLANET POSITIONS

NAME: ____________________

DATE: ____________ TIME: ________ ☐ DAYLIGHT SAVING

PLANET	ROW LETTER	KEY NUMBER	SKY POSITION		RETRO. (✓)
SUN			(1)	(SU) ____	
MOON	(2) ____	(3) ____	(4)	(MO) ____	
MERCURY	(5) ____	(6) ____	(7)	(ME) ____	____
VENUS	(8) ____	(8) ____	(9)	(VE) ____	____
MARS	(10) ____	(10) ____	(11)	(MA) ____	____
JUPITER		(12) ____	(13)	(JU) ____	____
SATURN			(14)	(SA) ____	____
URANUS			(14)	(UR) ____	____
NEPTUNE			(14)	(NE) ____	____
PLUTO			(14)	(PL) ____	____
ASCENDANT			(15)	(AS) ____	

WORKSHEET II—PLANETS IN SIGNS AND HOUSES

A PLANET SKY POSITION

SIGNS	SKY POS	PLANETS	HOUSES
ARIES ♈	1		
	2		
	3		
TAURUS ♉	4		
	5		
	6		
GEMINI ♊	7		
	8		
	9		
CANCER ♋	10		
	11		
	12		
LEO ♌	13		
	14		
	15		
VIRGO ♍	16		
	17		
	18		
LIBRA ♎	19		
	20		
	21		
SCORPIO ♏	22		
	23		
	24		
SAGITT. ♐	25		
	26		
	27		
CAPRIC. ♑	28		
	29		
	30		
AQUAR. ♒	31		
	32		
	33		
PISCES ♓	34		
	35		
	36		

WORKSHEET II

PLANETS IN THE SIGNS AND HOUSES

FOR: ______________ ______
DATE

PLANETS IN THE SIGNS

B NUMBER IN EACH SIGN

ARIES		A	LEO		E	SAGITT		I
TAURUS		B	VIRGO		F	CAPRIC		J
GEMINI		C	LIBRA		G	AQUAR.		K
CANCER		D	SCORP		H	PISCES		L

C ELEMENTS AND QUALITIES

CARDINAL	FIXED	MUTABLE
(A) ____	(E) ____	(I) ____
(J) ____	(B) ____	(F) ____
(G) ____	(K) ____	(C) ____
(D) ____	(H) ____	(L) ____

C __ F __ M __

☐ FIRE
☐ EARTH
☐ AIR
☐ WATER

D GENDER (MASCULINE/FEMININE)

FIRE	☐	EARTH	☐
AIR	☐	WATER	☐

☐ MASCULINE ☐ FEMININE

PLANETS IN THE HOUSES

F

HOUSE	NO.	TOT.
FIRST	____	A
SECOND	____	( )
THIRD	____	
FOURTH	____	B
FIFTH	____	( )
SIXTH	____	
SEVENTH	____	C
EIGHTH	____	( )
NINTH	____	
TENTH	____	D
ELEVENTH	____	( )
TWELVTH	____	

E FIRST CUSP — SKY POS

__ ASCENDANT ☐

or

__ SUN SIGN ☐

G HEMISPHERES

D ( )	( ) C
A ( )	( ) B

☐ SOUTH
☐ NORTH

☐ EAST ☐ WEST

WORKSHEET II—PLANETS IN SIGNS AND HOUSES

A PLANET SKY POSITION

SIGNS	SKY POS	PLANETS	HOUSES
ARIES ♈	1		
	2		
	3		
TAURUS ♉	4		
	5		
	6		
GEMINI ♊	7		
	8		
	9		
CANCER ♋	10		
	11		
	12		
LEO ♌	13		
	14		
	15		
VIRGO ♍	16		
	17		
	18		
LIBRA ♎	19		
	20		
	21		
SCORPIO ♏	22		
	23		
	24		
SAGITT. ♐	25		
	26		
	27		
CAPRIC. ♑	28		
	29		
	30		
AQUAR. ♒	31		
	32		
	33		
PISCES ♓	34		
	35		
	36		

WORKSHEET II

PLANETS IN THE SIGNS AND HOUSES

FOR: ______________________ ____________
DATE

PLANETS IN THE SIGNS

B NUMBER IN EACH SIGN

ARIES		A	LEO		E	SAGITT		I
TAURUS		B	VIRGO		F	CAPRIC		J
GEMINI		C	LIBRA		G	AQUAR.		K
CANCER		D	SCORP		H	PISCES		L

C ELEMENTS AND QUALITIES

CARDINAL	FIXED	MUTABLE	
(A) ____	(E) ____	(I) ____	☐ FIRE
(J) ____	(B) ____	(F) ____	☐ EARTH
(G) ____	(K) ____	(C) ____	☐ AIR
(D) ____	(H) ____	(L) ____	☐ WATER
C __	F __	M __	

D GENDER (MASCULINE/FEMININE)

FIRE ☐	EARTH ☐
AIR ☐	WATER ☐

☐ MASCULINE ☐ FEMININE

PLANETS IN THE HOUSES

F

HOUSE	NO.	TOT.
FIRST	____	A
SECOND	____	( )
THIRD	____	
FOURTH	____	B
FIFTH	____	( )
SIXTH	____	
SEVENTH	____	C
EIGHTH	____	( )
NINTH	____	
TENTH	____	D
ELEVENTH	____	( )
TWELVTH	____	

E FIRST CUSP — SKY POS

___ ASCENDANT ☐
or
___ SUN SIGN ☐

G HEMISPHERES

D ( )	C ( )
A ( )	B ( )

☐ SOUTH

☐ NORTH

☐ EAST ☐ WEST

WORKSHEET II—PLANETS IN SIGNS AND HOUSES

A PLANET SKY POSITION

SIGNS	SKY POS	PLANETS	HOUSES
ARIES ♈	1		
	2		
	3		
TAURUS ♉	4		
	5		
	6		
GEMINI ♊	7		
	8		
	9		
CANCER ♋	10		
	11		
	12		
LEO ♌	13		
	14		
	15		
VIRGO ♍	16		
	17		
	18		
LIBRA ♎	19		
	20		
	21		
SCORPIO ♏	22		
	23		
	24		
SAGITT. ♐	25		
	26		
	27		
CAPRIC. ♑	28		
	29		
	30		
AQUAR. ♒	31		
	32		
	33		
PISCES ♓	34		
	35		
	36		

WORKSHEET II

PLANETS IN THE SIGNS AND HOUSES

FOR: ______________________ ____________
DATE

PLANETS IN THE SIGNS

B NUMBER IN EACH SIGN

ARIES	A	LEO	E	SAGITT	I		
TAURUS	B	VIRGO	F	CAPRIC	J		
GEMINI	C	LIBRA	G	AQUAR.	K		
CANCER	D	SCORP	H	PISCES	L		

C ELEMENTS AND QUALITIES

CARDINAL	FIXED	MUTABLE
(A) ____	(E) ____	(I) ____
(J) ____	(B) ____	(F) ____
(G) ____	(K) ____	(C) ____
(D) ____	(H) ____	(L) ____
C __	F __	M __

☐ FIRE
☐ EARTH
☐ AIR
☐ WATER

D GENDER (MASCULINE/FEMININE)

FIRE ☐	EARTH ☐
AIR ☐	WATER ☐
☐ MASCULINE	☐ FEMININE

PLANETS IN THE HOUSES

F

HOUSE	NO.	TOT.
FIRST	____	A
SECOND	____	( )
THIRD	____	
FOURTH	____	B
FIFTH	____	( )
SIXTH	____	
SEVENTH	____	C
EIGHTH	____	( )
NINTH	____	
TENTH	____	D
ELEVENTH	____	( )
TWELVTH	____	

E FIRST CUSP — SKY POS

__ ASCENDANT ☐
or
__ SUN SIGN ☐

G HEMISPHERES

D ( )	C ( )
A ( )	B ( )

☐ SOUTH
☐ NORTH
☐ EAST
☐ WEST

WORKSHEET II—PLANETS IN SIGNS AND HOUSES

A PLANET SKY POSITION

SIGNS	SKY POS	PLANETS	HOUSES
ARIES ♈	1		
	2		
	3		
TAURUS ♉	4		
	5		
	6		
GEMINI ♊	7		
	8		
	9		
CANCER ♋	10		
	11		
	12		
LEO ♌	13		
	14		
	15		
VIRGO ♍	16		
	17		
	18		
LIBRA ♎	19		
	20		
	21		
SCORPIO ♏	22		
	23		
	24		
SAGITT. ♐	25		
	26		
	27		
CAPRIC. ♑	28		
	29		
	30		
AQUAR. ♒	31		
	32		
	33		
PISCES ♓	34		
	35		
	36		

WORKSHEET II

PLANETS IN THE SIGNS AND HOUSES

FOR: ____________________ __________
DATE

PLANETS IN THE SIGNS

B NUMBER IN EACH SIGN

ARIES		A	LEO		E	SAGITT		I
TAURUS		B	VIRGO		F	CAPRIC		J
GEMINI		C	LIBRA		G	AQUAR.		K
CANCER		D	SCORP		H	PISCES		L

C ELEMENTS AND QUALITIES

CARDINAL	FIXED	MUTABLE	
(A) ____	(E) ____	(I) ____	☐ FIRE
(J) ____	(B) ____	(F) ____	☐ EARTH
(G) ____	(K) ____	(C) ____	☐ AIR
(D) ____	(H) ____	(L) ____	☐ WATER
C __	F __	M __	

D GENDER (MASCULINE/FEMININE)

FIRE ☐ EARTH ☐

AIR ☐ WATER ☐

☐ MASCULINE ☐ FEMININE

PLANETS IN THE HOUSES

F

HOUSE	NO.	TOT.
FIRST	____	A
SECOND	____	( )
THIRD	____	
FOURTH	____	B
FIFTH	____	( )
SIXTH	____	
SEVENTH	____	C
EIGHTH	____	( )
NINTH	____	
TENTH	____	D
ELEVENTH	____	( )
TWELVTH	____	

E FIRST CUSP — SKY POS

__ ASCENDANT ☐

or

__ SUN SIGN ☐

G HEMISPHERES

D ( )	C ( )
A ( )	B ( )

☐ SOUTH

☐ NORTH

☐ EAST ☐ WEST

WORKSHEET II—PLANETS IN SIGNS AND HOUSES

A PLANET SKY POSITION

SIGNS	SKY POS	PLANETS	HOUSES
ARIES ♈	1		
	2		
	3		
TAURUS ♉	4		
	5		
	6		
GEMINI ♊	7		
	8		
	9		
CANCER ♋	10		
	11		
	12		
LEO ♌	13		
	14		
	15		
VIRGO ♍	16		
	17		
	18		
LIBRA ♎	19		
	20		
	21		
SCORPIO ♏	22		
	23		
	24		
SAGITT. ♐	25		
	26		
	27		
CAPRIC. ♑	28		
	29		
	30		
AQUAR. ♒	31		
	32		
	33		
PISCES ♓	34		
	35		
	36		

WORKSHEET II

PLANETS IN THE SIGNS AND HOUSES

FOR: ____________ ________
DATE

PLANETS IN THE SIGNS

B NUMBER IN EACH SIGN

ARIES	A	LEO	E	SAGITT	I		
TAURUS	B	VIRGO	F	CAPRIC	J		
GEMINI	C	LIBRA	G	AQUAR.	K		
CANCER	D	SCORP	H	PISCES	L		

C ELEMENTS AND QUALITIES

CARDINAL	FIXED	MUTABLE	
(A) ____	(E) ____	(I) ____	☐ FIRE
(J) ____	(B) ____	(F) ____	☐ EARTH
(G) ____	(K) ____	(C) ____	☐ AIR
(D) ____	(H) ____	(L) ____	☐ WATER
C __	F __	M __	

D GENDER (MASCULINE/FEMININE)

FIRE ☐ EARTH ☐

AIR ☐ WATER ☐

☐ MASCULINE ☐ FEMININE

PLANETS IN THE HOUSES

F

HOUSE	NO.	TOT.
FIRST	____	A
SECOND	____	( )
THIRD	____	
FOURTH	____	B
FIFTH	____	( )
SIXTH	____	
SEVENTH	____	C
EIGHTH	____	( )
NINTH	____	
TENTH	____	D
ELEVENTH	____	( )
TWELVTH	____	

E FIRST CUSP — SKY POS

__ ASCENDANT ☐

or

__ SUN SIGN ☐

G HEMISPHERES

D ( )	C ( )
A ( )	B ( )

☐ SOUTH

☐ NORTH

☐ EAST ☐ WEST

WORKSHEET III—NATAL ASPECTS

NAME: ______________________________ DATE: ________________

	SU ( )	MO ( )	ME ( )	VE ( )	MA ( )	JU ( )	SA ( )	UR ( )	NE ( )	PL ( )
SU ( )	--									
MO ( )	--	--								
ME ( )	--	--	--							
VE ( )	--	--	--	--						
MA ( )	--	--	--	--	--					
JU ( )	--	--	--	--	--	--				
SA ( )	--	--	--	--	--	--	--			
UR ( )	--	--	--	--	--	--	--	--		
NE ( )	--	--	--	--	--	--	--	--	--	

ASPECTS: Take difference between Sky Position numbers of two planets. Find the aspects that correspond with those differences below.

0	CONJUNCTION	☌		18	OPPOSITION	☍
6	SEXTILE	✱		24	TRINE	△
9	SQUARE	□		27	SQUARE	□
12	TRINE	△		30	SEXTILE	✱

WORKSHEET III—NATAL ASPECTS

NAME: ______________________ DATE: ______________

	SU ( )	MO ( )	ME ( )	VE ( )	MA ( )	JU ( )	SA ( )	UR ( )	NE ( )	PL ( )
SU ( )	--									
MO ( )	--	--								
ME ( )	--	--	--							
VE ( )	--	--	--	--						
MA ( )	--	--	--	--	--					
JU ( )	--	--	--	--	--	--				
SA ( )	--	--	--	--	--	--	--			
UR ( )	--	--	--	--	--	--	--	--		
NE ( )	--	--	--	--	--	--	--	--	--	

ASPECTS: Take difference between Sky Position numbers of two planets. Find the aspects that correspond with those differences below.

0	CONJUNCTION	☌		18	OPPOSITION	☍
6	SEXTILE	⚹		24	TRINE	△
9	SQUARE	□		27	SQUARE	□
12	TRINE	△		30	SEXTILE	⚹

WORKSHEET III—NATAL ASPECTS

NAME: ______________________ DATE: ____________

	SU ( )	MO ( )	ME ( )	VE ( )	MA ( )	JU ( )	SA ( )	UR ( )	NE ( )	PL ( )
SU ( )	--									
MO ( )	--	--								
ME ( )	--	--	--							
VE ( )	--	--	--	--						
MA ( )	--	--	--	--	--					
JU ( )	--	--	--	--	--	--				
SA ( )	--	--	--	--	--	--	--			
UR ( )	--	--	--	--	--	--	--	--		
NE ( )	--	--	--	--	--	--	--	--	--	

ASPECTS: Take difference between Sky Position numbers of two planets. Find the aspects that correspond with those differences below.

0	CONJUNCTION	☌		18	OPPOSITION	☍
6	SEXTILE	✱		24	TRINE	△
9	SQUARE	□		27	SQUARE	□
12	TRINE	△		30	SEXTILE	✱

WORKSHEET III—NATAL ASPECTS

NAME: ______________________ DATE: ____________

	SU ( )	MO ( )	ME ( )	VE ( )	MA ( )	JU ( )	SA ( )	UR ( )	NE ( )	PL ( )
SU ( )	--									
MO ( )	--	--								
ME ( )	--	--	--							
VE ( )	--	--	--	--						
MA ( )	--	--	--	--	--					
JU ( )	--	--	--	--	--	--				
SA ( )	--	--	--	--	--	--	--			
UR ( )	--	--	--	--	--	--	--	--		
NE ( )	--	--	--	--	--	--	--	--	--	

ASPECTS: Take difference between Sky Position numbers of two planets. Find the aspects that correspond with those differences below.

0	CONJUNCTION	☌		18	OPPOSITION	☍
6	SEXTILE	⚹		24	TRINE	△
9	SQUARE	□		27	SQUARE	□
12	TRINE	△		30	SEXTILE	⚹

WORKSHEET III—NATAL ASPECTS

NAME: ______________________ DATE: ______________

	SU ( )	MO ( )	ME ( )	VE ( )	MA ( )	JU ( )	SA ( )	UR ( )	NE ( )	PL ( )
SU ( )	--									
MO ( )	--	--								
ME ( )	--	--	--							
VE ( )	--	--	--	--						
MA ( )	--	--	--	--	--					
JU ( )	--	--	--	--	--	--				
SA ( )	--	--	--	--	--	--	--			
UR ( )	--	--	--	--	--	--	--	--		
NE ( )	--	--	--	--	--	--	--	--	--	

ASPECTS: Take difference between Sky Position numbers of two planets. Find the aspects that correspond with those differences below.

0	CONJUNCTION	☌		18	OPPOSITION	☍
6	SEXTILE	✱		24	TRINE	△
9	SQUARE	□		27	SQUARE	□
12	TRINE	△		30	SEXTILE	✱

WORKSHEET IV—SUMMARY OF NATAL PLANETS

NAME: ______________________ DATE: __________

PLANETS	RETR	(From WS I & II) SIGN	HOUSE	(From Worksheet III) NATAL ASPECTS
SUN				
MOON				
MERCURY				
VENUS				
MARS				
JUPITER				
SATURN				
URANUS				
NEPTUNE				
PLUTO				
ASCEND.			SCOUT PLANET:	

WORKSHEET IV—SUMMARY OF NATAL PLANETS

NAME: ______________________				DATE: __________
PLANETS	RETR	(From WS I & II)		(From Worksheet III)
		SIGN	HOUSE	NATAL ASPECTS
SUN				
MOON				
MERCURY				
VENUS				
MARS				
JUPITER				
SATURN				
URANUS				
NEPTUNE				
PLUTO				
ASCEND.			SCOUT PLANET:	

WORKSHEET IV—SUMMARY OF NATAL PLANETS

NAME: ____________				DATE: ________
PLANETS	RETR	(From WS I & II)		(From Worksheet III)
		SIGN	HOUSE	NATAL ASPECTS
SUN				
MOON				
MERCURY				
VENUS				
MARS				
JUPITER				
SATURN				
URANUS				
NEPTUNE				
PLUTO				
ASCEND.			SCOUT PLANET:	

WORKSHEET IV—SUMMARY OF NATAL PLANETS

NAME:				DATE:
PLANETS	RETR	(From WS I & II)		(From Worksheet III)
		SIGN	HOUSE	NATAL ASPECTS
SUN				
MOON				
MERCURY				
VENUS				
MARS				
JUPITER				
SATURN				
URANUS				
NEPTUNE				
PLUTO				
ASCEND.			SCOUT PLANET:	

WORKSHEET IV—SUMMARY OF NATAL PLANETS

NAME:			DATE:	
PLANETS	RETR	(From WS I & II)		(From Worksheet III)
		SIGN	HOUSE	NATAL ASPECTS
SUN				
MOON				
MERCURY				
VENUS				
MARS				
JUPITER				
SATURN				
URANUS				
NEPTUNE				
PLUTO				
ASCEND.			SCOUT PLANET:	

WORKSHEET V—TRANSITS (OR COMPANION) ASPECTS

NAME: ______________________

COMPANION: ______________________ TRANSIT DATE ________

(OTHER PLANET POSITIONS)	(YOUR NATAL PLANET SKY POSITIONS)									
	SU ( )	MO ( )	ME ( )	VE ( )	MA ( )	JU ( )	SA ( )	UR ( )	NE ( )	PL ( )
SU ( )										
MO ( )										
ME ( )										
VE ( )										
MA ( )										
JU ( )										
SA ( )										
UR ( )										
NE ( )										
PL ( )										

KEY: 0-☌ 6-✱ 9-■ 12-▲ 18-☍ 24-▲ 27-■ 30-✱

OTHER PLANETS	RET	IN YOUR HOUSE #	OTHER PLANETS MAKE THESE ASPECTS TO YOUR NATAL PLANETS
SUN			
MOON			
MERCURY			
VENUS			
MARS			
JUPITER			
SATURN			
URANUS			
NEPTUNE			
PLUTO			

WORKSHEET V—TRANSITS (OR COMPANION) ASPECTS

NAME: ______________________________ ______________ TRANSIT DATE

COMPANION: __________________________

(OTHER PLANET POSITIONS)	(YOUR NATAL PLANET SKY POSITIONS)									
	SU ( )	MO ( )	ME ( )	VE ( )	MA ( )	JU ( )	SA ( )	UR ( )	NE ( )	PL ( )
SU( )										
MO( )										
ME( )										
VE( )										
MA( )										
JU( )										
SA( )										
UR( )										
NE( )										
PL( )										

KEY: 0-☌ 6-✱ 9-■ 12-▲ 18-☍ 24-▲ 27-■ 30-✱

OTHER PLANETS	RET	IN YOUR HOUSE #	OTHER PLANETS MAKE THESE ASPECTS TO YOUR NATAL PLANETS
SUN			
MOON			
MERCURY			
VENUS			
MARS			
JUPITER			
SATURN			
URANUS			
NEPTUNE			
PLUTO			

WORKSHEET V—TRANSITS (OR COMPANION) ASPECTS

NAME: ______________________ ______________

COMPANION: ______________________ TRANSIT DATE

(YOUR NATAL PLANET SKY POSITIONS)

(OTHER PLANET POSITIONS)	SU ( )	MO ( )	ME ( )	VE ( )	MA ( )	JU ( )	SA ( )	UR ( )	NE ( )	PL ( )
SU ( )										
MO ( )										
ME ( )										
VE ( )										
MA ( )										
JU ( )										
SA ( )										
UR ( )										
NE ( )										
PL ( )										

KEY: 0-☌ 6-✱ 9-■ 12-▲ 18-☍ 24-▲ 27-■ 30-✱

OTHER PLANETS	RET	IN YOUR HOUSE #	OTHER PLANETS MAKE THESE ASPECTS TO YOUR NATAL PLANETS
SUN			
MOON			
MERCURY			
VENUS			
MARS			
JUPITER			
SATURN			
URANUS			
NEPTUNE			
PLUTO			

WORKSHEET V—TRANSITS (OR COMPANION) ASPECTS

NAME: ____________________________________ TRANSIT DATE

COMPANION: ______________________________

(YOUR NATAL PLANET SKY POSITIONS)

(OTHER PLANET POSITIONS)	SU ( )	MO ( )	ME ( )	VE ( )	MA ( )	JU ( )	SA ( )	UR ( )	NE ( )	PL ( )
SU ( )										
MO ( )										
ME ( )										
VE ( )										
MA ( )										
JU ( )										
SA ( )										
UR ( )										
NE ( )										
PL ( )										

KEY: 0-☌ 6-⚹ 9-■ 12-▲ 18-☍ 24-▲ 27-■ 30-⚹

OTHER PLANETS	RET	IN YOUR HOUSE #	OTHER PLANETS MAKE THESE ASPECTS TO YOUR NATAL PLANETS
SUN			
MOON			
MERCURY			
VENUS			
MARS			
JUPITER			
SATURN			
URANUS			
NEPTUNE			
PLUTO			

WORKSHEET V—TRANSITS (OR COMPANION) ASPECTS

NAME: ______________________________ ____________

COMPANION: _________________________ TRANSIT DATE

(OTHER PLANET POSITIONS)	(YOUR NATAL PLANET SKY POSITIONS)									
	SU ( )	MO ( )	ME ( )	VE ( )	MA ( )	JU ( )	SA ( )	UR ( )	NE ( )	PL ( )
SU ( )										
MO ( )										
ME ( )										
VE ( )										
MA ( )										
JU ( )										
SA ( )										
UR ( )										
NE ( )										
PL ( )										

KEY: 0-☌ 6-✱ 9-■ 12-▲ 18-☍ 24-▲ 27-■ 30-✱

OTHER PLANETS	RET	IN YOUR HOUSE #	OTHER PLANETS MAKE THESE ASPECTS TO YOUR NATAL PLANETS
SUN			
MOON			
MERCURY			
VENUS			
MARS			
JUPITER			
SATURN			
URANUS			
NEPTUNE			
PLUTO			

BLANK HOROSCOPE WHEEL

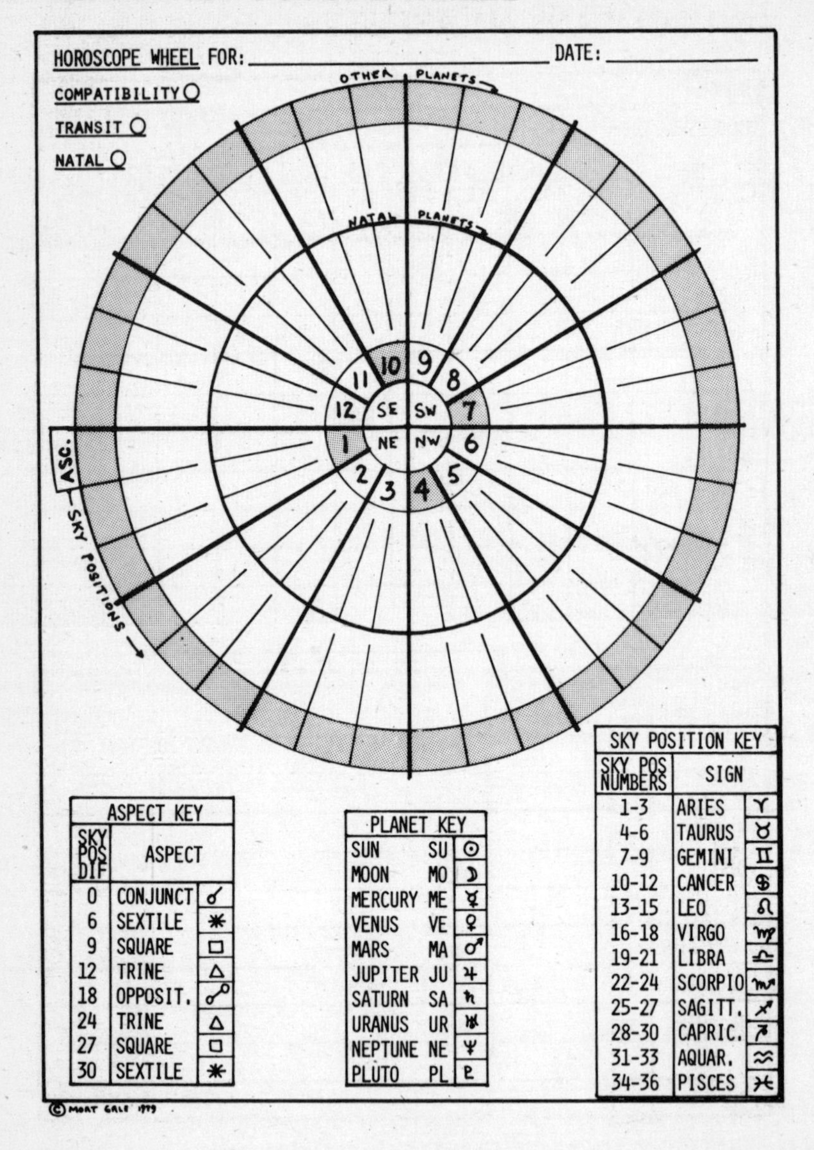

ASPECT KEY		
SKY POS DIF	ASPECT	
0	CONJUNCT	☌
6	SEXTILE	⚹
9	SQUARE	□
12	TRINE	△
18	OPPOSIT.	☍
24	TRINE	△
27	SQUARE	□
30	SEXTILE	⚹

PLANET KEY		
SUN	SU	☉
MOON	MO	☽
MERCURY	ME	☿
VENUS	VE	♀
MARS	MA	♂
JUPITER	JU	♃
SATURN	SA	♄
URANUS	UR	♅
NEPTUNE	NE	♆
PLUTO	PL	♇

SKY POSITION KEY		
SKY POS NUMBERS	SIGN	
1-3	ARIES	♈
4-6	TAURUS	♉
7-9	GEMINI	♊
10-12	CANCER	♋
13-15	LEO	♌
16-18	VIRGO	♍
19-21	LIBRA	♎
22-24	SCORPIO	♏
25-27	SAGITT.	♐
28-30	CAPRIC.	♑
31-33	AQUAR.	♒
34-36	PISCES	♓

BLANK HOROSCOPE WHEEL

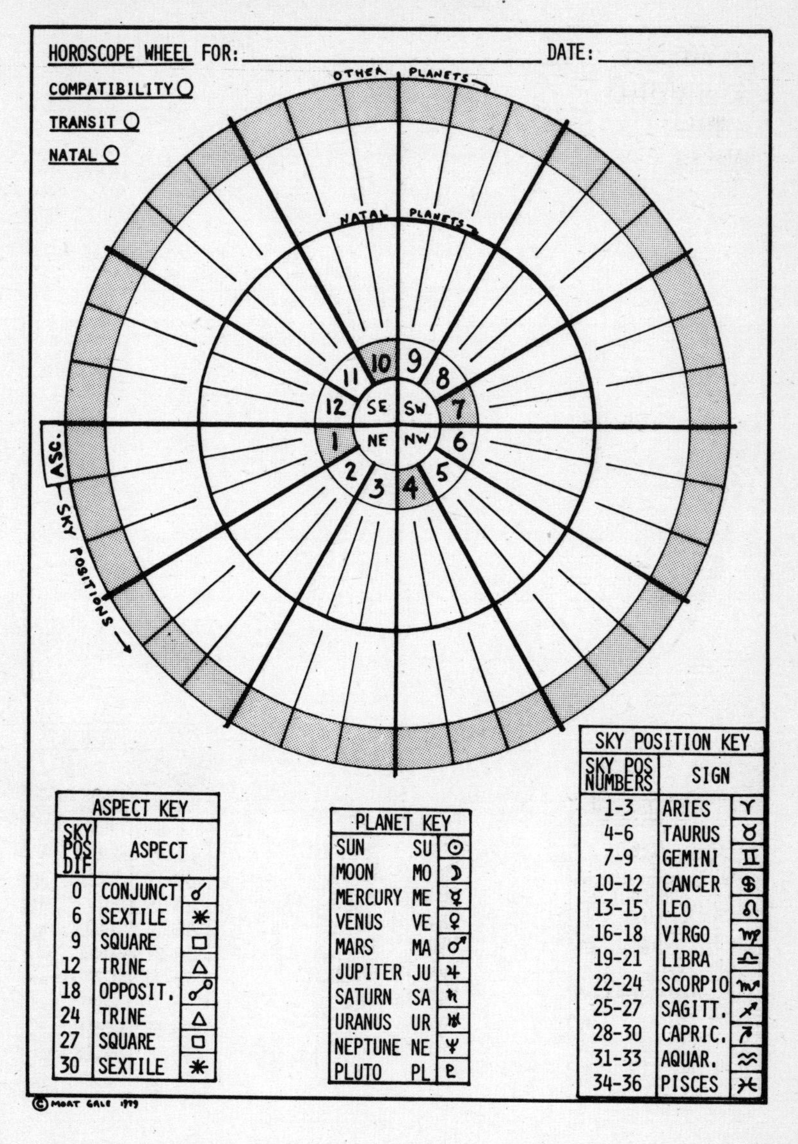

HOROSCOPE WHEEL FOR: ____________________ DATE: ____________

COMPATIBILITY ○

TRANSIT ○

NATAL ○

ASPECT KEY		
SKY POS DIF	ASPECT	
0	CONJUNCT	☌
6	SEXTILE	✳
9	SQUARE	□
12	TRINE	△
18	OPPOSIT.	☍
24	TRINE	△
27	SQUARE	□
30	SEXTILE	✳

PLANET KEY		
SUN	SU	☉
MOON	MO	☽
MERCURY	ME	☿
VENUS	VE	♀
MARS	MA	♂
JUPITER	JU	♃
SATURN	SA	♄
URANUS	UR	♅
NEPTUNE	NE	♆
PLUTO	PL	♇

SKY POSITION KEY		
SKY POS NUMBERS	SIGN	
1-3	ARIES	♈
4-6	TAURUS	♉
7-9	GEMINI	♊
10-12	CANCER	♋
13-15	LEO	♌
16-18	VIRGO	♍
19-21	LIBRA	♎
22-24	SCORPIO	♏
25-27	SAGITT.	♐
28-30	CAPRIC.	♑
31-33	AQUAR.	♒
34-36	PISCES	♓

BLANK HOROSCOPE WHEEL

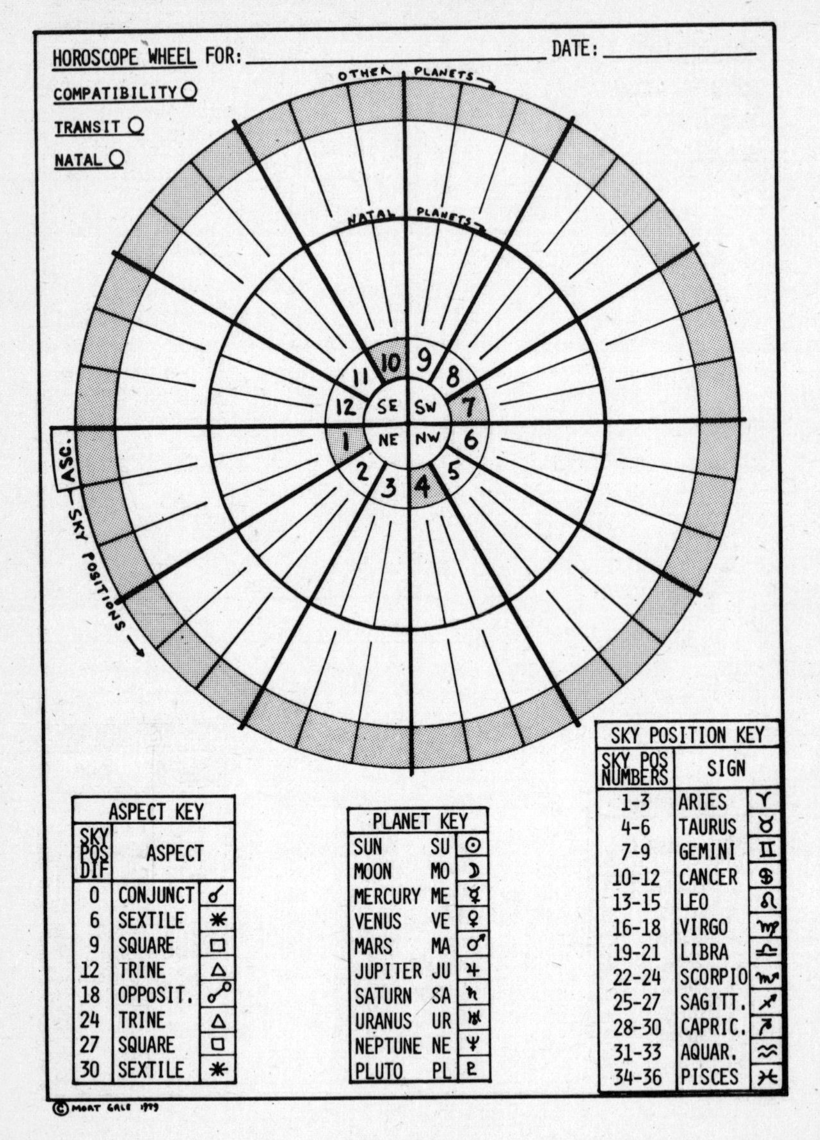

ASPECT KEY		
SKY POS DIF	ASPECT	
0	CONJUNCT	☌
6	SEXTILE	⚹
9	SQUARE	□
12	TRINE	△
18	OPPOSIT.	☍
24	TRINE	△
27	SQUARE	□
30	SEXTILE	⚹

PLANET KEY		
SUN	SU	☉
MOON	MO	☽
MERCURY	ME	☿
VENUS	VE	♀
MARS	MA	♂
JUPITER	JU	♃
SATURN	SA	♄
URANUS	UR	♅
NEPTUNE	NE	♆
PLUTO	PL	♇

SKY POSITION KEY		
SKY POS NUMBERS	SIGN	
1-3	ARIES	♈
4-6	TAURUS	♉
7-9	GEMINI	♊
10-12	CANCER	♋
13-15	LEO	♌
16-18	VIRGO	♍
19-21	LIBRA	♎
22-24	SCORPIO	♏
25-27	SAGITT.	♐
28-30	CAPRIC.	♑
31-33	AQUAR.	♒
34-36	PISCES	♓

BLANK HOROSCOPE WHEEL

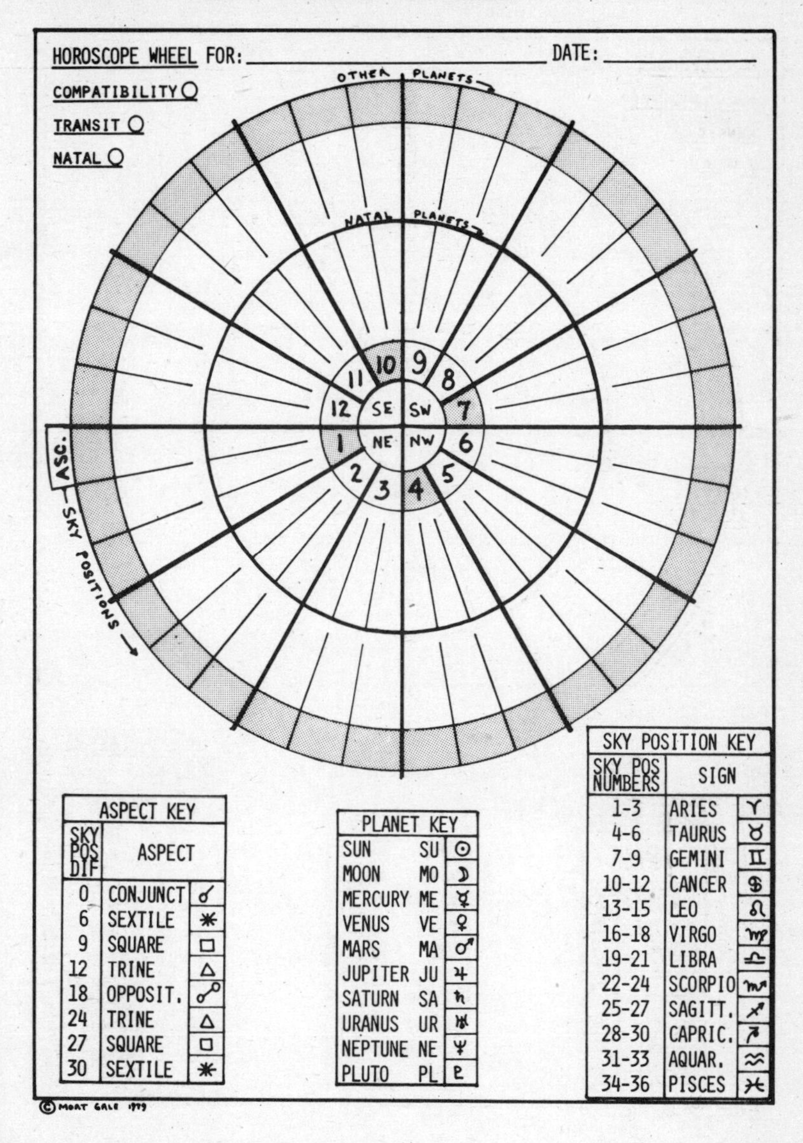

ASPECT KEY		
SKY POS DIF	ASPECT	
0	CONJUNCT	☌
6	SEXTILE	⚹
9	SQUARE	□
12	TRINE	△
18	OPPOSIT.	☍
24	TRINE	△
27	SQUARE	□
30	SEXTILE	⚹

PLANET KEY		
SUN	SU	☉
MOON	MO	☽
MERCURY	ME	☿
VENUS	VE	♀
MARS	MA	♂
JUPITER	JU	♃
SATURN	SA	♄
URANUS	UR	♅
NEPTUNE	NE	♆
PLUTO	PL	♇

SKY POSITION KEY		
SKY POS NUMBERS	SIGN	
1-3	ARIES	♈
4-6	TAURUS	♉
7-9	GEMINI	♊
10-12	CANCER	♋
13-15	LEO	♌
16-18	VIRGO	♍
19-21	LIBRA	♎
22-24	SCORPIO	♏
25-27	SAGITT.	♐
28-30	CAPRIC.	♑
31-33	AQUAR.	♒
34-36	PISCES	♓

BLANK HOROSCOPE WHEEL

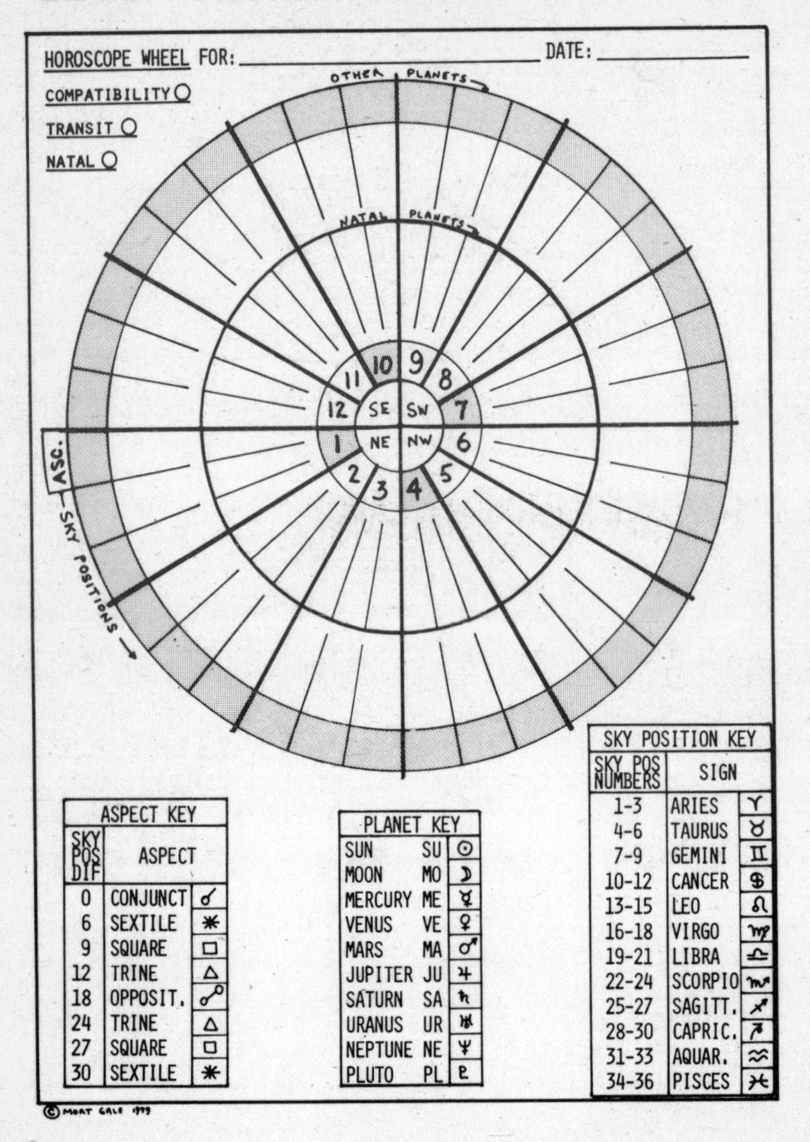

ASPECT KEY		
SKY POS DIF	ASPECT	
0	CONJUNCT	☌
6	SEXTILE	✱
9	SQUARE	□
12	TRINE	△
18	OPPOSIT.	☍
24	TRINE	△
27	SQUARE	□
30	SEXTILE	✱

PLANET KEY		
SUN	SU	☉
MOON	MO	☽
MERCURY	ME	☿
VENUS	VE	♀
MARS	MA	♂
JUPITER	JU	♃
SATURN	SA	♄
URANUS	UR	♅
NEPTUNE	NE	♆
PLUTO	PL	♇

SKY POSITION KEY		
SKY POS NUMBERS	SIGN	
1-3	ARIES	♈
4-6	TAURUS	♉
7-9	GEMINI	♊
10-12	CANCER	♋
13-15	LEO	♌
16-18	VIRGO	♍
19-21	LIBRA	♎
22-24	SCORPIO	♏
25-27	SAGITT.	♐
28-30	CAPRIC.	♑
31-33	AQUAR.	♒
34-36	PISCES	♓